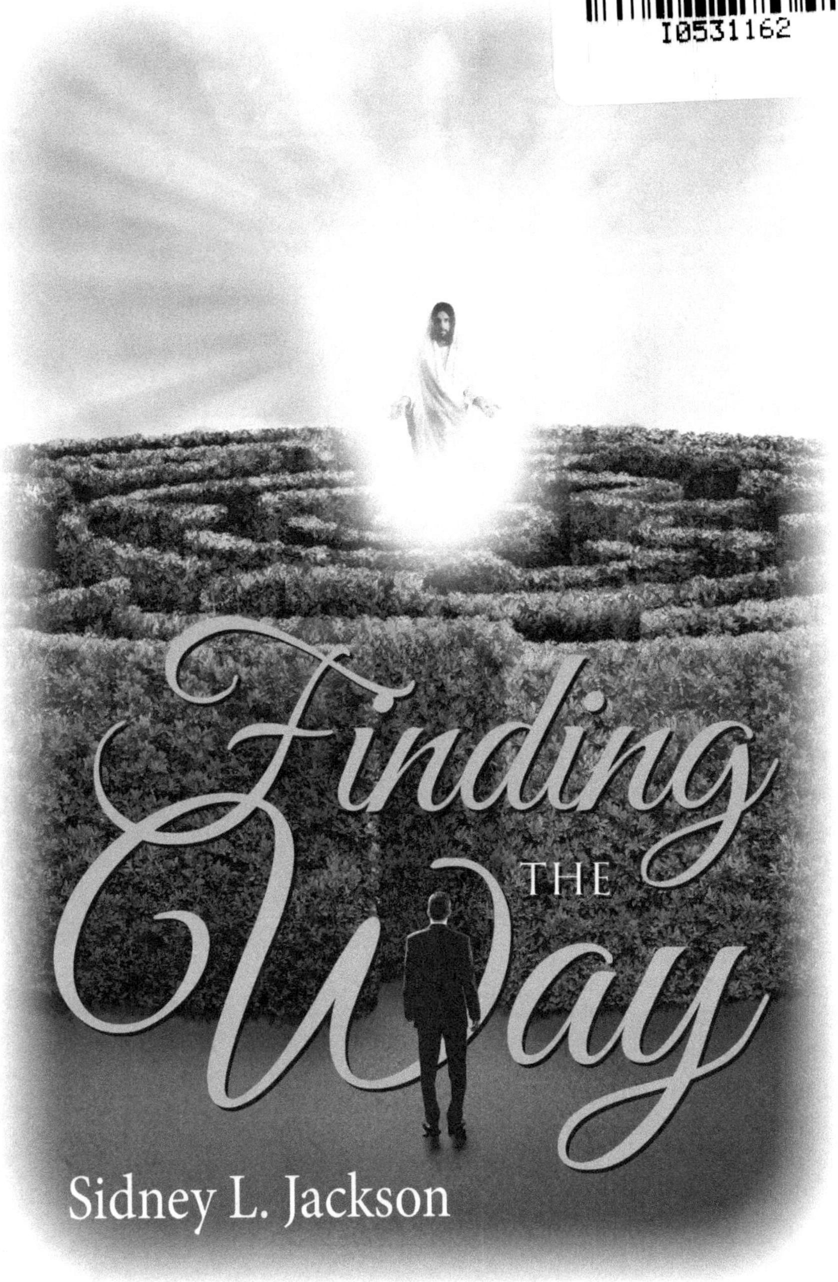

I0531162

Finding

THE

Way

Sidney L. Jackson

Finding The Way
Copyright © 2023 by Sidney L. Jackson

All rights reserved. No part of this publication may be reproduced,
distributed, or transmitted in any form or by any means, including
photocopying, recording, or other electronic or mechanical
methods, without the prior written permission of the author, except
in the case of brief quotations embodied in critical reviews and
certain other non-commercial uses permitted by copyright law.

ISBN
978-1-961601-77-2 (Paperback)
978-1-961601-78-9 (eBook)

TABLE OF CONTENTS

CHAPTER 1
The Genesis

Time and space are allotted to everyone equally and cannot be hoarded or exhausted. The opportunity to sin is equally made available to all. Down through the annals of time and across all spatial planes man's willingness to violate laws that are intended to harbor him from danger have caused a deep rift in the Creator's master plan. In one of the recognized physical laws it states that for every action there is an equal and opposite reaction. Scientists the world over have experimented with attempting to manipulate this law to achieve a different result than what was intended. Success in this effort has yet to be realized. Even as physical laws are immutable so are the spiritual laws provided by the Creator and are meant to be obeyed.

In life there are many choices to be made while traveling along the way. Many paths are presented with beckoning enticements that provide a lure that's hard to resist. Taking the wrong path, often leads to an undesirable end. When confronted with the proverbial fork in the road, it is sometimes difficult to know which prong to pursue. True guidance is not always revealed immediately. Fear of the unknown is a major factor in making a decision or a wise choice. It is not that one has to know what the end will be in order to make a wise choice, but rather placing a trust in something that will guide you eventually is where faith comes in. Having faith in and believing in a spiritual guide will lead to making the right decision or choice.

The many paths and roads in life are there to provide a way to reach a particular destination, but not all roads will lead to salvation. Only the wise and prudent shall know when the right road or path is taken. For one to make the right decision, it is helpful that the person be guided by spiritual Providence.

In the following story exposure to good and evil begins at birth and is like an ever present shadow that manifests itself based on decisions and choices made. From cradle to grave birth to death no one is exempt from the exposure. Although the circumstances that prevail at the time of birth may have a significant impact and influence on how one responds to good and evil, they cannot permanently darken the path for one who seeks the light.

* * * * * * * *

The cradle rocked from side to side and her cries grew louder as the infant sought immediate attention. Mama was in the next room, but was slow to respond. Exhausted from her heated argument with the baby's father she was having a hard time composing herself and be an attentive mother. Left alone as Norman had stormed out of the apartment, uncontrollably Elena's tears were rising to match those of the baby. As she desperately tried to regain self control and rein in her emotions enough to attend to the child's needs, the thoughts running through her mind were causing such anxiety that she was shaking when she entered the room. At the side of the crib she paused for a moment just looking down wondering about the change her life had taken as a result of this now bawling creature that lay before her. Finally giving in to her natural motherly instinct she picked up the baby and held her to her breast. The bawling now reduced to a whimper, but not completely gone was a sign that this was just a visual display of something everyone needs – to be held and loved.

In the three months since Elena came home from the hospital with Monica in her arms, the rift between Norman and her had grown wider. He blamed her for getting pregnant and wanted her to have an abortion. At the time when she told him of her condition, she was hoping he would be happy about it, but when he displayed such a violent reaction to the news, she was shocked. Having been raised by a moderately religious family who did not believe in abortion, Elena was not even considering his idea. She just hoped that over time he would adjust to the fact. They were married now almost three years, but had never talked about starting a family. Now that the time had come when she was pregnant she could not bring herself to believe what he was asking her to do. Elena had assumed he wanted a family since he came from a large one, but just never consulted with him about it. As it turned out during the early gestation months he seemed to have accepted the status so she believed he had acceded to the fact.

He didn't overtly proclaim that he was happy about it, but he just became distant from her. She tried desperately to love him and did all the things that she thought would please him. She went out of her way to cook the things she knew he would like, she wore, for as long as physically possible, nightwear that she hoped would arouse him and she even bought him gifts for no reason while she still worked. Try as she might his attitude did not change and her efforts were becoming fruitless so she stopped. They had reached the point where they were still living together and even sharing the same bed, but no love was in the room. Finally at the point of mental exhaustion she confronted him.

"Norman I am going to have this baby, your baby and there is no changing my mind. How long are you going to sulk and behave like a spoiled brat?" The time is growing short when it will happen so why can't you accept it and be a man about it?"

"You talk about being a man about it. Why didn't you tell me you were planning to become pregnant before you did so I could let you know how I felt. You gave me no warning or even hinted about what you were thinking. You just decided to spring the news on me after the fact and then you expect me to be happy. I am as much a man as any other guy, but I just hated to be surprised by your selfish action. It's not about my manhood or questioning me about sulking, I am just having a hard time accepting what you did. When this baby comes how am I supposed to feel when I never wanted it. I have been doing some serious thinking about this whole situation and believe me I've been struggling about what I should do."

When he finished, Monica was crushed by the words that were coming out of his mouth. Was he really even thinking about leaving me? Could he be that cruel? The tears were welling up in her eyes, but she was not going to allow him to see them so she got up and went into the bathroom and let it all out. It was not hard for him to hear her crying, but he turned a deaf ear to it and went to sleep. At this point she was emotionally drained of any love she had ever felt for this man and the effect it was having on her unborn child she could not have imagined, but she felt the violent stirring of the fetus in her womb. It was hard for her to return to the bed watching him sleep peacefully without thinking the most evil thoughts. However, for the sake of the baby she was going to persevere..

The next morning she got up early as she usually did and put on a pot of coffee. Several minutes later he got up and strolled into the kitchen like nothing had happened. Since it was a Thursday and he had to go to work first he ate his breakfast, which she had prepared, and without mentioning anything about last night's words went into the bathroom to get ready to leave. She was still working also, but did not have to leave as early so she just sat there pondering last night's word exchange. He finished dressing and without even saying goodbye or anything he walked out. She continued to sit there several more minutes wondering about what was going to happen to them, especially the baby, until she realized it was getting late and if she wanted to get to work on time she had better get busy.

Elena was employed by a telephone service company as a secretary to one of the mid-level managers. When she arrived at her desk, a bit late, she was not appearing at her best and her supervisor noticed. Being a married father himself, he was not insensitive to her condition, but it was not like her to come in late or even not look her best so he asked about her wellness.

"Good morning Elena are you feeling alright?"

She knew that he was picking up on the fact that she was late and she became a little defensive in her response.

"Yes I'm fine why are you asking?'

He sensed the slight irritation in her voice so he softened his tone when he continued.

"Oh I was just inquiring about your health. I remember when my wife was going through the same period, I believe about where you are now she would have some days that she wished she had stayed in bed. Is that how you're feeling?"

Elena was touched by the sincerity in his voice and her tone changed to match his.

"No I'm fine really it's just that adjusting to becoming this fat girl that I've never been is going to take some time."

They both laughed and before he went into his office he said: "You are a great secretary and I'm going to miss you when you go, but now anytime you think you need to take a day or so off, just let me know"

"Thank you. I know you mean that and I'll try to be here and on time as long as I can."

She finished speaking and watched him go then started addressing the work issues that needed attention for the day.

The rest of the day went along without any major issues and she was happy to see the clock exhibit the 5:00 O'clock hour. As she prepared to leave, her phone rang and she was hesitant in answering it because she didn't want to be drawn into some activity that would demand that she stay longer. She looked at the caller ID to determine whether it was someone that she needed to talk to or her supervisor, but it was neither. The name on the ID was not someone she recognized or any of the people that she would normally conduct business with so she was strongly considering letting it go and wait for a message to be left. As the voice message began to record she listened.

"Elena you don't know me, but I am a friend of Norman's and that's how I have this number. I want to let you know that I just left him at a bar on 49th street called Lenny's Watering Hole and he is drinking himself into a stupor. I've tried to talk him into letting me get a taxi to take him home, but he wouldn't listen and kept on imbibing. I had to leave, but I thought you ought to know. The telephone number there you can get from information. I suggest you call and try to get someone to convince him to go home."

The message ended and it sent a chill down her spine Had his negative reaction to her pregnancy driven him to this point? She called information received the number and called the bar.

Ring, ring, ring.

"Hello--Lenny's Watering Hole" the bartender answered.

"Hello my name is Elena Miller and I believe my husband is there. Can you tell me whether he is still there?"

The bartender, who knew Norman because he was a regular there, answered in the affirmative and told her he was just about to leave. Elena thanked him and hung up. Not sure what condition he would be in when he came home, if he came home, she wasn't sure just how to prepare for his entry. She left the office and went home wondering whether she should fix dinner or let him go to bed and sleep it off. Knowing that she had to eat something for her and the baby, she fixed a light dinner sufficient for their needs and then waited for his arrival. About an hour later the key turned in the apartment door lock and she heard him mumbling to himself as he entered. What he was mumbling was not comprehensible and she was trying hard to make some sense of what he was trying to say. As he staggered into the room, his movements from side to side prevented him from walking straight toward her, but he made an effort to sit down at the kitchen table and put his head down. Elena's whole demeanor went into a rage as she watched him pass out on the table. She could feel the baby reacting to her emotions as it squirmed and it was not comfortable so she just left him sitting there and went into the bedroom to lie down.

About three hours later, it was now about 11:00 O'clock and she had gone to bed when she heard him stirring. He walked into the room stared at her said nothing and started to undress.

"Norman we can't go on like this. Like it or not you have a responsibility for this child and you can't change the fact by trying to drink yourself into believing otherwise. I can't do this alone, but if you don't get yourself together then I will have to find some other way."

He stopped what he was doing for a moment looked again at her then responded.

"I'm having a real hard time accepting the idea that I'm going to be somebody's father. My father was never a real father to me and I don't see how I'm going to be a real father to this baby."

Even though his words were still somewhat slurred the message he was conveying was not difficult to understand. For the first time, Elena now understood why he was so against her having a baby. He was dealing with some childhood trauma of his own that had never been resolved. Confused and wondering why she had never been able to see this before even when she had been around his family several times before they were married. It was like a hidden secret that was protected by his whole clan and only those inside the inner, inner circle were privy to. Now that she was exposed to his secret she wasn't quite sure how to deal with it.

From that night on, as time passed, she at least was able to understand his position even while she had no remedy for how to console him. It seems that after he unburdened his weight that night, although his attitude was only slightly mitigated toward her condition, he no longer came home drunk nor did he do anything that would really upset her. When the time came and she had left her job to take her maternity leave she was at home. The pains were increasing as were the contractions so she knew it was time for her to get to the hospital. Arrangements had already been made and the next door neighbor called for a cab. Norman had gone to work, but when the neighbor called she reached him and said to get down to the hospital right away.

Upon arrival at Trinity Memorial she was admitted immediately and shortly thereafter went into labor. Norman got there soon after that and was met by the neighbor who told him about Elena's status. She was puzzled by the expression on his face that showed very little emotion one way or the other. He neither seemed to be happy or sad, but just accepting of the fact that the time had come. About another hour later the hospital nurse came out and announced to him that he was now the father of a beautiful healthy baby girl who weighed in at 7 lbs and 7ozs. Again the neighbor looked at him for some sign of emotion, but again surprisingly there was none. Both of them walked to the area where the baby's were on display and as he peered through the glass he exhibited for the first time a sign of some emotion. As he viewed the baby a slight smile came across his face which he had a hard time trying to hide.

That was the event three months ago that had now led up to this point. After Monica was born life in the apartment was turned upside down. A newborn baby presents a challenge to the most stalwart of parents, but when one of them refuses to participate in the duties that come with attending to the needs of the child then some type of disaster is bound to happen. From the time that Elena brought the baby into the house Norman acted as if he had nothing to do with whatever was required. Had it not been for the kind and friendly neighbor who doted on Elena as well as the baby, things might have been worse than what they were. For the first few weeks sleep was something that came at a premium. Norman had left the bedroom, where the crib was and started sleeping on the couch. Since the neighbor could not be there at all times, it was Elena who had to wake up whenever the baby cried.

His only contribution to the situation was that he continued to go to work and provided the necessities for the household such as groceries, baby products and the rent payments. Even though Elena was still drawing a modified paycheck during her leave, it was not sufficient to cover the unexpected costs of so many things. Frustration was building as she continued to try and be a good mother without his help, but the boiling point had now been reached. One day when he came home and she had had an extremely exhausting and challenging day she confronted him like he had never heard her before. Her voice was loud, but not quite a scream when she let him have it with nothing held back.

"Norman this can't go on like this. I am both mother and father to this child and it's got to stop. Now either you are going to help me raise her or there has to be some changes made. I know what your feelings were before, but now that we both have a responsibility to this baby, you can't pretend that there is nothing that you need to do to help. I can't help what happened between you and your father. The evil that he foisted upon you should not make you a carrier of that same sin. You have got to get over the hurt he put on you and begin to learn to love this child like a real father. Even while I was carrying her I could feel and sense the times when she was reacting to your diatribes and my emotional distress as a result. Now if you feel that you can't be the man that I married and the man I thought I loved then I have to do what I think will be best for her."

"Woman you brought all this on yourself. I asked you before she got here to do what would make the situation okay, but no you had to go on and have her anyway. Don't throw my father up in my face. He had some issues it's true, but he always put food on our table and we always had a place to sleep. He was never one to express any kind of love to any of us, not even to my mother that I could see, but that's the way he was. I don't know if that's the only reason that I didn't want this child, but you should have talked to me about having her before you did it. You talk about me not helping you with her. You're the one who is breast-feeding her, not me. You're the one who's not working and can sleep during the day. You're the one who is making my life a mess because of her. Now you talk about something must be done, yeah I agree with that and I'm about to make that decision for both of us."

When he finished talking, he stormed out the door failing to see the rage that was building up inside of her. The tears began to fall and the baby woke up adding her tearful contribution to the matter. After she composed herself enough to attend to Monica, she called her neighbot and asked her to come over.

"I know you must have heard us because these walls are not that thick."

"Yes I did and I really can't believe that man. Didn't you know what he was like before you married him?"

"I guess I didn't spend enough time observing his ways and most of all I believed I loved him. It never occurred to me that he had such a hatred for children especially since he comes from a large family. It was only recently that I found out what the reason was. His relationship with his father has caused him some real internal issues that I can't solve. He told me how he resented the lack of love in his household and how his father never showed any of them love. I know that must have been painful growing up, but he seemed to have managed it all the while we were dating. I never suspected how deep the hurt was and how much evil there must have been in that house. Anyway now I have to decide what to do about my situation and the baby's. I can't continue to do it all without some help. You have been a great help and I really appreciate you, but something has got to change."

"What are you going to do?"

"I don't know yet. That's why I called you over. What do you think I should do?"

"Girlfriend I love you like my own sister, but I'm really not the one you should be asking that kind of advice from, I have never been married, not even close and have never had to deal with what you're going through. If I can offer any kind of a suggestion at all it would be that you find someone who is qualified to advise you. What about your mother?"

"My mother is too far away and besides she's old and not in the best of health to be burdened with this kind of a problem. I wish my father was still living he would be here in a New York minute when I told him about what's happening, but then I would have to worry about what he would do to Norman. It would probably create a worse problem than what I have now."

They both laughed and for a minute they both relaxed. Then Elena continued.

"There must be some agency or somewhere I could go for help without exposing my deepest secrets. Since I'm not a battered woman I don't think that agency would be interested in talking with me and since I'm not on welfare yet they probably wouldn't be interested in me either. I really don't know where to turn."

For the next several minutes Trish, her neighbor, and Elena sat there not speaking but pondering her plight trying to come up with somewhere or some agency or institution that might be able to help her. Finally, Trish thought about a possible solution.

"You know now that I thought about it, there is a place that may be able to give you some sound advice if not even provide shelter should it come to that."

"Oh really and where is that?"

"A church."

"Church! What church you talking about?"

"You know – the one down there on Elmwood Avenue. I'm not a member and I don't go there, but there is a lady where I work who swears by it. She's always talking about how they help everybody and feed the poor and all that kind of stuff. Maybe if you try and get in touch with someone there they might be able to give you what you need.."

"I don't know about that. I haven't been to church since I was a little girl living with my parents. I wouldn't even feel right trying to get them to help me when I don't know anybody there. Besides it would be strange for me to just show up like I'm begging or something."

"From what this woman tells me it would not be like that at all. Tell you what Monday when I go back to work let me ask her what she thinks. Her name is Phyllis Ryder and she is one of the nicest people you want to know. At least let her talk with you and maybe you can work something out. If you don't mind I'll give her your number and ask her to get in touch with you."

"Yeah of course if you think she can do anything to help me then go ahead."

"By the way the name of that church is Holy Trinity Baptist Church and the pastor there is somebody named Reverend Dumas. She has been trying to get me to go with her there for I can't even remember how long, but it always seems that whenever I plan to go something else distracts me.. I will say one thing though, I have gone by that church many times late on a Sunday afternoon and judging from the size of it, if all the people that go there are really righteous people, like my co-worker, then someone should be able to provide some assistance."

"That sounds real promising and I look forward to hearing from her. You're sure it won't be an inconvenience imposing my burden on her."

:As I said she's always talking about how they help people so I have to believe she would love to have an opportunity to talk to you and I'll bet she will certainly try to get you to come to the church."

"Well if that's what it will take to get some help then that's what I will do for me and Monica."

Just as the two were ending their talk the sound of the key turning in the door was heard. Trish was startled at first and wasn't so sure after hearing the argument that happened before, that she might not be so welcome when he walked in. The door opened and he saw the two ladies sitting on the couch. It was late afternoon on this Saturday and it didn't appear that he had been drinking, but the way he looked at Trish gave her the feeling that she indeed was not welcome there. He didn't say anything to her and went straight into the bedroom, but from the look he gave she knew it was time for her to leave. Elena grabbed her hand as she got up to leave and told her how grateful she was for her just being there.

After Trish left, Elena wasn't sure whether she should go in there and confront him again, but since the baby was still in there asleep there really wasn't a choice. She walked in quietly and watched him for a minute reclining on the bed. Not saying anything she walked over to the crib and made sure everything was okay. It had finally reached the point where the baby was sleeping for long intervals and it was a welcome respite. When she turned around she was bracing to experience a continuation of the earlier argument, but she was surprised when he started talking with a slightly cordial tone.

"You know I've been doing some serious thinking about us and this baby. The things I said before I'm not sure that that's the answer to what's been happening to us since she arrived here. Leaving you is not really what I want to do and besides I don't have anywhere else to go anyway. Maybe we just have to figure out what it's going to take to make this thing work for all of us. I'm willing to try."

When he said that it was like a hundred pound weight had been lifted off her chest and she was able to breathe with an ease that she not been able to do for quite some time She continued to look at him without saying anything trying to see whether he was really being sincere or just stalling before the next storm could develop. It appeared after her assessment and looking deeply into his eyes that he might be telling the truth and some sort of reconciliation might be in order. She answered him with a mild tone of her own.

"You know I've been doing some thinking myself. When you stormed out of here just a little while ago, I seriously thought you might not be coming back. I was trying to decide just what I was going to do if that happened. You know Monica is all that matters to me and her welfare is my deepest concern. Whether you want to accept the fact that she is your child or not, I can't change how you feel, but you need to at least try to show her some love. Now if what you're saying about trying is true then I am ready and willing to do all that I can to make this a happy home for all of us. I don't need you to do everything, but I do need you to love me and her by doing what a good husband and father should. I know you are still hurting from your experience with your father, but that shouldn't carry over to how you treat your daughter."

"You're right and it's something I have to deal with."

When he finished talking she walked over embraced him then with a tender kiss she lay down beside him. It had been such a long time since they had had an intimate moment like this that it felt kind of strange for both of them.

It didn't lead to anything further because even though a truce had been achieved she was not quite ready to resume the relationship they had months ago. For her only time would tell whether he was really going to do what he said and if so then the deep intimacy could return.

After that exchange of some sorely needed honesty about their relationship and their situation it gave them a mutual feeling of relaxation. For some time the unspoken tension throughout the apartment was like the shadow of evil that hovers over a dying unconverted convict. The release of that tension gave them a feeling of joy even though both of them were not quite sure if this was to be an everlasting sensation. "Enjoy the moment while it lasts" he said to himself and maybe a lasting solution may come soon. She also had some inner thoughts that reflected on the joy of the moment, but for her it all depended on him how long it would last.

They spent the rest of the day playing with Monica in a fashion that they had not done since the baby entered the house. Watching her do some of the things that a now six month old does that makes anyone with a human spirit laugh, seemed to unite the family with a new bond that had not been shared before. To see each other smile at the baby's antics and to witness her attempting to imitate sounds she heard was gratifying. However, hearing Monica's first attempts at saying things like stop, no, bad and even hate were a stark indication to them of how much this baby's recording mechanism, which was always on, was taping their adult conversations. It was clear that what was being said by them in a heated moment was taken in word for word and now being regurgitated back in a mocking fashion. Although the baby could not yet formulate the words as clearly as she heard them the fact that she was trying to made them realize what impact they were having.

Recognizing that what they say to each other within the baby's hearing was going to be recorded, they both began making an effort to say only the things they could expect to be repeated. Since this pattern of behavior was something they had not practiced for a long time, it was taking some effort to be conscious of what they were saying and where it was being said. Not only did it have a positive impact on their relationship, but now they realized it was something they should have been doing even before the baby's arrival.

Now that it appeared they were moving in the right direction for becoming good parents there was something new that demanded their attention. Within a week Elena was going to have to return to work and they had not yet made any arrangements or provisions for what to do with Monica. It wasn't as if they were not aware that this was coming, but it seems that the time to act slipped up on them too quickly. Now that both of them had become so attached to watching the baby's development it was going to be hard to let her out of their sight for even a few hours. Even Norman who had seemingly made a transition from total rejection to learning how to appear to love the child was having a difficult time in agreeing to letting the baby leave their home. It had to be done, but who would they trust enough to give the job to.

Elena went to work searching the internet for services, while Norman talked to one of his sister's, who had three children. What they came up with was a short list of places they felt would be a good fit for their work schedule. The next step was to, after checking the credentials and reputation of each place, go and visit. Upon arrival at the one that topped their list, Happy Learning Center (let your child grow with us) from the outside it appeared to be just what they were looking for. It had a beautiful front façade that pictured several happy children playing. However, when they entered and were shown around the facility, the accommodations were less than sanitary and they observed what appeared to be a lack of monitoring the behavior of the many children who were there. Monica whispered to Norman "they have more kids then they have staff to watch them. Look at that one punching the other one." They walked around with the director for a few more minutes, asking questions about staffing and enrollment and of course the cost, then asked if they could have some privacy for a minute so they could make a decision. The director said "sure" and left them alone.

Elena told Norman she would be worried all day thinking that one of those bigger kids was punching on Monica. Norman readily agreed and a rejection decision was made. They called the director over and explained that there was one more place they wanted to look at then they would get back to him. Of course the director, not wanting to lose a potential enrollee, told them that there were only two slots left and they may be filled even today. The couple ignored his words bid him goodbye and walked out.

The second facility on the list was called "Precious Foundations (let us help build your child). When they arrived there although the outward appearance was not as nice as the first, it appeared to be well maintained. Once inside a much nicer presentation was given. While being shown around they noticed that the place was exceptionally clean and the number of children did not exceed the ratio to the staff. The kids appeared to be well behaved and the teachers were paying attention to the play of all. Elena told the director that their child was still in diapers so how do they handle that. The response was just what she wanted to hear so she asked him if he could give her and Norman a minute to discuss enrollment. After he left Elena said to Norman she felt good about this one, but they had not inquired about the cost. When they called the director back they told him they really liked the facility and asked what the cost would be. When he quoted them the price, the couple tried hard to hide their disappointment, but it was clearly out of the range of what they had considered they could afford. When they told the director the price was somewhat higher than they expected, he offered no sales pitch to engage them, but just said they carry an insurance policy that not only totally protects all of the children, but the staff as well This was great to hear, but it did not change the affordable factor

At the third place called "Dream Builder Academy" (We make it happen) neither Elena nor Norman were impressed with the outside. The advertisement they ran did not look anything like the actual place they were looking at. Norman immediately suggested they turn around because this can't be good. Elena said that since they were there they may as well take a look inside. Once inside the inward appearance belied that outward one. It was spotless. The director showed them around and introduced them to one of the teachers. Like the second place the children appeared to be well behaved and there seemed to be enough staff to properly oversee them. Elena was willing at this point to dismiss the outside appearance and she tried to convince Norman that this could be it. They called the director over and asked the cost. This time she also asked about insurance coverage. When the director responded he quoted them a price within their range, but when he referred to their minimal insurance coverage, it gave the couple pause. The question for them now was did they want to leave their child in a place that if something should happen they would have to pick up most of the bill. They finally decided to pass on this one also and go home and rethink their strategy.

Disappointed and frustrated at not being able to find an immediate solution to their child care problem they arrived at the apartment without any sense of new direction. Elena knew that there was always the internet to do a new search, but deep inside she felt that they would just run into the same type of issues they just experienced so that was out. Norman agreed but was unable to offer a new way to go. To add stress to their situation, Monica now decided to become cranky and unresponsive to being cuddled. The pacifier was ineffective and gentle rocking didn't help either. For once in a long time Norman had a positive suggestion. He remembered something from a long time ago when he watched one of his sisters deal with her baby who was about this age that teething may be the problem. Elena was surprised at his insight, but at this point she was willing to listen to any possible solution. Quickly she got back on the internet to find out what to do and immediately had more answers than she knew how to handle. The one that seemed the most feasible for her right now was the one that said for her to wash her hands then look in the baby's mouth to see possibly where the new growth might be happening. When discovered then gently massage the area until the relief the baby is seeking occurs. It was easy to tell where the pain might be because of the redness and swelling in the area. Elena was quick to apply the remedy and sure after a few minutes Monica ceased crying and began to suck on Elena's finger. At that point she realized the pacifier could now take over.. Then she continued to read more of the answers and found out that there were some Over The Counter (OTC) baby medications that could help ease the pain of this new stage of baby development. Norman left quickly to go out and find what they needed.

While this problem seemed to be solved temporarily, there was still the issue of what to do about a baby sitter or child care. There was no one in either family that was near enough or even trustworthy enough to be considered for letting a family member handle the task. So now what else was there to consider. For some reason whenever she got to this point she felt the need to call Trish because she always seemed to come up with a good answer. Although Trish, whose real name was Patricia Ramey, was not a favorite of Norman's because he thought she was too meddlesome in their business and she was always over at their house, because he had no other solution had to concede that she might be able to help.

The call was made and within the hour Trish came knocking at the door.

"Just a minute" Elena answered. "Trish is that you?"

"Of course – were you expecting somebody else?"

Elena opened the door and as Trish walked in Norman said a mild "hi how you doin'" and before waiting an answer immediately faded into the bedroom.

"Don't mind him we've just had a very challenging day trying to find someone to keep the baby when I go back to work next week. He's just tired."

"You know I don't pay much attention to him anyway. I'm just glad to see that you two are on much better terms now. It's good that I don't hear much screaming coming through my wall anymore."

They both laughed.

"Yes it seems like he has had an Epiphany or something because he has really mellowed over the last few weeks. Whatever it was that changed

I'm just glad about it. Anyway I called you over this time because as I said before I'm about to return to work and we need to get someone to care for Monica when I do. You got any suggestions?"

"You know I hate to keep bringing her up, but my co-worker Phyllis, who I told you about, has even talked to me bragging about the nursery they run at that church and how good it is for children in the community. Since you called me off from talking to her when you were having your other troubles, maybe this time I can get her to call you and talk to you about this. I don't know who runs it or what and how they charge, but I'm sure she'll be able to provide you with all the details. Why don't I talk to her on Monday and get her to call you. How's that?"

"That's great. It may be the answer we've been looking for."

"Okay then let me do that and we'll see what happens next. So what else is going on?"

"Well let me tell you about the latest thing with Monica. I believe she is teething because when we got back home earlier she started having a fit and there was nothing I could do to sooth her. I tried everything I know how to do but.........."

The two women continued talking for about another hour and a half with just the usual girl talk and Elena was glad to have her company. After their talk Elena felt more relaxed especially now feeling she had a possible solution to the child care problem so she went in to tell Norman. Since the baby was sleeping soundly Norman took advantage of the silence and took a nap also.

Quietly she tipped into the room and nudged him to wake up. It was only about 9:30 so she knew he wasn't in bed for the night.

"Wake up Norm I have something important to tell you."

He stirred turned over a couple of times and finally responded to what she was saying.

"Is that woman still here?"

"No she's gone home. She did leave us with some good information I think you'll be glad to hear."

"Good information coming from her – that would be a first."

Stop that, you know she does try to help – me at least. If you would be a little nicer to her you might see that clearer. Anyway what she gave us is a way to solve getting some child care for Monica. She said there is a co-worker of hers that belongs to that big church down there on Elmwood Avenue, you know the one I'm talking about."

"Yeah I do, so what?"

"Well she said the church has a nursery that we may be able to enroll the baby there. On Monday she will talk to her and get her to call me giving me the details. This may be the answer we need."

"Okay that sounds good as long as in the details she tells you that their nursery provides all the things we saw in all those other places - especially in the insurance area."

"I feel good about this and I think a church would have thought about that and made provisions. At least it sounds like a plan we could use but we won't know anything for sure until after I talk with the woman."

"I'm good with that so let's see what happens."

They both agreed with what could be the answer to their problem so the rest of the night was pleasant and relaxing.

On Monday late that afternoon Elena received a call from Phyllis.

Ring, ring, ring, ring.

"Hello."

"Hello is this Mrs. Miller?

"Yes it is who's calling?"

"Hi my name is Phyllis Ryder a friend of Trish Ramey. She asked me to give you a call about the nursery at my church. Are you busy now or do you have a few minutes to talk?"

"No I'm not busy and so glad you called. I don't know how much Trish told you about us, but we need to find somewhere to place our baby quickly because I am about to go back to work, Trish suggested that your nursery might be a good place for her. Can you tell me about it?"

"I would be happy to give you all the information you need. As far as getting the baby in quickly, you are blessed because of the timing. It just so happens that for the next couple of weeks we are having an open enrollment for two slots that have just become available. Let me start by telling you about what our mission is."

Phyllis went on to tell Elena all about the nursery, what they provide, who are the teachers, maintenance of the facility etc. The part that was most appealing to Elena was the cost. It was well within what she and Norman could afford and as it was explained to her the church receives a renewable grant from the federal government every two years that helps pay for a lot of the expenses.

This was certainly the answer they were looking for and she couldn't wait to tell him when he got home. After that phone call she tried to call Trish to thank her, but she was unavailable. Feeling very excited about what they were going to be able to do for Monica, she started looking at all of the things the baby would need before entering the nursery. There was just one thing that she had to discuss with Norman before anything was finalized however. Although it was clearly said that they did not have to join the church and become members in order to enroll Monica, Phyllis mentioned it more than once that they would encourage it. Elena was not sure how Norman would react to this because they were definitely not church going people.

As it turned out when he got home and after she fed him a nice dinner she brought up the question. To her surprise he was not totally against it, but he said "if that's what it takes to get her in that place then that's what they will do." With that hurdle crossed they both began to prepare to go down to the church and take care of the final arrangements for enrolling Monica.

The following week after Elena returned to work and Monica was enrolled safely in the church nursery the weeks just seemed to fly by. Monica was now approaching her first birthday and it was an exciting time for the couple. Elena wanted to throw a big party and invite all of the nursery children and parents to the event, but Norman was solidly against it saying they didn't need to do all that. He just wanted to have a quiet celebration with just the three of them. Sadly, Elena gave in.

One week before the birthday celebration was to take place Norman received a telephone call from his sister in South Carolina. She informed him that his father had become very ill and was now under hospice care at the local hospital. Unbeknownst to Norman his father had left the city about a year and a half ago to go down and live with his oldest daughter. Until now she had not told any of the other children about this status because it was his wish. Emily, the daughter, was the only sibling who had a good relationship with him and the other siblings could never understand why that was. Even when their mother passed away a few years ago it was never made clear. Now that Robert Miller, the father, was at the end of his life, when Emily talked to Norman she told him that the father only wanted to see him, not the others. Norman was having a hard time processing this because he felt that least of all he would be the one requested to attend.

When Norman discussed the matter with Elena she said this may be a good opportunity for him to be reconciled with his dad and maybe clarify some things he never knew about him. Norman listened and after giving her words some thought he agreed and started to make arrangements to go. He was still confused though about why his father did not want the others to know about his condition and it really bothered him. Deep inside, he wrestled with defying Emily's instruction about not getting in touch with the other five siblings and decided he was going to do it anyway. When he reached each one individually and told them they were just as surprised as he was, but none of them committed to go and see him.

Norman received the bad news on Wednesday and booked a flight for the following morning. He arrived at Charleston International Airport about 11:00 O'clock and within the next hour he was on his way to the hospital. He had reserved a hotel room, but didn't stop to check in just went straight to the hospital. Staying with his sister was not an option for him because he hadn't seen or talked to her for a long time and it would be an uncomfortable visit. When he got to the hospital and identified himself he was given a brief explanation regarding his father's condition and then escorted to the section reserved for hospice patients. Just outside the room he stopped for a minute or two trying to prepare himself for what was about to happen. When he finally walked in there was his sister Emily sitting by the bed holding their father's hand. She greeted Norman warmly and then turned to Robert and said: "look whose here." The father in his very weak condition managed to raise his head and through somewhat glazed eyes looked at Norman intently and tried to raise his right hand. Norman stepped forward took hold of it and gently shook it. After that the old man motioned to Emily that he wanted to be alone with Norman so she got up and walked out.

What happened next was the last thing Norman could ever have imagined or expected. His father began speaking in some kind of dialect that Norman had never heard before and the words, though more mumbled than clear, sounded like a curse rather than any kind of blessing. The old man's final gesture was to raise his left hand and point it at Norman. After that he dropped his hand closed his eyes and departed this world. Norman was shocked because he felt like all the evil that was in the man had been somehow passed on to him. He shuddered and had to sit down looking at the peaceful expression on his father's face. Moments later he got up went outside and found Emily to bring her back into the room. She was not surprised and told her brother she guessed that's all he was waiting for. She then kissed her father's forehead then went out and found the attendant nurse who took over.

Norman went home with Emily and they talked extensively about what kind of a funeral they should try to have. He was still very uncomfortable about not having told their siblings about this and how could they not have them come to whatever arrangements are made. After listening to her brother's concerns, Emily got up and retrieved a piece of paper from a dresser drawer. On that paper Robert had specifically instructed in his last wishes that only the two of them be at his funeral and he wanted to be burned. He didn't use the word cremate but specifically said burned. Norman thought this very strange, but that gesture that his father did at the hospital to him was even more strange. The two siblings spent the next few hours going over who to call and how were they going to get it done.

At that point, Norman needed to call Elena and let her know what had happened so he asked to use the phone and said he would reverse the charges because he was calling home. Emily told him he didn't have to do that so he just made the call. Norman explained to Elena that his father had passed and he was going to have to spend a few days here to take care of the funeral. Elena asked him if he was alright and wanted to know if had gotten anything resolved about their relationship. Norman hesitated answering, but finally said he would tell her all about that when he got home.

The next day after all of the necessary calls had been made and the final arrangements were set in place, there was nothing else for them to do. The cremation was to take place on Saturday at a local mortuary and his ashes would be given to Emily. Norman spent the rest of his time in his hotel room pondering what that hospital ritual was all about and whether anything had been done to him. Although he was not a believer in that kind of thing he was well aware that in certain parts of South Carolina, especially the islands where his father was from, they practiced a kind of mock religion that took into account some evil practices. His mind was putting him in a rather confused and nervous state so to relieve the tension he took a few drinks of the whiskey he purchased earlier, to settle him. Before long he was nodding and then went to sleep.

The next day, the day of the cremation, he got up early even though he was experiencing some ill effects from last night's indiscretion. The funeral director gave a brief eulogy and then proceeded to show them to the crematory where the final act was performed. The ashes were gathered and placed in an urn then handed to Emily. That was it - it was done. After the ceremony, Norman wasted no time in making a hasty exit headed to the airport. There was no long goodbye exchange between him and his sister, neither was there any commitment to visit again or even call to stay in touch. The taxi ride for him seemed to take forever in getting there as his anxiety was building up. He was able to board in plenty of time and the flight took off as scheduled which was a pleasant relief from his recent ordeal.

Arriving at EWR (Newark International Airport) around 1:00 O'clock he proceeded to hail a taxi for the ride home. About 45 minutes later he walked through the door to the apartment immediately unpacked and sat down on the bed staring out the window. Since it was still early Elena had not come home yet so he had time to ponder the events of the last three days. Three hours later when she walked in with Monica in her arms she found him still sitting on the bed staring out the window. It appeared like he was in some kind of hypnotic state and when she called to him he did not respond immediately.

"Norman, Norman are you alright?"

Several minutes later he finally answered.

"Yeah I guess I am it's just that these last few day have been a real weird experience and I can't get it out of my mind."

"Let me put Monica in her bed then we can talk okay? Are you hungry?"

"No I'm fine. You go ahead."

Once his response seemed to her like he had regained his sanity, she went and took care of Monica. When she returned he had gotten up from the bed and was now sitting at the kitchen table She looked him over again and repeated her words about his condition. He assured her he was okay and started telling her all about what happened. When he finished though

Elena agreed it was kind of weird she didn't think any more about it and started to prepare dinner.

For the next few days everything occurred as it normally would and life seemed fine until he started to exhibit some strange behavior. Normally he would be the first one up in the morning and also the first to arrive at work. Now he was late in getting up and when he did he was starting to mumble to himself words she couldn't understand. Even when he came home he had no time for the baby and would ignore watching her playful ways. There were other small behaviors that also bothered her, but she thought he just needed to adjust to the loss of his father and time would take care of that. The odd behaviors however, were increasing as were her concerns. She didn't take any action to confront him about it hoping it would go away and he would really return to normal soon.

However, It was late one night when she felt him get up out of the bed and go into the room where Monica was now sleeping. At first she thought he was going to the bathroom then she heard Monica's door open. Out of curiosity she got up and followed. When she peered into the room, only the night light was on, but the shock on her face from what she saw made her gasp as she watched what was about to happen.

CHAPTER 2
The Incident

Global Communication Technologies (GCT) the telephone service company where both Elena and Norman worked was a large corporation that employed over 30,000 people worldwide. He had been employed there now almost ten years and she came on a few years later at seven. As a line utility worker he was often asked to work several hours overtime handling emergency call situations. Before the baby arrived this was not a problem for the couple and they came to enjoy the extra bonus income. When Monica arrived things became a little different because of the amount of undue stress it was placing on Elena. Often she was the one who had to pick up the baby from the nursery and perform many other errands that she would like for him to do. The extra money was good, but the strain on her personal life style was becoming a concern.

They had met at one of the company's annual team building picnics where it was like a day off for the whole mid-town office. During one of the exercises she was partnered with him and it seemed like they just enjoyed each other's efforts at the task so much that even after that day they continued to see each other. They began dating and it was not long before the relationship took on a serious turn. It was only a little over a year before he asked her to marry him and she said yes. They had never really gotten to know each other. Of course there were intimate times when they shared what they considered real love, but it was not as if they were able to get to know the person that was inside of the outward façade. Even though Elena visited several times with his family there were secrets about them she was never made privy to.

Elena's family consisted of her mother and father and one brother, who all lived far away in two different states. Her parents resided in Atlanta, Georgia and her brother in Chicago. Originally they lived in Brooklyn,

New York where both of the children were born, but after the children finished their education, mom and dad decided to move south. Her brother went west on a football scholarship playing for the University of Illinois and after graduation decided to remain in Chicago. For the early years of her life she remained close to her family, but as time passed the relationship waned. Then her father passed and her mother started experiencing some health issues. She visited her mother as often as she could, but once she married even the visits became fewer and far between. Norman never got to meet any of them.

For the first three years they enjoyed each other life was good and the future seemed promising. It was not until she became pregnant that there was a rude awakening for both of them. Elena never realized how much he didn't want children and the pregnancy created a serious problem for the couple. After the baby was born it took quite some time before he made an adjustment and learned to at least try and love the baby. As time passed and Monica, the baby, was now about to enjoy her first birthday, Norman received a telephone call from his sister who told him about the condition of his father. A short time later his father passed, but not before performing a ritual that changed him.

After his father's passing, Norman began to exhibit strange behaviors and Elena was becoming greatly concerned. She would observe him doing and mumbling odd things, but she was hoping that it was just a phase he was going through as a result of his father's death. It was not until one night when he got up in the middle of the night and entered the baby's room that she thought something was wrong. She felt him get up and out of bed so she followed him. When she got to Monica's room she was horrified at what she saw. Even though only the night light was still on she could see him holding the baby high up in the air and mumbling some incomprehensible words. Elena screamed and rushed at him, but before she got there he threw the baby down into her crib and ran out of the room. Elena picked up the crying child and examined her intently. There were no outward signs of any physical damage, but the trauma the baby must have felt would be life scarring. Elena gently rocked the baby for several minutes until it appeared she was okay and gently placed her back in the crib. Then she went out to confront Norman.

There he was sitting at the kitchen table as though nothing had happened. Elena sat down in one of the chairs opposite him and for a moment just looked at him. He appeared to be different. There was no life in his eyes and the darkness in them frightened her. She tried speaking softly to him hoping to get him to tell what was wrong and why did he do what he did to the baby.

"Norman what is happening to you? Do you even know what you just did?"

He did not respond, but just sat there staring into space at nothing. She tried again.

"Norman talk to me. I need to understand what you're going through. I can't let you harm our child. Please tell me what's wrong. We need to get you some help."

Again he did not respond, but continued to sit there staring at nothing. At this point she was at a loss as to what to do. She considered calling the emergency number for help but then because it was so late she decided to just let him sit there and watch him. Eventually he put his head down on the table and went to sleep. She went and got a blanket threw it over him and let him continue. Then she went picked up Monica and put her in the bed with her. The rest of the night was uneventful, but her sleep was not peaceful because she was always listening for him to get up. .

It was only a few hours later when the sun was making its appearance, she awakened from what was a very disturbing night. Fortunately the baby slept through the rest of night and when Elena woke her up she did not appear to have suffered any effects from what happened. She left the baby in the bed and went to the kitchen to see about her husband. Apparently, without her hearing it he got up and left the apartment. When she saw him last he only had on his nightclothes and that really worried her. It was only a few minutes later that the phone rang. At first it startled her wondering who would be calling at this hour, but then she composed herself long enough to pick up the receiver.

"Hello."

"Hello is this Mrs. Miller?"

"Yes it is who's calling?"

"This is Sergeant Gibson down at the 5th police precinct. We have a man here who says he's your husband. We found him wondering around the street in only his pajamas and when we questioned him at first he couldn't recall who he was or where he lived. We brought him here gave him some hot coffee and eventually he started to speak. That's when he said you are his wife and gave us this number. Is your husband missing?"

"Yes officer that is probably him. He must have gone out very early this morning without me knowing anything about it. He's been going through some stressful events lately and has not been himself. Did he do anything wrong? Has he been arrested?"

"No ma'am the only thing we could charge him with is indecent exposure which we're not going to do since you corroborate his story, but we want to know whether we should bring him there. Is everything alright at your house?"

"Yes officer we're okay. Please just bring him home and we'll handle it."

"Okay Mrs. Miller Within the hour one of our officers will bring him there."

The conversation ended and Elena now had a decision to make. When he got home what should she do? It was a weekday and she had to go to work. She could take Monica to the nursery as she normally did, but should she leave Norman here by himself, not knowing really what was wrong with him. There was not a lot of time for her to figure out what to do before the doorbell rang.

Brrring, bring.

"Who is it?"

"Police we have your husband here with us."

"Just a minute."

Monica put on a robe and wrapped it around her tightly, then answered the door. There he ws standing between the two police officers looking like a humble street beggar. The officers had wrapped a blanket around him which they asked that he give back. They walked him into the apartment and sat him down on the couch. Then they asked her if there was anything she wanted them to do before they left. She answered no and they went. Now unable to decide what should be done next she had to figure out what first to do with Monica then Norman. There was still enough time for her to get dressed, take the baby to the nursery and get to work on time, but what about him. Even now she was afraid to leave him alone with the baby while she showered and got dressed. Could he be trusted alone with her even that short period of time? She took a long look at him sitting there and decided he was not a threat. He was just sitting there staring at the ceiling. There was no expression on his face it was as if his body was there, but his mind was somewhere else. Given the appearance of this docile state, she went ahead and prepared to take Monica to the nursery and then go to work.

As she was about to leave the apartment, he stood up and asked her where she was going with his baby. His eyes were fixated on Monica as if he was going to cause harm. Elena held the baby closer and left without answering his question. After getting Monica settled at the nursery, Elena arrived at work and the first call she made was to the apartment. The phone rang for several minutes with no answer. This meant he had turned off the machine or disconnected it. She waited for about an hour then tried calling again. Same result. This time she was afraid that he had done something rash. She could have had no idea how right she was.

About a half hour after she left the apartment Norman went to the nursery demanding that the teachers hand over his child. The head supervisor looked at his disheveled appearance and especially the sinister look in his eyes and refused to comply with his demand. He was still clad in his pajama top but had at least put on pants. When he was denied even access to the nursery his belligerent attitude became exasperating and the supervisor was frightened. A teacher standing nearby heard the loud heated conversation and called the police. Within minutes a patrol car arrived and took Norman into custody. Strangely, it was the same two officers who had picked him up earlier that morning. This time he was arrested and charged with disorderly conduct and making violent threats against a church worker.

The police did not have Elena's work number so she could not be contacted there and calls made to the number they had used before went unanswered. It was only because Elena was suspicious about what he might do that she called the nursery and was told the whole story. At work she told her supervisor that she had an emergency at home and needed to take some time off. He didn't hesitate in granting permission and said he hoped everything would be alright. She bolted out of the office building headed for the precinct and arrived shortly thereafter. After identifying herself she spoke to a Lieutenant there who explained what the charges were and what she needed to do. He also cautioned her because he was acting very strange and talking incoherently. Elena asked the officer what he thought she should do and he advised that she should contact someone in the psychiatric unit at the hospital and ask for him to be seen. Elena said she would do that, but what would happen to him now. The officer told her they couldn't hold him much longer on the charges he was booked under and unless there was some intervention by the hospital they would have to release him. Elena thanked him and left without seeing Norman.

She arrived at Trinity Memorial within the hour and asked at the reception desk if there was someone she could talk to about a situation she was having with someone who may be having a mental breakdown. The receptionist was very helpful and directed her to a social service component of the hospital where she was able to talk with a service person right away.

"Come in, come in may I help you?" said the male specialist.

"Yes I hope you can. It's regarding my husband who I believe is having a mental breakdown."

"Okay please sit down and let me take some information about the matter. What is your name and his?"

Elena went on to provide the specialist with all the information he required and after him hearing where Norman currently was he quickly pointed out that unless she was willing to have him brought here to the hospital and consent to him being examined, then there was not much they could do.

"If that's what it will take to get him some help, then I'm certainly willing to do that. How soon can he be picked up and brought here?"

"Well I have already assigned you a case number but since this is not an emergency it depends on who is available to go and get him."

"Elena explained to him that the police are going to release him back on the street shortly because they can't hold him longer. In his present state of mind I don't want him coming back to the house. I have an infant that he may try to hurt."

"Oh! In that case and under those circumstances I can have the police bring him here and we can set up an expedited examination."

"That would be the right thing to do. What do you need from me?"

"Nothing - you've already provided me with the information I need to get started. I just need for you to sign these forms and I personally will call the precinct and ask them to escort him here. What was the name of the officer you spoke with so I can deal directly with him or her.?"

"It was a man and his name was Lieutenant Childress. He gave me his card so here is his direct reach number."

Elena handed the card to the specialist and sat there when he made the call. He was able to make contact with the Lieutenant and the process for getting Norman brought to the hospital was started. Next the specialist made arrangements for a staff psychiatrist to examine Norman as soon as possible upon his arrival. At this point Elena felt a great relief that something was going to be done to help her husband. In the back of her mind though she couldn't help from thinking about whether all this was a result of his visit with his father at the funeral. He had tried to tell her about the thing his father did, but she dismissed it and didn't give it any more thought until now.

The arrangements were carried out and two hours later Norman was brought to the hospital in restraints. Apparently his condition had worsened and he started acting violently toward the policemen. The hospital security received him and he was placed in the psychiatric ward. Elena was still there and she witnessed how he was brought in. He seemed like he was in another world except for his attempts to get free. He continued to mumble incoherently and even when he saw her it appeared he had no recollection of who she was. This really bothered her and the tears started to well up in her eyes.

Once he was placed in the examination room she was not permitted to go in, but the doctor talked to her at length before he started and asked her for any details she could provide that may have lead up to this condition. She was reluctant to tell him about the funeral episode because she had not believed yet that could be the cause. When she finished giving everything else she felt may have contributed, including his reaction to the baby, the doctor went in and began his examination.

Norman was still in restraints when the doctor had him placed in a comfortable chair and he started to question him. For the first several minutes Norman just looked at him with an evil stare and refused to say anything. The doctor, despite Norman's stare, kept on talking to him and asking questions. Eventually Norman's eyes seem to clear up and he started to answer the questions.

"Do you know who you are?"

"Yeah I know and what the Hell am I doing here tied up like some kinda animal?"

"Can you tell me your name?"

"Yeah – it's Norman Miller. What's yours?"

"I'm Doctor Danforth and we need to talk about you not me. Do you remember why you were brought here?"

"Kinda – I went to visit my daughter at her school and they gave me a hard time when I wanted to take her home."

"It was early in the morning and she just got there. Why did you want to take her back home?"

"'Cause she don't belong there. She belong with me."

"Can you tell me why you think that is?"

"They got bad people there who are trying to hurt her. I want to protect her."

"I've been told that you're the one who wants to hurt her. Is that true?"

"Nah – not me I've been sent to protect her."

"Who sent you to do that?"

"The angel with the black wings and funny looking face. He told me I need to get her."

"Okay now where did you see this angel?"

"I see him all the time. He walks and talks with me."

"When did you first start seeing this angel?"

"A month or so ago he come to me when my father went away.

"You say your father went away. What do you mean?"

" You know - he went to that other place."

"No I don't know. Can you describe what that other place is?"

"Man – you know. That place where men like him go to be forever." The same place where the angel come from."

"You mean your father died don't you?"

"No he don't die he just went to that other place."

" Okay - now does this angel who talks to you have a name?"

"Yeah he told me to call him Massa-Baal."

The questioning went on for about two and a half hours when the doctor finally came out and talked with Elena.

"Your husband is definitely delusional and suffering from some type of trauma he may have experienced, perhaps recently. How long has he been like this?"

"He started behaving strange ever since he came back from attending his father's funeral two month's ago. "

"Yes I got that impression that something like that may have happened. Was he very close to his father?"

"No they have been estranged for some time ever since he was a young adult. Why do you ask?"

"I believe whatever happened at that event he must have suffered some type of trauma that has left an indelible impression on him that is causing an escape from reality."

"I want to keep him here for at least two more days so I can examine him further. I believe possibly exposing him to what we call Regression Hypnosis Therapy may determine how deep his psychotic state is. Of course you need to consent to this and you're welcome to attend the session."

"If it's going to help him certainly I agree to whatever it takes. When will you do it?"

"As I said I want to talk with him a little more without the procedure, then I will determine if that may give us a better insight into his condition. If I decide to go ahead with it, I will schedule it for Wednesday at 9:00 am. I will have someone contact you the day before to confirm. Can you be here?"

"Yes I can come. Now I think you said us. Who else is going to be involved?"

"We have a team here that I would like to consult with regarding this case. From what your husband has been saying there may be more to this case than what is obvious."

Elena went on talking with the doctor asking more questions for a while longer, then satisfied with all of his answers she left the hospital. Her next stop was at the nursery. She wanted to know exactly what happened. The head instructor gave greeting and invited her into his office.

"I'm glad you came. I called your house a little while ago, but there was no answer and I couldn't leave a message. We have never had anything like what happened this morning here. Is your husband alright?"

"I apologize for his behavior it must have been a little scary for your staff. He's been going through some rough times lately ever since his father died a couple of months ago. He's at the hospital now getting some treatment I hope will be able to help him. Anyway I wanted to thank you and your staff for how you handled the situation without him or anybody else getting hurt."

"We did what we're supposed to do. Our first priority is to protect these children and do whatever it takes to ensure that happens."

"Well again I thank you. I'm going to look in on Monica now and I'll pick up her at the usual time. "

"Okay fine Mrs. Miller I will see you later."

Elena left the office and went into the nursery. Monica was there looking as happy as could be playing on the carpet with one of the other kids. Elena felt a sigh of relief knowing that things could possibly have turned out very differently this day if Norman was able to carry out his intent.

When she arrived home it was still early before she would have to go back to the nursery and pick up her child, so she decided to take a nap and refresh. Just as she was just getting into a sleep state, the phone rang. Not wanting to get right up she let it ring thinking the answering machine would activate. When the ringing went on for more than the programmed number of rings, she remembered that Norman must have disconnected the machine so she got up. By the time she got to the phone it had stopped ringing. She looked at the caller ID to see who it was and it said name unavailable. This started her wondering who it might have been that would not have a name recognition. Moments later it rang again while she was still there and she looked at the caller ID which again said name unavailable. At first she hesitated answering thinking whoever it was that wouldn't have an ID she may not want to talk to. Curiosity made her pickup.

"Hello."

"Hello is this Elena Miller?"

"Yes – who's calling?"

"Hi my name is Beverly Winstatt Norman's sister. You may not remember me, but we met a few years ago when you came to our house while you and my brother were still dating. I was Beverly Miller then, but

I've since married. Did I catch you at a bad time or can you talk for a few minutes?"

"Oh hi, no I'm okay to talk for a few minutes, but I do have to go and pick up my daughter soon. I do remember you. It seems you are the one that's just a couple of years older than Norman is that right?"

"Yes I'm the one closest to him. The reason why I'm calling you now is that the rest of us, that is his other siblings are wondering what happened with my father. Norman called us and said he was in bad shape, but that's the last we heard from him. We just would like to know whether he passed or not, so we can put this thing to rest. Is Norman there?"

"No I'm sorry he's not here now, but I'll give him your message and ask him to call you. Does he have your number I notice it did not come up on the caller ID?"

"No we have a private listing because of some of the calls we had been getting a while ago. I'll give it to you. Are you ready?"

"Yes just give me a minute to get something to write with. Okay what is it?"

"The telephone number here is (906) 637 - ****. Please ask him to call me soon as he can so I can talk to him then let the others know what the situation is. Not that we want to send flowers or anything - we just would like to know what happened."

"Okay I'll give him your number when he returns."

Elena didn't want to let her know what was happening with her brother just yet. She wanted to wait until the doctor could give her some more definitive information about what really was wrong with him and will he be alright after some treatment. As far as Beverly was concerned, she would just have to wait. Elena looked at the clock and it was now time for her to go and pick-up Monica.

The following day, late that afternoon while she was still at work, she received a call from the doctor's office. The day nurse told her that the nurse practitioner who was on duty overnight had reported that Norman had some kind of psychotic episode and had to be sedated. This call was to advise her that the doctor wanted to go ahead with the procedure he discussed with her early tomorrow morning. Could she come to the hospital at 9:00 am? Elena was alarmed by the report, but said she would be there.

Promptly at a few minutes before 9, she arrived at the hospital and was escorted to the area where the doctor was. He thanked her for being on time and gave her a brief overview of what was about to happen. She nodded her understanding and followed him into a semi-lit room where Norman was sitting in a reclined position in a chair. Although he had restraints on his upper body his legs were free. He didn't appear to be fully conscious, but rather in a semi-alert state. The doctor asked her to be seated in a far corner and not to say anything unless she was asked to. Again she nodded her head in agreement and the session began.

The doctor then administered a needle into Norman's arm and asked him to begin counting backward from 100.

"100, 99, 98, 97, 96, 95 94, 9………… "

By the time he reached 94 whatever medication that had been administered was taking effect.

"Norman can you hear me?"

"Yes I hear you."

"I want you to listen only to the sound of my voice and nothing else. Will you do that?"

"Yes."

"Now I want you to go back to the time and place where you began feeling troubled."

A few seconds passed then Norman clenched his fists violently and although his eyes were closed they started blinking rapidly. The doctor waited a few more seconds then continued.

"Norman I want you to completely relax."

Seconds passed again then Norman unclenched his fists and the blinking stopped.

"Do you know where you are now?"

"Yes."

"Where are you?"

"At the hospital."

"What hospital?"

"Carolina General."

"What day is it?"

"Thursday."

"What do you see?"

"Nothing. It's very dark."

"Can you see any light at all?"

"No. Only darkness."

"Now I want you to focus and find the light. There must be a light somewhere. Can you do that?"

"Yes, yes now I see a light, but it's very dim."

"Okay now move toward the light. Is there anyone else there with you?"

"Yes. There's a man with black wings and a distorted face."

"What is he doing?"

There was no answer. The session went on for two hours and at each interval with certain questions, Norman became agitated and violent pulling at his restraints.

Norman's fists again clenched and his eyes blinked rapidly. The doctor felt it was time to end this session. Finally the doctor awakened him.

"Norman I'm going to count to three and when I finish I want you to slowly come back to the present – today. Will you do that?"

There was a short pause.

"One - two - three."

Norman's fists unclenched, his eyes stopped blinking and opened. He was awake, but his stare was blank. The doctor then pressed a button on a wrist band he was wearing and the door opened. Two large male attendants who were waiting outside walked into the room.

"Please take Mr. Miller back to his room, put him in his bed and let him sleep. Be sure to keep him restrained."

The doctor then led Elena into his office.

"Something really bad happened at that hospital before the funeral that is deeply embedded in his psyche. I'm afraid I am going to have to recommend that he be held here for some time. This is not going to be an easy case to resolve."

Elena was totally not prepared to hear the words coming out of the doctor's mouth.

"When you say some time what exactly does that mean?"

"It could be days, weeks or even months. Until I'm able to discover what it was that happened and pinpoint the source, he will continue to have these psychotic episodes and he may be a danger to others or even himself. For some reason he is protecting the source and I can't get in yet. I think though with a little time I will be able to break through that barrier. Now I will need you to sign some forms allowing us to commit him for an extended stay here."

"What is all that going to cost?"

"From what I understand he has very good insurance and for something like this it should be fully covered."

At that point Elena wasn't sure how she should feel. Should she be glad that insurance will cover his stay or should she be concerned that the doctor still really didn't know what was wrong with him. Either way there was nothing more she could do now. She signed the necessary forms and went home. The rest of the day until it was time to go to the nursery and pick-up Monica, she began pondering what she was going to do about their bills. It was good that insurance was paying the hospital, but what about the rest of the bills if he had to be gone for months. Her mind's eye saw no clear picture on what solution was available. Anxiety was building up and her strength was going down.

For the next few days that turned into weeks and finally four months from the time Norman wa admitted, Elena was barely able to make ends meet. She had delved into their meager savings until that resource was just about depleted. Then the notice came advising her that the insurance coverage was about to end. Her frustration level had reached its zenith and she was at a loss as to what to do or where to turn for help. She was doing the best she could to shield Monica from her emotional distress and tried to keep on a happy face in her presence. Each day however, seemed to present a new challenge and her own mental health and stability was at risk. She finally reached the point where as a last resort and in her mind what would be best for Monica, decided to investigate giving her up for adoption.

Time continued to move on and Norman had been transferred to a long term mental institution where the state was footing the bill. Monica was now 5 going on six and about to reach the stage where she would complete her pre-school training and age out of the nursery where she had been raised. She would be ready to enter the public school kindergarten. For Elena this was a joy and a sad state. The thought of having to give her up to adoption after she had observed, as well as her nursery school teachers, that she was an exceptionally gifted child, but needed close nurturing and guidance because of her ability to pick-up on things so quickly, was depressing.

As she usually did when she was burdened with a difficult problem she consulted with Trish.

"I just can't do this anymore. I am out of ideas on how to keep up this front for her sake. I know she's beginning to pick-up on how things are changing. There's no telling when or if Norman will get better and I have maxed out every credit card we have. I've reached the point where I don't have any solutions at all. Adoption seems like the only answer. I have investigated how to start the process and now I think I'm ready to do it. I just can't see any other way that would be best for her."

"I can't say that I know how you feel, because honestly I don't. Nothing like this has ever happened to or for me. Wish I could be of more help. But if there's anything I can help with, besides give you money which I don't have, then I'm willing to do it. I have watched Monica grow and there is no question she is a beautiful girl and smart also. She's going to be a heartbreaker somewhere along the line. Her future can have great possibilities if the fates don't get in the way and spoil it. I really hate to see you have to give her up for someone else to finish raising her, but like you I don't have any solutions either. Maybe that's the best thing for her. Perhaps she'll get adopted by some wealthy family who will love her like we do and give her the kind of life she deserves. What's your next step?"

"Tomorrow I'm going down to the social service agency and talk to one of their counselors about what I need to do. Would you like to come along?"

"Girlfriend you know I got your back, but that's one thing I just can't bring myself to help you do. I would probably fall apart just thinking about what is happening and mess up you getting the best advice from whomever you talk to. No I think you need to do this one alone."

"Okay then that's what I have to do."

That conversation ended and they moved on to a different subject.

The next day Elena was able to get off a little early and keep her appointment for 3:30 pm at the social service agency. Arrangements had been made for someone at the nursery to keep Monica a little longer than normal and Elena was thankful for that courtesy. The teacher who agreed to stay was not going to charge any extra because all of them at the school had fallen in love with Monica and were willing to do whatever they could to assist Elena. It was no secret what she was going through in light of her husband's condition so most of them were happy to help in any way they could. At the agency Elena was directed to an office on the third floor of the building that seemed to be crowded with many people. She wondered how many of them were there for the same reason as she was. Her curiosity was answered quickly when she saw most of them lining up in a line that led to unemployment registration. The others headed toward a smaller line leading to immigration assistance.

When she got to the office of the person she was scheduled to meet with she was a bit surprised at how young the service provider was. To herself Elena was saying how much could this person know about adoptions. She looked like she could be ready for adoption herself. Getting past that first thought she was impressed with the pleasant greeting offered and was invited to take a seat next to the desk.

"Hi Mrs. Miller my name is Cassandra and I'm going to try and help you. I know this must be a very difficult decision for you and I will be as accommodating as possible."

When she said that Elena's perception of her changed and she was looking forward to working with her.

"We need to do some preliminary paper work to get things started so why don't I just give you the forms that need to be completed and you can take them to that table over there and fill them out. There's no rush so please be as accurate as you can with your answers. It's very important that the information you put on these forms be correct because they will be looked at by legal services and sometime they can be a bit testy when it comes to these proceedings. Monica took the documents went over to the table and started filling them out. The first two pages were basically asking for her personal bio so she had no problem with the answers. However, when she got to page 3 the questions became a little more inquisitive about the reason(s) she wanted to give up her child. The deep probing in this section seemed to continue on forever, but in reality it was just for the next five pages. To her the questions now appeared to be analyzing her motives rather than asking for a statement. She took her time considering her answers and after several minutes she finished and went back to the staffer's desk.

"Okay here it is now what?"

"Just one more thing. Do you have a recent picture of the child that you are willing to part with? It is for our files and cannot be returned. If you don't have one you can bring her here and we will provide that service."

"I have a recent nursery class picture that she is prominently featured in. Will that do?"

"Oh no I'm sorry Mrs. Miller it must be a full body image of the child by herself. As I said I can set up an appointment for you now and you can bring her here for the shot. Or you can have it done wherever you like, but we do need the picture for the file before we can present the case for adoption. Would you like for me to schedule an appointment with our photographer?"

"Yes I would like that, but it would have to be around this time because I can't take off from work any more days. Because of my situation I've had to use several days that I never thought I would have to."

"Okay let me see what his schedule looks like."

She went to her computer and pulled up the photographer's availability.

"Wow! Look at that. The fates must be on your side today. He has an open window from 4-5 pm tomorrow here. Would you like me to put you in that slot?"

"Yes I believe I can do that. I will try to get here again around 4 or possibly a little after. Is that it?"

Yes you're all set for now. What's next is that my department will review your file, then the legal department will take a look at it and then once the case is approved it will be made available for all perspective adoptive parents. Once that's done and we have an interested party then of course they have to be screened, an intense background check and mandatory qualifications must be met. With any stroke of goodwill you are probably looking at approximately 4-6 months before an adoption can be finalized."

When Cassandra finished talking and the words final adoption came out of her mouth, a chill ran down Elena's spine. At this point it hadn't really sunk in what that really meant. Up to now it was just a process, a procedure she was considering, but now those words put a sense of finality for something deep inside she really had not prepared for. Elena thanked her and asked whether she would see her tomorrow when she came? The answer was probably not because the photographer's office was down on the second floor and there was no need for her to come up here unless there were some unanswered question that needed attention. After that exchange, Elena exited the office and the building.

From the time that she arrived at the nursery and thanked the teacher for staying late with Monica, the thoughts kept going through her mind about how she was going to prepare her child for what is about to happen in her life. When they got home Monica went to the living room to watch TV and Elena to the kitchen to fix dinner. Since the time when Norman was no longer there to eat with them it had become a kind of strange routine. From time to time Monica would ask where he was and when he was coming back to eat with them. Over the months Elena had gotten very creative with her excuses and they seemed to postpone further inquiries.

As scheduled Elena was again able to get off a little early. This time however, she went straight to the nursery and picked up Monica. She arrived at the photographer's studio at 4:20 and he was there waiting for her. The picture was taken promptly shown to Elena for her approval and then placed in a folder to be delivered to Cassandra. He asked Elena whether she would like a copy of the photo that was going to be placed in her file. She hurriedly said yes and thanked him when he said there would be no charge.

From that point on the time just seemed to fly by while Elena was making every effort to find ways to tell Monica about what was coming up. She and Trish started taking the child everywhere they could – to the movies, to the playground, to the library and even to the children's section of the local museum. The time they were spending together was something that would create a lasting memory for each of them. Trish whenever she could would take Elena aside and would ask her whether she told Monica what was going to happen. The reply was a shameful no and always with her head down she would say that she was waiting for the right time. It seems though that the time was never quite right and the clock just kept on ticking.

Finally that day came when the phone rang at home and Elena answered.

"Hello."

"Hello Mrs. Miller it's Cassandra from the agency. How are you?"

Just hearing her voice sent a chill down Elena's spine because she now feared the worse

"Oh I'm okay how about you?"

"I'm fine thank you. I have some good news for you. We have found a lovely couple who have qualified to adopt Monica and it will be just a short time now before we can complete the proceeding. If you want I can give you all the background on the couple if you want to stop by my office. For now I'll just tell you they are in their early thirties and have two other children, both boys who are a little older than Monica. I believe this is going to work out fine. "When can you come in so we can schedule a date for the adoption?

Now this was it There was no turning back at this point. Elena set the date for Friday when she would meet with Cassandra and they could set up the adoption schedule. Of course legal counsel would also have to be present so Cassandra mentioned that to Elena. Now it was absolutely no time left before Monica had to be told. Elena was having difficulty trying to come up with the words that would make sense to the child. Her life would be drastically changing and the world she knew would never be the same. Elena slowly went into the living room where Monica was watching TV.

"Sweetheart I need to tell you something that's very important. You know that mommy loves you very much don't you?"

Monica was a little disturbed at being pulled away from one of her favorite children's shows and she wondered why. But when she saw the tears beginning to form in her mother's eyes she knew something wasn't right

"What's wrong mommy you don't feel so good?"

"No honey mommy is fine it's just that I have to tell you something that I've been putting off for too long. Do you remember when daddy first went away how things started to change. We didn't have all the things we had before and we couldn't buy as much. Do you remember that?"

"Yes mommy okay."

"Well that was because mommy can't afford to do all the things we did before by herself and now it has reached the point where I have to let you go."

"Where am I going?"

"You are going to live with another family who will be able to take care of you better than I can. They will be able to give you all the things you need that I can't."

"Mommy I don't want to go. I want to stay here with you. I won't eat much and I won't ask for any new clothes. I can wear whatever you can give me."

"I'm so sorry honey, but arrangements have already been made and it will happen soon."

After their tearful embrace Monica was made to realize that things might be better for her where she's going. It took some time, but she finally accepted it.

All of the necessary papers were signed and all the reviews taken care of and the day was set. Elena never did get to meet the couple because she said that she didn't want to. On the day that the exchange was to happen Elena brought her to the agency and after a long tearful goodbye she left. Shortly after her departure the couple arrived and were introduced to Monica. It was rather awkward at first, but with the skillful intervention of Cassandra things started to go well.

When it was all said and done the couple with Monica in tow left headed for her new home.

The neighborhood they lived in was a middle class one with well maintained houses and attractive yards. Inside the four bedroom house there was plenty of space for easy living and it was equipped with all the latest modern appliances and entertainment devices. However, that old saying all that glitters is not gold was certainly applicable here. From all outward appearances the couple presented an image of a loving and happy family. On paper they had all of the proper credentials to convince any one of their value to society. However, it did not take long before Monica was exposed to the evil that was present within these walls.

At first and after she was shown to her well appointed room that had all of the things a young girl would want, Monica appeared to be happy. Although expectedly withdrawn and shy in the beginning, once she got acclimated to the routine of the household she started to warm to the ways of the family. For the next month or so she was starting to adjust to her new life when things began to change. The older boys started teasing her with little annoying things that made her feel inferior. They would tell her she didn't belong there because she was adopted and other mean sayings like that. The parents knew this was occurring, but failed to do anything to admonish the boys so it was allowed to go on. The real reason the family wanted to adopt was finally beginning to show. It was to gain access to additional income that was provided by the state. Neither of the parents had any real love for her and it didn't take long before Monica was able to sense this.

There were times when it was obvious that the two boys were given preferential treatment over her and the mean things they did were done out in the open right under the parents observation. Monica was beginning to feel a strong sense of rejection and the lack of true love in this household made her wish she had never left her real mother. As time passed the little things that were done to her became more than just little things and she started to become afraid. At night she would make sure her door was fully closed and the big teddy bear she was given became her protector. Even the father began to look at her in a different light and it frightened her.

There was no way for her to contact her real mother or even get in touch with the agency that made all this happen so she decided to try and make the best of what she had. It was not until late one night when she was in bed, but not quite asleep yet, that the door opened and the father stood just inside. He had been drinking and he was clad only in his pajamas. Monica was scared because she didn't know what he was going to do. At first she tried to pretend that she was sleeping, but in the next instance she knew that she was wide awake because it happened.

CHAPTER 3

Miseducation

From the time she left the social service agency leaving Monica behind, Elena's life seemed to have lost its meaning. On the job she was there, but not as attentive to her work as her work record would attest to. Her visits to see Norman were becoming less frequent and the fact that the doctors still could not determine a treatment that would lead to his full recovery caused her despondency to elevate. Finally she just stopped going when the visits reached the point where he would barely recognize who she was. As a result of the number of days she would miss work completely, because she was an hourly wage earner, her paycheck suffered. This led to her falling months behind in rent payments and other critical household bills. Even her supervisor who was lenient as he could be reached the point where he had to warn her that she had to improve or be let go.

There were times when thoughts of what could be happening to Monica would drive her to just sit at her window and stare into space. Trish was aware of her downward slide and as often as she was allowed to even enter the apartment she would attempt to provide some encouragement and motivation to prevent a total breakdown. Being away from Monica, the bond they had shared especially toward the end when the adoption was imminent, was causing Elena to internalize what she perceived as her failure as a mother. She had been restricted from knowing where her daughter lived and consequently had no way to make contact with her. As badly as she wanted to know the fate of her child it was not to be.

Eventually she was evicted from the apartment and was forced to find lodging somewhere else. At first she considered going south to live with her mother, but when she assessed her own emotional state, the idea of burdening her health challenged parent with new troubles was a deterrent to the move. For a short while she was sheltered by Trish, but even that could not be a lasting solution, because there was just not enough room in that apartment for the two of them. So she left there and began to wander from homeless shelter to homeless shelter until one day she turned up missing. The search for her over several months did not turn up any positive results and was finally abandoned and entered into the cold case files.

Somewhere on the other side of the city the fate of her daughter was also being tested. For many months Monica was acclimating to her new living quarters and even though it was obvious that she was not accepted as a whole member of the family, she was learning to cope with the situation. The lack of love shown caused her to begin to develop coping mechanisms that helped her to survive. She would pretend that her stepfather really loved her because he would buy her clothes and give her other things, but he never showed any genuine affection toward her. The stepmother was even less affectionate. She only provided what was absolutely necessary to keep from losing the state financial support if it ever came to be known that they were not keeping up their end of the adoption agreement. The two older boys teased her unmercifully and whenever possible taunted her for no reason. Monica learned to defend herself from these taunts by developing ways to ignore them and created a fantasy world where her existence was okay. Time was passing and she was moving ahead with her development despite the challenges.

It was not until one night in late summer as she lay in bed with her teddy bear wrapped tightly in her arms that her bedroom door opened. It was late, well past the time that the family normally retired for the evening, that her step father, Harold entered and closed the door behind him. He had been drinking and he was clad only in his pajamas. Monica was scared because she didn't know what he was going to do. She held onto Teddy even tighter as he approached the bed. He snatched the bear from her arms and threw it aside. Monica was paralyzed with fear as she stared up at him unable to move, cry out or even shed tears. He leaned over and began unbuttoning her pajama top exposing her budding eight year old breasts. He started to fondle her breasts and then proceeded to remove her pajama bottoms. Spreading her legs wide open he moved on top and was about to complete his mission when suddenly the door opened and another figure entered. The light came on and a loud scream, a shriek that could be heard throughout the house was coming from Laura, his wife. Startled, shaken and rendered sober he rolled off the bed onto the floor then got up and ran out of the room. He never penetrated Monica.

The next day it was early in the morning, around 6:30 when Laura came into Monica's room. Monica had not been able to go to sleep for hours, just lying there seeing in her mind's eye his face above hers. Finally and mercifully nature took over and the sandman graciously closed her eyes as she drifted off to a sound sleep.

"Are you hurt?" the mother said.

Unable to even speak at first Monica finally calmed down enough to respond.

"I, I, I'm not hurt I don't think, but what did he try to do to me?"

"Monica sometimes men, especially after they have been drinking, start to do unforgiveable things. He really wasn't trying to hurt you, but you are becoming so pretty I guess he wanted to make love to you. You don't understand that quite yet and I will tell you more about it when you are a little older. For now just try to put what happened out of your mind and forget it ever did."

"Will he be coming back here again?"

"No Monica I assure you that won't be happening again in this house. Take my word for it you are going to be alright. Now you can go back to sleep for a little while longer and I'll call you for breakfast in a little while."

Laura after consoling the child to the best of her ability left the room and went downstairs to the kitchen. Harold, who had fled to the couch in the living room where he spent the balance of the night, had not yet awakened from his drunken stupor. She walked in and looked down on him just shook her head and returned to the kitchen.

When he finally awakened not too long after and meekly entered the kitchen he was so embarrassed that the words would hardly come out of his mouth. She just stood there staring at him.

"I don't know what got into me last night. I guess the liquor told me it was okay and I succumbed. Believe me I never intended to hurt that child, but it just seemed like I couldn't help myself. Can you forgive me?"

"I watched you and it looked like you were getting ready to violate that young girl. If I hadn't stopped it, you would have committed an unforgiveable sin. It's not about my forgiving you, but it is about whether you realize what you did. That kind of behavior can never happen again while I'm here. I know she is becoming very attractive, but remember she's just a child and you're a grown man. I know we've lost that loving feeling for each other even to the point that our sex life has disappeared, but you can't satisfy your evil lust with that young girl. I'm going to be watching you like a hawk every hour of the night so that it doesn't even look like you're headed that way. Do you understand me? I will not put up with that."

"I am so ashamed I really don't know what to say. There is no way I can undo what happened, but I will try to do something to make up for it. You're absolutely right whatever evil got into me came from that bottle and I promise I won't be doing that again."

"See that you keep that promise."

That conversation ended but the thought of what he had seen in the promising naked body of Monica remained. His lack of self control, in that instance, boosted by his yielding to the liquid spirit that had entered his body was only a harbinger of what possibilities were yet to come. He left the kitchen and wanted to go to her and apologize, but what could he say. No words could ever diminish the emotional scarring he knew he must have caused, so he left the thought lingering in the atoms of his mind and went to his room. It was his hope that time would be the ultimate healer and if he just treated her with kindness not making any inappropriate advances toward her, day or night, then even she might one day forgive him.

For months after the incident the atmosphere throughout the house was somewhat guarded. The boys who must have heard the scream during that frightful night never acknowledged it, but knew that something had happened that was not right. They continued with their ill conceived treatment of Monica, but by this time the effect was minimal because her defenses were honed to a high level of self protection. Whenever he could Harold would give her little gifts that he hoped would hasten her forgiveness. Although she accepted them, it was always with a cautious hesitation believing that he even now had bad intentions. It was not until when she reached the fifth grade that he gave her a rather expensive computer laptop. The boys, Michael the older one and Ricky his younger brother had already received an expensive desktop one that they shared. Now that her classroom studies required it, he provided one without hesitation.

The laptop provided a new outlet for her to escape into a broader fantasy world. She was a very bright and quick learner that was confirmed by all of her teachers to this point. She excelled academically in all of her studies and was highly praised by all except her surrogate family. They never intended it to be that mechanism that opened a door for her to gain knowledge that was far greater than what her young mind should have had access to. Although they placed parental restrictions on what she could access via the internet, her clever and astute curiosity allowed her to discover ways to bypass the restrictions. What she found on line were subjects that were intended for more mature adults. These subjects, even pornographic materials, began contributing to the development of a dark side within her psyche that she wasn't even aware of it happening.

Throughout the remaining years of her elementary school requirement, she remained at the very top of her class. While she was recognized for being academically gifted, there was something else developing within her persona that was not seen. Her physical development on becoming a young lady was maturing faster than the average and her attributes would not go unnoticed by all who saw her. Her male classmates, also maturing at that age, were conspicuously aware of what she had and all of them, without fail were making an effort to incur her favor. She also was aware of what she had and now was learning how to use it for her benefit. Manipulation to gain advantage became her modus operandi and she became very skilled at it.

By the time graduation came her teachers all praised her accomplishments and recommended that she be placed in one of the gifted and talented high schools in the region. High praise was given by most, but conspicuously absent from that fan club were her surrogate parents. They attended the graduation, but failed to praise her for anything even for the fact she was the number one student in the class. Monica sensed this and the lack of any adoration or genuine love did not go unnoticed. Since it was not unusual, over the years since she was with them, that they wouldn't give her credit for any accomplishment, no matter how small or great, she was hurt, but not surprised. When the letter came that she had been accepted to the number one regional high school for the gifted and talented programs, she was the only one in the family to be excited. As a result of the high recommendation by the principal and the number of corroborating teacher signatures on the letter that was sent to the Board Of Education her acceptance was almost a sure expectation for them. Included with the acceptance was the provision that all necessary transportation would be arranged at no cost. Since the school was some distance away from where she lived, this proviso was an outwardly welcomed stipulation. However, inside, her surrogate parents were hoping that they would be receiving some additional income if they provided her ride to school.

The summer months passed quickly, without any major household incidents and the September school entry period was about to begin. Monica's excitement grew with each passing day. The obvious jealousy on the part of her step brothers was on full display, but as usual she was able to ignore it. She had heard so much from her elementary school teachers about what she was going to learn in the high school, she was looking forward to starting right away. What they did not or could not tell her was about the social side of this new experience or how to prepare for it. This was something she would have to learn on her own. .

Day one at Kimberly Clark Regional High School (named after one of the major donors) was no different than the usual first day series of mishaps, especially with the new students. Finding the right classroom for the right subject was a bit of a challenge for some who had never been to a school building that was as large and spread out as this relatively new facility. It didn't help their cause that mischievous seniors would intentionally misdirect them. Monica was also among those who sought help in finding her way, but rather than misdirect her two seniors who were immediately impressed with her assets took it upon themselves to personally escort her to her first homeroom. Thus her new introduction to a different world had begun.

Within the first month after learning the routine for changing classes, she settled in and started to focus on her academic pursuits. Some of the other girls who were first year students as she was befriended her and she felt like this experience was going to be great. However, there were other girls in her class who simply were envious of the obvious talents she displayed, that made it their goal to make student life difficult for her. From the time she entered and was discovered, word began spreading primarily amongst the upper class boys about this new pretty girl who had arrived. In the cafeteria during lunch period several of them would find a way to sit near or even next to her whenever possible. It didn't take long for Monica to become aware of what was going on so she would often surround herself with her new girlfriends who could act as shields at her table.

Between being challenged by the new academic subjects she was given in an accelerated learning program, she was also challenged by the pace at which things were starting to happen. Handling the subject matter was easier for her than negotiating the swarm of upper class boys who would always find a way to get near her. She was finding out that manipulating the boys to do what she wanted them to do in the lower grades was not so easy now with this new group. There was one female teacher, Mrs. Rabinawitz very attractive herself, who noticed what was happening and one day called Monica into her classroom after the school day. To Monica this was a blessing even when she really didn't know much about what blessings were.

"Monica you are a very pretty girl and I know what you must be going through here as a new student. Believe me when I was about your age I went through the same thing at my high school. Remember this. You were accepted here because you have the brains to become anything you set your mind on becoming. Don't let those boys whose adolescent hormones are right now raging out of control upset your focus on the work you need to do. Being at this school is a golden opportunity for you to develop into someone who will do great things. Don't squander the chance. If you ever need someone to talk to about anything while you're here, you can always come to me. I'll be here for you."

Monica sincc the time she was separated from her real mother had never had anyone talk to her like this. Someone who was genuinely interested in her welfare and she started to tear up while listening. The teacher was true to her word and throughout her academic career at the school this was her closest ally and confidant.

Freshman year passed and Monica after learning how to avoid being overrun by boys at every turn used her talents under the guidance of her favorite teacher to become solidly entrenched academically near the top of her class. There was one thing however that she was also learning. Even though she skillfully repelled most of the boys, there was one who stood out among them and she felt differently about him. He didn't follow her around like the others and whenever she saw him the feelings she had made her want to follow him, but she couldn't let him know that. She was afraid to tell Mrs. Rabinawitz how she felt because she didn't think it would meet with her approval.

Over the summer there was no change in how she was treated even though she had completed an excellent academic year. No one acknowledged her accomplishments and love was definitely missing from her life. Her step father was keeping his distance under the watchful eye of his wife and her brothers seemed to not care that she even existed. More and more she poured herself into the world that she created via her laptop and as she discovered new ways to survive, not all of them were beneficial for her. The dark side she was nurturing started to manifest itself in ways that would soon lead her into trouble. When she was allowed to go to the store alone, she would shoplift little things at first, then as she felt more emboldened in the act, the booty grew larger. Stealing and getting away with it, somehow gave her the feeling of invincibility and as she practiced it her skill level increased. Lying also became a part of her persona. Often when she came home and was asked about where she got the things she had, her creative imagination would render such a plausible lie that it was accepted.

It was not until near the end of summer when it was almost time to return to school that she wanted to return with some pretty new clothes so she decide to go shopping without any money. The things her father usually let her get were very inexpensive and of low quality and none were to her true liking. Her desire was to fit in, more this year with the social crowd who were generally made up of the students coming from wealthier families. She visited Kleins Department Store on several occasions and went shopping without any monetary resources. Picking out the best of what was pretty and available in her size she would find a way to cleverly walk out unchallenged. However, as the old saying goes, don't go to the well too often, on her last visit one of the store's security officers noticed that she was carrying a large shopping bag when she came in that appeared to be almost empty. When she started to leave, the bag was no longer almost empty. He signaled to another officer and they caught her just as was about to exit.

When she was confronted and asked to produce receipts for the merchandise, even her glib responses could not provide what she needed. She was escorted into the rear of the store and examined. Even then she felt no remorse or guilt, but only a sense that next time she would do it better and not get caught. By the time both her step father and mother came to the store she had totally confessed to the misdemeanor. The store manager who recognized the couple as regular shoppers was very gracious and agreed not to file any complaint, but either they would have to pay for the garments or leave them there. There were three outfits in the bag totaling a rather large amount. After looking at the price tag for each, there was no question about what their disposition would be. Even when they left the store Monica did not know what to expect because nothing was said to her.

Upon arrival at the house and once inside, judgment was finally rendered. The scolding issued by Harold was tantamount to a whipping, but even then she remained recalcitrant and returned his evil look with her own stare. The dark side was fully entrenched now.

"Do you know what you have done to this family? Did it ever occur to you while you were stealing what it would do to our reputation?" he hollered at her.

"I just wanted to have some nice things like the other kids, not that stuff you let me get."

"Why you ungrateful little tramp. I give you what you deserve. If it was not for us taking you in, you would probably still be stuck in some orphanage hoping for a family like this. From now on you will wear only what I provide for you. If you ever go back to that store and do again what you did, I will allow them to lock you up and then you will see what life on the other side is like."

Monica's defiant look, even though she didn't say anything further, infuriated him even more and he wanted to strike her, but his wife who was standing there stood between them. He brought his hand down and walked away. Nothing else was said by either parent or Monica as she just stood there for several minutes more thinking about all he said. It was no secret that they didn't really love her, but had taken her in only for the money. But some of the things he said were absolutely true and she realized it. It had been a long time since she thought about her mother and truly missed her, but now if ever she needed her more this was it. She left the living room, went to her room, lay down on her bed and wanted to cry, but she couldn't.

There was only one week left before school started so she spent that time organizing what she thought she would need, in spite of the clothes she was relegated to wear. The relationship between her and her foster parents had sunk to an all time low, and communications throughout that period was minimal. She did what she had to do and they did the same. The two boys waffled between the options, talking to one side or the other only when necessary. It was a strange situation and no one in the house had any inkling on how to bring peace to a tense atmosphere.

The week passed and it was time for Monica, as well as the boys, to go to school. She was still receiving special transportation and the boys were still jealous of this because they had to walk to the public high school. Tensions lessened when they all separated from each other and started their day. Going to school and getting away from that house was a welcome respite for her and she looked forward to reuniting with the few friends she had made in the last school year. Her bus arrived on time as it usually did and she was off to a new adventure.

At Kimberly Clark High School, which was well known for the high success rate of it's graduating students, it was no surprise how orderly was the procession that entered on opening day. At the front main entrance stood the principal welcoming the returning classes and doling out words of encouragement and motivation to all who passed by him. Monica played her part in the procession like a talented actress and smiled as she walked by him and on to the next line of the teachers who stood like a military formation just inside the doors. She was greeted by all of them, but especially the ones who had her as a student last year. When she came before Mrs. Rabinawitz her smile got broader as the two of them paused the line for a moment. Sarah Rabinawitz whispered in her ear that she should stop by her classroom after school because there was something she wanted to talk to her about. Without the slightest hesitation Monica nodded her head in acknowledgment.

After the procession ended and the students were sent to the gym where they received their schedules and locker assignments for the year, the next stop was to go to their assigned homerooms and wait for the bell signaling the start of the new school year. When Monica arrived at her homeroom, she got excited again when she saw the two other girls who befriended her during their first year when many of the other girls snubbed her. The three of them had formed a bond that continued to gel throughout the year and now was ready to unite again. Reilly O'Donell, whose father was one of the city's largest building contractors was a few months older than the other two so she was considered the leader. Soun Li's father was a heart specialist at the hospital and she was hoping to follow in his path. Monica could boast of no high esteem for her parents and made no attempt to do so. The girls gravitated toward each other almost from day one when they sat together at lunch in the cafeteria and talked. Since they shared for the greater part of schedules the same academic track for classes they would often end up with the same lunch and study periods. Early on in their first academic year it became clear to the teachers, as well as the other students, who the academic stars were going to be. This may have been the common denominator that brought them together.

For Monica seeing them again was a great relief knowing she had at least two friends who she could rely on. The fact that she was not of the same social ilk as the other two never seem to enter into their conversations with each other. Although deep inside she felt a bit inferior and would sometimes make up little lies to balance out the imbalance. They became like the three Musketeers, all for one and one for all was their motto and it seemed to create a genuine hedge of mutual protection for each of them.

At the end of that first day, as she was requested to do Monica happily went to see Mrs. Rabinawitz. There was another student there ahead of her so she was asked to wait outside for just a minute. Moments later she was invited in.

"Well how was your first day back?" Sarah asked.

"I loved it" was the quick reply.

"May I see your schedule?"

Monica was quick to pull out the document and show it to her.

"Well I see they have you taking some challenging courses which I'm sure you will be able to handle. What I want to talk to you about is not so much the academic portion of your stay here, but the other opportunities that are available. Monica you could have a very bright future beyond these doors after graduation. One thing you have to accumulate as you build your portfolio is the other things that will contribute to your success."

"What's a portfolio?"

"Ah! Glad you asked. The portfolio is the sum of all your activities and accomplishments brought together in a file that can be shown to the world. That's why I want you to consider some of the activities I'm about to suggest to you. I don't know whether you have even considered going to college or not, but if and when you do you need to have more than just a high grade point average. Most colleges look at other things you do to become a well rounded individual. With that in mind let me ask you if you have any hobbies now? What do you like to do when you're not studying?"

The question kind of caught her off guard because at home in between all of the turmoil and strife, there was not much she liked to do accept stay in her room out of the way and log in to her computer.

"Oh I don't know. I guess I don't have any hobbies or things like that, but I do like to stay on my computer a lot and search for things. You know discover new subjects."

"That's all well and good, but you need more than that. I'm going to suggest three clubs here I think you should join that will give you a chance to use your academic talents as well as your creative abilities. The first one is the Debate Club. Last year under the guidance of one of our very fine instructors, the club was able to go to several competitions. They did very well. I think you would be a welcome entry there. The second one is the Young Entrepreneurs Club that will provide you with exposure on how to succeed in business. I don't know if that's your interest, but it will be good to have, as I said, in your portfolio. And finally I'd like to see you in the Political Science Club. This will help you to develop your leadership skills and learn how to negotiate and manage people. As I looked at your schedule for now there's not room for some of the courses offered here in these areas, but perhaps by the time you reach your senior year you may have some time to take one or more of them as an elective subject. But you don't need to wait until then to get the experience. Okay what do you think?"

"Wow that's a lot to think about. I know I should do more than just study, but I want to be really good in my courses. Thank you for telling me about these clubs and I will consider joining at least one of them. Will I have to stay after school long if I join them>"

"You will have to spend some time after school yes, but I can't say for how long because each one will require a different amount of time. Why don't you look on the bulletin board and see when each club will be meeting next and go to one of the sessions. Then you can ask all the questions you need answers for."

"Okay I'll do that. Well thanks again Mrs Rabinawitz for your advice."

"You're quite welcome. Remember anytime you need to talk about anything I'm always here."

Monica left the office and went outside to meet her bus. However, because of the extra time she spent with Sarah, her bus had already gone. Fortunately for her, Reilly's father was late in coming to pick her up so she was still there. When Reilly saw her she waved and called her over.

"You missed your bus?" she saud.

"Yeah. I know they have to keep on schedule, but he knows I ride that bus all the time you think he could have waited a few minutes longer. I don't know what I'm going to do now. I can't call my father because he's probably not even there now or my mother either for that matter."

"Don't worry about it. My father just sent me a text and he's on his way. I'm sure he'll give you a ride home.".

Within minutes the sleek SUV pulled up and Reilly's father was driving it.

"Come on, come on that's my father" she said to Monica.

"Hi dad. This is my friend Monica and she missed her bus. Can you drive her home?"

"Sure thing angel. Monica nice to meet you – where do you live?"

Monica hesitated for a minute telling him because she didn't want Reilly to see where she lived after some of the stories she had told. However, now was not the time for vanity so she provided her address.

"It's nice to meet you too sir. Thank you for the ride. I live at ...."

When they arrived at her house she quickly got out of the vehicle then looked back at Reilly to see what expression might be on her face. To her surprise saw nothing indicating a surprise. Satisfied that her living quarters were not an issue for her friend she went inside the house.

Both of her brothers were already there and as usual the bantering began.

"Well the family princess has arrived shall we kneel now" said the older boy.

Monica tried to ignore him like normal and just walk by, but this time he persisted in trying to engage her in some form of conversation.

"Your highness exactly what is it that they're teaching you at that school that we aren't getting to know? Do they give you special meals or special chairs so your butt don't get sore from sitting? Really, I'd like to know what it is that makes you so special?"

Monica sensing he was not going to let her by until she confronted him got ready for the battle.

"Well since you asked and really want to know, I'm going to tell you. However, I don't think your little brain is going to understand anything I tell you. First off I'm studying geometrical progressions for mathematical solutions. Did you get that? Secondly, I'm engaged in the study of anti-social behaviors. That one you may understand because you are a prime example of the subject. Finally I'm learning how to get around having to associate which ignorant imbeciles like you who have no idea of what they want to do or how to go about doing it. Does that answer your question?"

The boy got so mad because he didn't understand most of what she was saying and didn't know how to react that he resorted to the tactics of all those who are placed in that situation. He clenched his fists and started toward her when suddenly the door opened and in walked their parents together. To see the children together and in a confrontational stance was not an unusual sight, but to observe the anger showing on the boy's face and his clenched fists ready for battle deserved an explanation.

"What's going on here?" the father demanded an answer.

"Dad she thinks she's so much better than we are because she goes to that haughty taught school. Tell her she ain't no better than me and Ricky. Go on dad tell her."

"Son I'm sure whatever gave you that idea she didn't intend for you to feel like that. Now what did she say or do to make you think that way?"

"She didn't say anything, but it's just that she gets a ride to school and we have to walk. I also heard in my school that they get to go to special events that we don't and they also say that some of those kids are rich. Why is that?"

"You can't blame her for what the teachers at that school are able to arrange and as far as getting a ride to school, if we lived a little farther away you could get a ride too. Now you go on upstairs and I don't want to hear anymore about this matter – you understand me?"

"Yes dad."

Meanwhile Monica was just standing there observing how the father handled the matter and she thought to herself – he's a prime example of the behavior I'm studying.

"Now as for you I know you must have done something to provoke his anger. Whatever it was I want you to stop it. Because you are able to go to that school, don't try to lord it over your brothers."

Monica burst in.

"They're not my brothers and they will never be. I know why you brought me into this house. It was not because you wanted a girl, a daughter to love and cherish, but because you are greedy for more money than you make."

Pow! The slap came across her face with such force that it knocked her down. As she lay on the floor looking up at him, she still refused to cry, but rather got up and ran upstairs to her room. Lying on her bed she promised herself that as soon as she was able she was going to get out of this house.

"You shouldn't have done that. Now that she's getting older and meeting some of those important people up at that school if she shows up with bruises don't you think one of them will start asking questions?" .

"Yeah I know that, but she just irks me with her defiant ways and she never seems to cry when hurt. Is that normal?"

"I don't know if its normal or not, but if you want to lose that extra money we get for her, the quickest way to do that is to have one of those social service people start snooping around here."

"Yeah, yeah I know I'll have to be more controlled with my temper. Now what are we going to eat?"

The rest of the night was uneventful and during dinner nothing was said that would provoke a repeat of what happened earlier. Very little conversation was had except for asking for a certain element to be passed at the table. Monica had come down showing no signs of relinquishing her attitude about what she said not only to the father but to the boys also. On her face was a large bruise as a result of the slap, but no one at the table mentioned it or seemed to acknowledge it. Later after the meal was finished and each member went to his or her respective area of the house to do what was regularly done, Monica who had been given the one luxury that was afforded her used the phone and called Reilly.

Ring, ring, ring.

"Hello."

"Hi Reilly this is Monica are you busy?"

"Oh hey girl no I'm not doing anything important, just trying to figure out how I'm going to balance this new study schedule and also work in my father's office after school. He asked me if I wanted to learn something about the business a while ago and I agreed to do it, but I had no idea what my new schedule was going to look like. What are you doing?"

"Well I just had another confrontation with my brothers and even my father. I don't know if I ever told you this or not, but he's not my real father – he's a step father."

"No you never mentioned it. What happened to your real parents?"

"I'm not actually sure. I do remember my mother a little, but I was brought here when I was very young and they never told me where my parents are. These folks seem like they don't want me to know. Maybe it's because they get money from the government to support me. I don't know the whole story about that, but anyway they don't really care about me, but they have to shelter and feed and clothe me as long as they get that check."

"Wow that's heavy. What did you fight about?"

"It's not a new thing it's an ongoing battle and it's just getting worse. With my brothers it's all about their jealousy of me going to our high school. Today it started with the brothers talking about how they have to walk to school while I get a ride and how we get to go on trips and they don't. I've about had it with them and my so called parents, but right now there's nothing I can do about it."

"There's nobody you can talk to and get help with your situation?"

"No, no one that I can think of. I guess I'll just have to tough it out here until I graduate and get a job."

"You shouldn't have to live like that. Maybe I can talk to my dad and see what he says. He knows a lot of people and maybe one of them can bail you out."

"No, no please don't do that. I only told you because you are my close friend and I needed someone to tell it to before I lose my mind. I don't want anyone to know about it until I can figure out how to work things out myself. Please just keep it to yourself."

"Okay sure if that's what you want, but I think you need to get some help."

"Yeah I know, but I have to be sure whatever or whoever is going to help me can definitely get me out of here safely."

"Well if there's anything you want me to do just say the word."

"Thanks I'll keep that in mind. Thank you for listening I feel better already. I'm going to crack a book or two now and then go to bed. By the way did you understand the assignment for our geometry class, it seems in all the confusion here I have misplaced my notes."

"Yeah let me get mine and I'll tell you in a minute."

The girls continued to talk for another hour about everything, but what Monica had called about. When they finished talking she open the geometry book and tried to do the assignment, but just did not have the will to do it so she went to bed.

The next morning everyone followed the normal routine and left the house at different times. When Monica got to her school she met her two allies in homeroom and the first thing they both noticed was the bruise on her face. Although Reilly had some idea of what might have happened, Soun had no clue so she started the interrogation.

"Monica what happened to your face, did a truck hit you?"

Although she said it playfully she was serious about the inquiry.

"Oh does it look that bad? I thought the make-up had covered it up pretty good."

"Well the disguise isn't working. Here look."

Soun took out a small hand mirror from her purse and showed it to Monica. When she was dressing this morning she had used a dressing mirror in her room that did not provide enough light to give her a good look at the bruise even with the make-up she applied.

"Um I see what you mean. I can't go to classes looking like this. What am I going to do?"

At this point Reilly chimed in.

"Maybe you ought to go see the nurse. She may have something that can cover it up better than that poor make-up job."

They all laughed. Monica heeded Reily 's advice and headed to the nurse's office. But before she got there Mrs. Rabinawitz was coming the other way and stopped her. She was going to follow up on the conversation they had yesterday after school. However, when she got close to her she also noticed the bruised face.

"What happened to your face?"

"Oh I just had a little accident."

That looks more like the mark of a hand print to me. Is everything okay at yur house?"

"Yes, yes I'm fine and everything there is fine. I was just going to the nurse to see if she can cover it up."

Mrs. Rabinawitz continued to look at her for another minute or so then let her go.

"Okay if you say so. But remember what I told you. If there's ever anything you need to talk to me about don't hesitate to stop by and see me."

"Yes I remember and I will do that. Thanks I'll see you later."

Monica continued on into the nurse's office where she was greeted with a warm welcome.

"Good morning I believe it's Monica right?"

"Yes that's me. Can you do something about this?"

"Well let me take a look at that. I think we can fix it but will you tell me how you got that bruise?"

Monica hesitated for several minutes trying to think up some clever answer that would not give away the actual cause, but couldn't.

"Please if you don't mind I would rather not say."

The nurse respected her answer and although her suspicion was raised she did not pursue the issue. She treated the mark with some special cover up for burn wounds and the mark became hardly visible when Monica looked in the nurse's mirror.

"Thank you that looks much better. Can I go now or do I have to get a slip or something for my class?"

"No just tell your first class teacher where you were and if she needs any confirmation have her call me."

Monica walked out and went to class.

Her first class was the geometry class for which she had not completed last night's assignment. Reilly was also in the class and tried to cover for her when the teacher asked why the work had not been done. She told the instructor that Monica had not been feeling well and had called her to get the assignment, but she gave her the wrong information. The teacher, a bit suspicious about this story, however was in a lenient mood and told Monica to make it up along with tonight's assignment. Monica breathed a sigh of relief then looked at Reilly, who sat next to her, smiled and winked.,

On Tuesdays and Thursdays Monica had a swimming class the next period and since this was Tuesday she headed there. By now as she was approaching her sixteenth birthday her body had developed into the young woman she was destined to be. Her hour glass figure that was accentuated by her large shapely breasts was to become both an asset and a liability as she moved through the remainder of her years at the high school. When she arrived in the pool locker room and was changing into her bathing suit, she noticed that one of the other girls was staring at her. At first she tried to ignore the stare, but the girl did not turn away but continued to ogle her body. Slightly embarrassed and unsure what she should do next, she quickly finished changing and entered the pool area. Upon her entry and after seeing her, even the male thirty something swimming instructor was having a hard time keeping his mind on only teaching her how to swim. The other girls in the class were also aware of her impact and wondered whether they would get the same swimming attention she got.

On Mondays, Wednesdays and Fridays a gym class would be in the same period as the swim class. For the second time in the locker room while she was changing that same girl, who happened to have the same class schedule, just stared at her. This time rather than changing quickly she took her time and watched the expression on the girl's face. Although the girl said nothing or tried to approach her, this was a new experience and she couldn't wait to tell her other two Musketeers about it.

For the rest of that day nothing unusual happened. She had been thinking about what Mrs. Rabinawitz had advised her to do about joining a club, so now was the time to begin checking it out. On the main hallway bulletin board was a list of all the clubs and organizations and their meeting schedules. It just so happened that today was the time for the debate club to have their first meeting. Before she decided to attend she consulted with Reilly to see whether her father would again be able to take her home. Reilly not only agreed, but said she was thinking about joining that club also and she would call her dad and let him know.

It was just before three O'clock when the two comrades found the right room and entered. To their surprise sitting there waiting for the meeting to start was the third Musketeer - Soun Li. As they met each other and embraced the laughter could not be ignored by the other members of the group who wondered what the joke was. Moments later in walked Mr. Ottenhoffer, the director of the club. He was a stern looking man of about fifty something years of age and muscularly built. He walked to the front of the room placed his briefcase on the desk and for the next few moment just stared at the group. After what seemed like forever to the girls, he started speaking. For the old members of the club, which was four, this was nothing new, but for the new prospects it was rather strange.

"Now that I have your attention wondering just what is this guy all about, let me begin by saying welcome to the greatest debate club in the eastern region. For those of you who qualify to become new members I promise it will be one of the greatest experiences of your young life. I hope that you who are new have become acquainted with these four over here who represent the award winning team from last year. In any event I'm going to ask them to introduce or reintroduce themselves to you."

The four former team members, three boys and one girl, one by one stood up and gave their name and a short bio. It was interesting for the Musketeers to watch them display such confidence and bravado that they were thoroughly impressed. There was no doubt in either of their minds that this was a club they wanted to be a part of. After the introductions Mr. Ottenhoffer went over some of the rules and requirements of membership and when he finished he asked the question addressing the three new prospects– "Do you want to join?" The answer was quick in their response and he was pleased. Then he handed each of them a sheet explaining what the next steps were to become members. When this was completed he asked whether they had any questions then walked out ahead of the group leaving the new girls to mingle with the current members.

When the meeting ended the three comrades spent a few more minutes together discussing the requirements of the club and a consensus was taken whether they wanted to go ahead. They all agreed and the work was begun. Reilly then called her father to let him know they were ready. Soun Li's older brother was coming for her. While they waited for their respective rides Monica thought about what happened in swimming class and again in the gym and started to tell her friends. The girls' name was not known to the other two and the questions immediately started coming.

"Did she try to do anything to you?" Soun Li asked.

"Was she naked when she was looking?" Reilly chimed in.

"No. She had on her bathing suit in swimming class and her gym suit at the gym. She didn't do or say anything – just stared. It was kind of creepy. I didn't know what to do. Have you had anything like that happen to you?"

"No not me" said Reilly.

"Me neither. Are you going to tell the teacher or what?"

"I'm not sure. She didn't really do anything so what do you think I should do?"

"My mother told me about some girls and women like that, but I never thought we would find them here" said Soun Li.

"Yeah my mother told me also. She called them some kind of a name which I forgot, but I'll ask her and let you know. I think you ought to let the teacher know that we have one of them among us."

They all laughed.

"I don't know. I don't want to get her into any kind of trouble because as I said she hasn't done anything. Think I'll just let it go and try to stay out of her way. Unless she tries to do something to me I think that's the right thing to do."

"Well if you think that's right go for it, but don't say we didn't warn you ahead of time" Soun Li offered.

"Yeah I agree with Soun. Better to be ahead of the game than behind the eight ball as my father always says."

"Okay I got your advice now let's move on. I will consider your words of wisdom."

As the girls waited outside for their respective rides almost simultaneously both pick-up vehicles arrived. Two got into Mr. O'Donell's SUV and Soun into her brother's.

When Monica got home all of the others were already there. Except for the second incident in the gym it had been a good day. Now that she was home her whole demeanor changed. First she was challenged by her step mother Laura asking about why she was so late in getting home and then her brother offered that she must be fooling around. It didn't take long before all of the positive feelings she had earlier disappeared and the negative ones entered.

"I think I told you that I was going to join one of the after school clubs. So today I went to a meeting to find out about how to join. That's where I was>"

"How did you get home?"

"One of my friend's father brought me."

"Do we know this friend?"

"I don't think so, but she is one of my classmates. Her name is Reilly 'ODonell she's good people."

"Well you let me know next time you're going to be this late. Also this club you are joining is it going to cost us any money?"

"No I don't think so. The instructor hasn't said anything about that."

"Well if it does remember you don't have any money to spare for that kind of thing."

"Yes I know that can I eat now?"

"Go ahead. Your plate is in the microwave."

"I think she was out there fooling around if you ask me" Michael chimed in after listening to the conversation.

Monica gave him a dirty look then went upstairs to deposit her school bag. A few minutes later she returned to the kitchen to eat. All the while she couldn't help thinking about how much she wanted to get out of this house and what she was going to need to do it.

There was no further conversation about her wanting to join a club or her coming in later than usual at that time. However a short time later Harold knocked on her door and said he wanted to talk to her. Reluctantly she invited him in.

"You know you are getting to be quite a good looking young girl and I'm sure the boys at that school have already taken notice of that. Your brother seems to think that you may be doing something else after school than what you said about some club. You're not fooling around with any of those boys are you?"

Monica stared hard at him for several minutes before answering.

"No I'm not fooling around with any boys nor anything other than what I told her. What are you so concerned about you think I might be getting pregnant?"

The response caught him off guard because he really wasn't prepared for this near sixteen year answering him like that. He stopped momentarily before continuing with a lighter tone.

"No, that wasn't what I was thinking, but since you brought it up that's not the case is it?"

"I can't believe you are really asking me that. From the time that I first came into this house you have treated me like property rather than a daughter. It didn't take long for me to realize what your reason was for even bringing me here. Now that I have a little bit of freedom you want me to report my every move to you like I'm some kind of prisoner on probation. You know I'll be sixteen very soon and I'm going to start researching how to get away from you."

"You do that, but as long as I'm housing and feeding you here, you will not bring any disgrace upon this family. Do you understand me?"

"I hear you and believe me I will leave here before I give you the satisfaction of gloating over something I do wrong."

"Good. I think we understand each other very well."

The conversation ended and he walked out. After he left, for the first time since she came here Monica felt like she wanted to cry, and the tears were welling up in her eyes. She caught herself and thought I'm not going to give him the satisfaction of besting me. She was hurt by his words and suspicions, but most of all by the lack of love that she was so desperately craving.

That night after she finished doing all of her school assignments she got in bed with the earlier conversations still on her mind. For a long time she just lay there unable to sleep because of the emotional barriers that were preventing a restful entry into REM. Finally though, after locking her door getting back in bed and turning out the light she must have succumbed to the sandman and drifted off. There was no way for her to tell how long it was after that when she apparently awakened and noticed that there was a presence in the room. She saw a figure clearly standing just inside the door which she knew she had locked. Rubbing her eyes hoping to gain some visual clarity for what she was seeing was ineffective. The more she rubbed the more the figure became more pronounced and the thought of what had happened to her when she was a young child returned. Could this be happening again?

CHAPTER 4
The Search

The three Musketeers finished their sophomore year, weathering all of the trials and challenges that come with competing against other very bright and talented students male and female, with great success. Soun Li as expected soared to the top of the class with Monica following close behind. Reilly, who was more playful and less committed to studying seriously than her buddies, was not among the top ten, but definitely within the top 5%. Although all three had started out becoming members of the debate club, it didn't take long before Reilly realized this was not where her strong suit lay so she resigned and looked elsewhere. What she found out was that she had a talent for athletics so she tried out for the volleyball team and was accepted. That's where her gift was and she soon became one of the stars.

One of the other areas that the three were developing an interest in had to do with their social life, especially the boys. Year one found Monica and the other two, who were also quite attractive and well formed, repelling the attention of their male counterparts. This year perhaps due to the continued maturation and physical development of the girls made repelling the boys less desirable. More often they found themselves interacting with the boys and enjoying the new relationships. Monica who, of the three, had garnered the most attention and spent much of her time trying to figure out ways to keep the boys at bay while she pursued her studies, also changed her attitude. There was one boy however, who she was attracted to, but never let on that she had an interest in him. This young man was in the class one year ahead of the trio and did not pay much attention to her or her partners. Whenever Monica had occasion to cross paths with him she would linger a little longer than necessary just to be around him. It was difficult to make him notice her without being overly aggressive and she was puzzled since the other guys were lining up to get her interest. She wondered, at one point, whether there was something wrong with him or was it that he had somebody else. She was diligent in doing her investigation to see when he was with that other person, but her search turned up negative. At no point did she ever see him with another girl.

His name was Anthony Underwood and to her he was the most handsome guy she had discovered since she arrived here. He was about six feet four inches tall and had wavy black hair along with a bronze complexion that was flawless. It didn't hurt his cause with her that he was now a Senior and also captain of the basketball team. Whenever she could, between her other activities, she would find a way to attend the home games so she could watch him play. Soun and Reilly were aware of her affections for the boy and began to hash a plan to get the two of them together. Reilly came up with the idea that she should invite him to her sweet sixteen party and make sure that Monica had a chance to be with him. Reilly's father had rented out space in one of the local hotels and it was going to be a grand affair. Of course, when Monica was told about the plan she was all in and looking forward to it. Invitations were extended, RSVP's collected and so the party was set.

It was planned for a Saturday night in mid October and as many of her student friends as her father would allow were going to attend. Mr. O'Donell spared no expense, because he doted on his daughter, in getting a good band along with a local DJ and it was going to be an outstanding catered extravaganza. The problem that came up with Monica was that her father was not in favor of her going and it was causing the trio some concern. If Monica was not there the plan Reilly concocted would be a failure. Even though she fully planned to enjoy herself sincc it was her party, the plot to hook up Monica and Tony would be destroyed. When Monica told the trio about her issue the week before the event the girls set their brilliant minds working on an escape plan out of the house should that become necessary. It was well under way in development when one day Monica came to school and told the group that for some reason she had yet to figure out, her step father changed his mind and was going to allow her to go. They were all puzzled about this sudden change until Monica found out later that her father when he learned who was sponsoring the affair was going to try and get to know the man through his daughter for his own personal monetary gain. This was no surprise to Monica and when she explained it to the trio, they were now more understanding about what she was going through living in that house.

Saturday night came and the party was underway. The band was in high spirits and the music was loud just the way the kids wanted it. Mr. O'Donell and his wife along with a few of the other parents were there as chaperones, but they tried to remain as inconspicuous as possible without totally disappearing. Even though Harold had tried his best to finagle a way to get invited, Monica was having no part in assisting him to that end and she let him know that. Their relationship had sunk to an all time low and he knew it.

Anthony arrived along with some of the other members of the basketball team and Reilly made it a special point to have the band acknowledge their entry because of the championship they won last year. The social game was also well underway and now coach Reilly was busy making her point to join Monica with Tony. She introduced them and even suggested he dance with her. He looked at Monica as if seeing her for the first time and she was almost embarrassed at how his eyes took in every inch of what she had to offer. She had selected the most provocative dress in her meager wardrobe and the effect she was going for certainly now was working. Reilly got out of the way as the pair went on to the dance floor.

"Hi I know I've seen you around the school a lot of times, but I never really paid much attention. I'm sure sorry for that. I've never seen you looking like this. You look absolutely beautiful" he said.

Monica was almost giddy hearing these words coming from the object of her affection. She was trying to think of some clever response, but for the first time in her shool career she was at a loss for the right words. When she did answer it was almost as if she were about to stutter.

"You may not have noticed me, but I certainly paid attention to you every chance I got. You know I think I must have gone to every home game. I even watched you when you won that award. What was it the most something or other?"

He laughed then answered her question.

"It was the most valuable player award. Guess you don't know much about sports do you?"

"No. Other than making my way to your games I try to keep my head in the books so I can get a good job when I graduate. That occupies most of my time."

"You said go to work after leaving here. Aren't you going to college?"

"I don't think so. Unless I get some great scholarship offer my parents certainly aren't going to spring for sending me anywhere. In fact I am so anxious to get out of that house I will take any job or anything else to make it happen."

"Wow sounds like that's not a happy home you live in."

"You don't know the half of it. It will take me all night to really fill you in on what goes on there, but that's not why we're here so let's just enjoy the night."

They continued with that dance and then several others until the night was slipping away. Near the end of the function everything stopped and the bell of the ball Reilly was given center stage as a super large cake was brought out with sixteen candles on it. She did the traditional thing and blew them out, but not before making her wish. When asked by one of the oher girls what she wished for she smiled and said "wouldn't you really like to know?" The rest of the night was as much fun as Mr. O'Donell envisioned it would be and he was pleased there were no squabbles or incidents to mar the celebration. As for Monica and Tony, Reilly's strategy was working out just the way she planned it. At the end of the affair he asked if he could take her home since he had a car. She hesitated for a moment thinking about what would happen if and when her father found out, but then she mustered up her courage and said "sure."

On the way home Tony told her that he enjoyed the night and really liked her. He wanted to continue seeing her and maybe take her out sometime. She cautiously started to elaborate on what she started telling him earlier about her home life and how dating for her might cause a problem. He wasn't quite sure just how bad things were that she was trying to explain, but he said he understood and didn't push it. When they pulled up in front of her house it was about 11:30 pm and she could see that the lights were still on. He opened the car door for her and walked to the stairway. He started to try and kiss her, but she turned away knowing that her father was probably watching from his window. She apologized and said "maybe next time" then turned and entered the house all the while bracing for what she suspected might be coming.

She tried to quietly walk up the stairs and go to her room, but before she got there out he came.

"Do you know what time it is?" he said.

"Yes its 11:30 and the dance just ended.

'How did you get home? Did that highfalutin Mr. O'Donell bring you?"

"No he didn't. One of the other students did."

"You mean one of those boys has a car?"

"Yes and all he did was take me here. I don't want to argue about it. He was very nice and that's all he did. Now I'm going to bed."

He didn't try to stop her, but she knew that he was still staring at her when she entered her room.

That night just as she was getting into a sound sleep reminiscing about the wonderful evening again she saw the presence she had seen before. This time she knew she wasn't dreaming and the image became clearer as she continued to watch. It was a woman dressed in a long white robe and holding a black book to her chest. Her fingers were covering most of the title, but the part she could see it said Holy. The woman was trying to tell her something, but although her mouth was moving the words coming out were inaudible. Monica strained to hear what she was saying, but the image lingered for just another minute or so then disappeared. Monica was not afraid and felt she had some kind of connection to the image. Then she thought – could that have been my real mother?

The next day when she got to school she couldn't wait to find Tony and again thank him for last night. Looking around where she thought he might be was unsuccessful and time was running out before her first class. Quickly she bolted to homeroom to wait for the bell. Soun and Reilly were there so she greeted them and then again thanked Reilly for her successful plan that got her and Tony together. Reilly acknowledged her gratitude and asked her about whether he wanted to see her again. Just as she was about to go into a long explanation about his wanting to date and the problems it would cause in her house, the bell rang and the girls had to split up.

Later that day when they came together again during their common lunch period, Reilly curious about where the relationship she had fostered was going to go asked her again to finish her story.

"Well on the way home he started talking about how much he enjoyed being with me and then asked if he could continue to see me. You know start dating. I had to pause for a minute to catch my breath before answering because this is what I hoped for. Then I had to tell him about my step father and his evil ways. I told him the whole story about my being adopted and how strict he was. Dating on a regular basis would probably cause a lot of problems for me."

"He said he understood and felt kind of sympathetic for my situation, but we could see each other at school and for a little while after since his season had not started yet and she had time for her club meetings.

"It was so sensitive I had a hard time believing this was coming from a boy because all of the other boys I had ever talked to were all about just one thing regardless of my needs. After that it just made me feel more dedicated to finding a way out of that house. Of course when I walked in the house you know who was still up and waiting for me to come in. Right away he started questioning me about the time and who brought me home. When I told him that set him off and the bickering began. I was in no mood to listen to his diatribe after having such a wonderful time, so I just said goodnight went in my room and locked the door. But wait a minute let me tell you about something really strange that happened later last night. Just as I felt like I was going into a deep sleep, an image appeared just inside my door. I know I locked it because that's what I've been doing lately, but anyhow there it was plain as I could see. It was a woman dressed in a long white robe holding a black book to her chest. I could only see part of the title because her fingers were covering the rest of it, but it looked like it read Holy something or other.

Now what do you think about that?

"That man has got you flippin' out and seeing things" said Reilly.

"No wait a minute" Soun responded. "My parents used to tell me about how in the old days when they were still living in China their parents used to worship and idolize their ancestors even to the point where they were able to conjure up their spirits. Monica did you ever see this image before and if so under what circumstances did you see it?"

"You know now that you ask me that yes I believe I have seen it before not too long ago, but then I thought I was just not fully awake and partially dreaming. It also happened one night after I had had another altercation with my father. Okay what are you getting at?"

"Well like I said if there's any truth to what my parents have been telling me you may be experiencing some visitations from one of your ancestors who's trying to protect you or even warn you about something I don't know. Who of your people were you really close to?"

"I wasn't close to anybody besides my father and mother. I never got to meet any of their relatives when I was just a little girl. Then when I got older and perhaps could have been introduced to some of them, my father became sick and went into some kind of long term hospital. I was still very young so I didn't get to know him that well. So that leaves just my mother. As far back as I can remember it was just the two of us."

"Monica where is your mother now?"

"I don't know. When she left me at the place where I was adopted that was the last time I saw her."

"Do you have any way of finding out where she might be?"

"No. That agency may be my only hope, but I'm not sure whether they know either if she doesn't want to be found. Wait a minute I'm remembering now there was a close friend of my mother's who used to live in the same apartment building that we did. She's the only one I can think of who might even have a clue."

"Do you remember her name?"

"Yes, yes I do. I used to call her Aunt Trish. I believe that was a nickname for Patricia, but I'm not really sure."

"There you go. That's a start. You just need to find a way to get back to where you used to live and see if that Trish lady is still living there. If she is then you may be able to find your birth mother and if you do then the visitations might stop."

"You know you two are starting to sound a bit spooky here" Reilly interjected.

"Monica are you really going to try to find your mother because you think she's haunting you? That would mean she's dead wouldn't it?"

"Not necessarily " said Soun.

"If she's still living, but can't get to her then the only way to communicate is through the spirit." .

"Okay, okay Soun you're beginning to creep me out" said Reilly.

"But Monica I think I might be able to help you. If you want to try and find your real mom then I can ask my dad if he will take you there when you get an address."

"Thank you, but no thanks Reilly, I don't want your father getting involved in the search because he's too well known and it would probably somehow get back to my step father. Soun what about your brother you think he might help me?"

"I don't know, but I'll ask him? First find out where that apartment building is then I can tell him and see what he says."

"Okay I'll do that and get back to you."

The trio broke up and headed to their respective next classes. Now that Monica had some idea of what her visions could be all about she was determined to find out whether this was really possible. So next she started her address search. It didn't take long to accomplish this mission because the social service agency kept a record of where the birth parents lived. After making the call and identifying herself the service person asked a few more questions about the reason she was seeking the address, since the birth mother had requested anonymity. This took a little more convincing, but finally Monica was able to get the address. She wrote it down and made a point to find Soun at the end of the school day. When the bell rang ending the last class for the day Monica rushed out to the spot where she knew Soun's brother normally picked her up. She was there waiting as usual and the exchange was made. Soun looked at the address and noted that it was on the other side of the city.

"You used to live over here?" she said.

"Yes for my early years until I got adopted. I believe my first schooling started at a nursery in that neighborhood. Why did you ask?"

"Because my father always talks about a church somewhere around there where the preacher is well known for his work in the community and even some of my father's patients refer to him as a healer. My father even attended a service once, so he says. I don't remember ever going there myself, but he was impressed with the man's Bible knowledge on healing."

"I can't remember my parents ever going to any kind of church and certainly not taking me to one."

"Well no matter. I'll talk to my brother on the way home and see if he will take you. I guess you would like to do this as soon as he can right?"

"Yes the sooner I can go visit Aunt Trish, if she's still there, and get any information regarding my mother's whereabouts then I may be able to actually find her. You can't imagine how much I would like to have that happen. There are so many questions I need answers to."

"Okay I got it. I will emphasize the urgency of your quest and maybe he will listen. Sometimes he does, but most of the time he doesn't. He only picks me up because my father won't let him use the car on weekends if he doesn't. I'll let you know tomorrow his decision."

"Okay great. Hope he's in a good mood when you ask him."

For several months after Elena lost her job, finally her apartment and had to move in with Trish because she had no place else to go, the two of them were struggling to make ends meet. In the one bedroom unit space became a real issue and being cramped together they knew couldn't last. As much as they liked each other it was just a matter of time before the strain on their personalities reached a breaking point. When they started to bicker over little things almost on a regular basis common sense told them it was time to separate before something serious happens.

Elena left and went to a shelter for homeless women. After only a few days, she was not satisfied with her life there so she found another one. Even that one did not meet her needs so she thought and then the parade started. She moved around from one facility to another until there were no more places to go to. That's when she took to life on the streets rummaging around on a daily basis just to survive. She who once was a beautiful woman had sunk to the level where her appearance didn't matter to her anymore. In the morning she would walk the streets panhandling to try and get enough for at least one decent meal for the day. At night she would find an alley or a vacant building to squat in. Life on the street, she soon learned came at a high cost. Too many times she was subjected to a merciless beating of another homeless derelict who demanded sex or whatever else she could offer. Finally one day it reached the level where she thought life was no longer worth living, she had totally lost her way so she decided to end it all. Suicide to her was the only answer and an attempt was made.

Fortunately for her at the hospital where she was taken they were able to revive her. Ironically it was Trinity Memorial where Norman had been first treated years ago. As with all suicide patients there when she was recovered enough to talk with someone she was referred to the same Psychiatrist who treated Norman.

"Mrs. Miller, how are you feeling today?"

"I don't know I guess I'll survive."

"You know you are fortunate that help got to you when they did or you would not be surviving today as you say. Can you tell me why you decided to take those pills and end your life."

"Yes that's easy. I'm tired of living."

"Well now there must be a reason you feel that way can you give me that reason?"

"Now where would you like me to start. There are so many reasons."

"I'd like for you to start at the time and place when you first began to feel that way."

"That's easy too. When the only thing I had a reason to live for was taken away that's when it started."

"And what was taken from you?"

"My daughter, my only child was taken."

"Do you mean she was kidnapped?"

"No, no, no she wasn't kidnapped she was given to another family that could raise her because I couldn't. She was adopted by them."

"So you mean you had to give her up she was not taken, right?"

"To me she was taken and that's the way I see it then and the way I see it now. That's when life started to have no more meaning for me."

"Where is your daughter now? Do you know?"

"No I don't know and they won't tell me."

"Who won't tell you?"

"The people that took her."

"If you could get her back would that make you stop wanting to die?"

"Yes. I would have something to live for then."

'Mrs. Miller where are you living now?"

Sidney L. Jackson

"Nowhere, I don't have any home and I ain't going back to one of them so called shelters."

'Why do you call them so called shelters?"

"Because they don't shelter you from nothing. Some of the people in there are just as bad as the people on the street that I know."

"Now you must live somewhere. I can't release you and send you back to living on the streets of our fair city that wouldn't be right. Do you agree?"

"Yeah I know you're trying to do the right thing, but the street's the only place I know I can survive."

"Well Mrs. Miller that's not quite true. Remember you came here because living on the street made you do what you tried to do. I have a suggestion. Will you listen to what I have to offer and consider doing it?"

"Yeah that depends on what you offer?"

"First let me ask you do you believe in God?"

"Well yeah I used to when I was young, but I don't think he ever did anything for me that I can think of. Why you asking?"

"Because I'm going to recommend that you stay here for a few days under my supervision and then I'm going to invite somebody here, who is a friend of mine, to talk with you who may be able to help you see that life is worth living. I'm going to give you a mild sedative to help you relax now while I make arrangements for you to stay here. Is that alright with you?"

"Yeah I'm okay with that> Are they going to feed me? Who going to pay for me staying here?"

The doctor laughed.

"Yes they will feed you and don't you worry about who pays. Now I'm giving you this shot and you will feel a little drowsy so just relax, then I'll be back shortly."

The doctor injected her then left the room and went to check her in for a short stay. While he was out it occurred to him that he had seen this woman before and treated her husband some years ago. He wasn't going to bring that up with her now, but he kept it in the back of his mind. The important thing to do now was to get his friend to come in and talk with Elena.

The next day at school when the trio gathered in homeroom Monica was anxious to find out what happened with Soun's brother.

"Did you ask him? What did he say?"

"He said he would take you this weekend if you want to go then, but he will only take you there he's not going to wait around for you to bring you back."

"Okay that's only half good. Assuming that I find Aunt Trish still living in that building, and also assuming that she's still living at all how am I supposed to get back home?"

"You ever heard of taxi's girl?" Reilly said.

"Very funny buddy, yes I've heard of them, but I never heard of a free taxi ride have you? Going to that side of town from my house should be a little costly don't you think?"

"Don't worry about that. Since I've been helping my dad out in his office he's been paying me on top of my allowance so I have a few extra dollars to spare if you need it."

"That sounds great Reilly but I can't ask you to do that when I don't know when I could pay you back."

"Like I said I'm working so don't worry about paying me back. What are friend s for?"

"That sounds like a good plan Monica so I should tell my brother you will go with him this weekend. What time do you want to go and should he pick you up at your house?"

"No absolutely not at the house, I'm sure my father will be watching. Why don't I just walk around the corner from my house and he can meet me there. Around 1:00 O'clock would be good if that's okay with him. By that time my brothers and father will be so into video games and TV they won't even miss me."

"Okay so that's what I'll tell him. Unless you hear anything differently from me, then it's all set."

"Okay good."

The girls broke up and started their daily schedule.

It was only Wednesday when the plan was solidified so Monica spent the next few days anxiously awaiting the weekend anticipating a successful rendezvous with Aunt Trish. When Saturday arrived and just as she predicted, the guys were totally involved in games and her mother had gone shopping, at a few minutes to 1:00 she managed to slip out unnoticed and walked around the corner to the meeting place. Soun's brother was already there waiting so they were on their way quickly. Not much was said in route, but he was curious about why she was so anxious to get to this place. She gave him a very brief synopsis of the story that seemed to satisfy him and the rest of the way was quiet.

When they arrived at the apartment building Monica seemed to recall some fond memories of the place, but there was not a happy ending when she left there. He asked if she wanted him to wait until she made her connection and at first she said no, but then thought about the possibility of Trish not even being there so she asked if he would come in with her for a few minutes. He reluctantly obliged her and they went inside the vestibule. Looking at mailboxes Monica searched for a name beginning with P. She didn't recall her last name because she didn't think she ever knew it. Fortunately of the assortment of several mailboxes there was only one that had a P. in front of the name. It was P. Ramey. That certainly didn't ring any bells in Monica's memory, but there was no alternative at this point so she rang the bell to gain entry.

The speaker responded.

"Who is it?"

"Aunt Trish this is Monica."

There was a long hesitation before the voice continued.

"Monica, Monica Miller is that you?"

"Yes Aunt Trish may I come in?"

Almost immediately the entrance door buzzer sounded and the door unlocked. At this point he asked if she wanted him to go up with her and she said 'yes please for only a minute." When they got to Trish's door there was another bell which apparently wasn't working so she gently knocked. When the door opened the woman standing there with a head full of gray hair and a thin frame looked carefully at the couple. Here was this handsome Chinese young man and this gorgeous black girl wanting to come in. The woman stared in disbelief for more than a minute before inviting them in. Monica then turned to him and said thanks and she would be okay from here so he left.

"Monica is this really you? I have worried more about you for so long I can't even remember when I stopped. How are you and what are you doing here?"

"Aunt Trish I know you know I was adopted and I've been living with the most awful family for all those years. It's been like living in a nightmare that I can't wake up from. I missed you and my mother so much I can't even express it. Now I'm just trying to find her and maybe see if there's a way she can get me back. Do you know where she is or how to contact her?"

"Monica you are such a beautiful girl I can't believe my eyes looking at you. You know I said from the time you were born that you were going to be a looker and now here you are. I'm sorry to say though I don't know where your mother is or how to even begin to find her. You know she lost that apartment next door a long time ago and then lived with me for a while, but that didn't work out because as you can see this place is just too small for the two of us so she left. After that I know she lived in some shelters, but when she left the last one I lost touch with her and don't know where she went. What about my father what ever happened to him?"

"As far as I know he is still in that mental hospital, but there's no use in trying to talk to him because the last time I visited him with your mother he didn't even know who she was. It's such a shame. I'm afraid I can't be any help to you in that way. Have you tried the social service agency they might know where she is?"

"Yes I started there, but if they know they won't tell me. I don't know what else to do, I have to get out of that house I'm living in before they drive me crazy or I hurt somebody there."

"It's that bad?"

"Worse. Well if you don't know I'm at a dead end."

"Well now wait a minute there is one other possibility. You know I have joined that church where you went to nursery school and they have a group called the Missionary Guild who do a lot of work with the various shelters and group homes. They might have come across your mother at some time. It wouldn't hurt to find out. Tomorrow I'm going to the 11:00 am service. Would you like to come with me? I can introduce you to one of the guild members and they can maybe answer your question or even guide you to her whereabouts."

"That would be great except I have no way to get to that church. As a matter of fact I don't even have a way to get back home now. The boy who brought me here is the older brother of one of my friends from school and he's not likely to repeat my transportation."

"Oh I thought maybe you had an international thing going on and he was your beau."

"No not hardly I'm not into that he just did me a favor because his sister asked him to for me."

"Okay no problem. As far as you getting home, I'll be glad to take you. I'll even pick you up tomorrow if you want to go with me to church. Just tell me whre you live."

"That sounds great I'm so glad I at least found you maybe this could lead to finding my mother."

"Okay I will pick you up at 10:30 am please be ready so I don't have to wait. I don't like to be late for service.

"I'll be ready."

Trish drove her home and saw where she lived. Before Monica got out of the car she thanked her and told her this was an evil house.

It was now about 4:30 in the afternoon and as soon as Monica walked in the house the interrogation started. This time it wasn't from her father, but her mother who wanted to know where she had been for so long without telling her. Monica who had now become a rather skillful liar to them, thought of a wonderful excuse for not only being out so long, but also for not telling her. It seemed to pacify her mother and the interrogation ceased. Once inside her room, her sanctuary, she lay across the bed and wondered how long could she continue to tolerate this family.

On Sunday morning it was a bright and clear day with not a cloud in the sky. Monica had already told her mother that she was going to church with a friend who was picking her up. Although the Evans family were not church goers themselves they could not in good conscious prevent her from going. To them letting her go they believed would possibly enhance their perception to the neighbors of how good they were. Trish arrived on time just as she said she would and they were off.

It had been so long since Monica had been inside a church except for her days at the nursery that it seemed almost strange to her. The service was a traditional one and the choir was in excellent form. Monica was thoroughly impressed with all that took place and said to Trish she would love to come back, but that might be a problem going forward. Trish didn't quite understand what she was saying, but didn't pursue it. At the end of the service, as promised, Trish found one of the guild members and introduced Monica to her. She was happy to meet the young girl and commented on how pretty she looked. When Trish explained why they sought her out she was sympathetic with the search, but said she could not recall having come across anyone matching the description of Monica's mother. She did however, offer that the members did not all visit the same places and it was possible that one of the others may have seen the woman. She asked if Monica had a picture of her mother. Monica bowed her head shamefully and softly said she did not. Trish however said she did have a nice picture of her although not one that was recent, but clear enough to get a good idea of what she looked like. Trish reached in her purse and went through some photos that she kept in a wallet. Sure enough there it was. She handed it to the guild member and the member told them she would circulate it among her group at the next meeting which happened to be this Tuesday evening. Satisfied that they at least had a possibly good lead on finding her mother Monica and Trish left the church.

When Monica got back home at about 3:00 O'clock the family was not there. Apparently one of the boys had some kind of accident with his bike and they were all at the hospital. A note was left on the refrigerator door briefly stating what happened and that they hoped to be back soon. The note did not specify what the nature of the accident was so Monica speculated on what it might be. First she thought he might have been hit by a car because Ricky was the one who thought he was a daredevil and took all kinds of chances on his bike. Then she moved on to Michael. Perhaps he was also hit by a car because he was always talking on his phone and not looking where he was headed. Either way she had a hard time feeling any genuine remorse for their condition regardless of what it might be or who.

She was able to grab something out of the fridge and had just sat down to eat when the front door opened and the family walked in. She was right in her mind's speculation. It was Ricky who did indeed get run over by a car. He had a long cast on his right leg and limped in on crutches. They all saw Monica sitting at the kitchen table and for some reason they were very hostile toward her for no apparent reason. Harold just looked at her before saying anything as if he was trying to blame her for what happened to Ricky. Since she was not even around when it happened so logically there was no way she could have had anything to do with it, but that didn't matter to him. When he finally spoke he asked her how long she had been there and did she see the note on the refrigerator door. His next diatribe went in to the fact that she did not care enough about her brother to even call the hospital to inquire about his welfare. Monica just dropped her head and shook it which infuriated him even more. Without finishing her sandwich at the table she grabbed it and left the kitchen walking right by him without uttering a word in response.

For the rest of the afternoon she stayed in her room on her laptop searching and researching ways to find an exit from this house. Since she was still under eighteen and in school there were not a lot of options. At dinner that night she came down and all of the talk was about how the driver of the car was so much at fault that they were going to sue the pants off of him. Not once did they ever consider the possibility that it was Ricky's fault. When Monica looked at Ricky during his parents rant, even he looked down showing some sign of guilt. She noticed it, but no one else did. Well she thought at least they had something else to talk about besides everything being my fault and it took the pressure off of her temporarily.

That night as she prepared to go to bed she did one final thing. She made sure that her bedroom door ws locked. Once again as she was getting to the point where the REM state was about to occur the image that had been visiting more frequently appeared. This time it was so clear that it could hardly be mistaken for a dream. The woman was again dressed in a long gleaming white robe still holding the black book to her chest. But this time Monica could see all of the title and it said Holy Bible. Although her mouth was still moving, but again the words continued to be inaudible. With this new clarity Monica could clearly tell that this was not the image of her mother, as she thought, but it was someone else.

CHAPTER 5

On Becoming

H oly Trinity Baptist church on the corner of Elmwood Avenue and Spruce street took up more than five square blocks of land. It was a complex that contained not only a modern nursery, a recreational center, a large auditorium with ample off street parking, but it also provided temporary housing for men and women who were in the midst of some type emergency displacement crisis. Under the leadership and pastoral care of Reverend Doctor David Dumas, the church was a beckon of light throughout the community. As the shepherd of the congregation, the holy flock, he had led them through many tough times, trials and tribulations over a period of twenty-five years in building up this sanctuary to finally reaching this pinnacle of worship. The membership role now boasted a number in excess of four thousand members and on any given Sunday there would be over two thousand worshipers in the house.

There were several ministries within the organizational structure of the membership and their service throughout the community was exemplary. Over the years the church had been recognized and awarded many accolades for their work. Even a few major magazine had placed the church in high esteem and one even gave them a four page spread in a monthly issue. Often the local newspapers would highlight an event or affair that brought national attention to something or someone who had exceeded the expectations of the city. Of all the ministries that met regularly and dedicated their service to God, there was one that focused on helping the poor, the indigent, the hopeless and all those who had lost their way that received the greatest praise from the so called grassroots people. It was those battered women, those victims of rape and or incest, those who had been tossed aside by society and suffered from low self-esteem and especially those who for an assortment of reason had given up on living, who offered the greatest praise and gratitude.

The Missionary Guild was the title given to this ministry and it served the whole city regardless of who the person in need happened to be. They worked with the hospital system, boarding homes, group homes, various shelters and all those places dedicated to helping the sick become well. It was at one of these places that a member of this ministry had occasion to come across Elena for the short time she resided there. Elena was particularly despondent and in conversation with this member of the ministry expressed an intense desire to be reunited with her daughter. When the Missionary Guild held their bi-weekly meeting and the member who received the picture from Trish circulated the photo among the group, the member who had been with Elena recalled talking with her because of her heartfelt desire to get back with her child.

When Trish received the telephone call from the missionary member telling her that Elena had been located she could hardly wait to get in touch with Monica to give her the good news. However, it was not known at that time, which was several weeks ago that Elena had left that shelter and taken to the streets. So it was when Monica was able to get the information on that specific shelter and made contact with the head administrator, although they did have a record of Elena having been there, she was gone and when she left there was no forwarding information regarding her current whereabouts. From the highest of heights to the deepest depths of despair Monica went from feeling totally elated about the possibility of reuniting with her true mother to the sinking feeling of absolute disappointment. When she told Trish about the result of her contact with the shelter and the disappointing news, Trish had no words of consolation that could lift up Monica's head. However, she did offer one more encouraging possibility and that was Elena may have been at one time in a hospital and it might be worth checking into. Monica gladly received that advice and set off on a new research direction.

Ring, ring, ring.

"Hello, Holy Trinity church how can I help you?"

"Hello is pastor Dumas available now?"

"No I'm sorry he's in a meeting and not expected back until this afternoon. Would you like his voice mail?"

"No that's okay I'll try contacting him again later. When you see him would you just tell him that Doctor Danforth called. He's an old friend of mine and I would like to talk to him about a patient I have."

"I will deliver the message as soon as he comes out."

"Thank you goodbye."

"Goodbye."

Doctor Danforth hung up and proceeded to go into the ward to see about Elena. It was only yesterday that he had examined her and arranged for her to stay. But when he walked in and didn't see her anywhere he questioned one of the nurses.

"Nurse where is Mrs. Miller? She was admitted yesterday, but I don't see her anywhere now."

"Oh doctor the night nurse said she had the hardest time with her last night and Mrs. Miller said she wasn't going to stay here long. The nurse, after some pleading and cajoling convinced her to stay at least for the night because it was late and very cold outside. Mrs. Miller allowed her to give a shot to help her sleep and that was it for the night. However, early this morning when she woke up she wanted to leave. There were no instructions or provisions for us to restrict her so we had to let her go."

"Did she tell anybody where she was going?"

"No as far as I know she was going home."

"Nurse that's a problem. She's homeless - doesn't have any home to go to. Why didn't someone call me when all this was happening?"

"When I came on this morning she was feeling fine just wanting to go home so I didn't see the need to call you. You know now that I think about it I believe I did hear her say she was going to her daughter's house so we didn't inquire any further."

"Nurse her daughter is an illusion in her mind. She doesn't even know, if she really has one or where her daughter is. That's one of the reasons why I had her admitted here. We've got to find a way to get her back."

"I'm sorry doctor I didn't know all of the particulars about her case. How can I help find her?"

"Well there's not much you can do now so just go on with your regular duties. I'll take it from here."

The next thing he did was to go back to his office and call the police department asking to speak with the officers who brought her in. According to their records there was no permanent address in the files for her either. What they did have was a picture that could be used to pick her up if they found her. The sergeant that he spoke with said he needed a reason for them to bring her to the hospital. Milton Danforth, the doctor, explained to him that she was under his care and never should have been released from the hospital. The sergeant's next question was whether she was to be considered dangerous. Milton assured him she was not, but she may be a bit reluctant to go with them. The sergeant said he understood and would put out a bulletin to all patrols immediately to be alert for her and if spotted take her to the hospital. The doc thanked him for his cooperation and said he hoped it would be soon when they found her.

Later that afternoon as he promised Doctor Danforth placed a call again to the church.

Ring, ring, ring.

"Hello Holy Trinity Church how can I help you?"

"Hi this is Doctor Danforth again I called earlier this morning. Is the pastor available now?"

"He's on his phone right now, but when I talked to him before he said he was anxious to talk with you so let me buzz him and let him know you're holding."

"Thank you that will be fine."

A few minutes later she came back on the line.

"Okay sir he's free now I'm going to transfer the call."

"Milton is that really you? I was wondering what happened to you since we last met at that golf tournament in Hilton Head."

"Yes it's me and I played so badly during that outing I thought it best that I disappear for awhile until the team got over it."

"Come on now none of us was having a great game that day so don't feel like we lost because of you. We all looked for you at the clubhouse after and no one could find you. It was all in fun and believe me no hard feelings were kept. Where are you now?"

"Oh I'm back at the hospital and that's one of the reasons why I'm calling you. I don't know if you remember some years ago I was treating a young man who had delusions of being indwelled by some evil spirit who his father had foisted on him."

"Yes now that you mention it I do remember him because you asked me if I would talk to him about his beliefs. I don't recall having much success in exorcising any of his so called demons, but whatever happened to him?"

"Well his condition got to the point it was becoming far beyond my capacity to continue to treat him here so I had him transferred to that mental facility over in Jersey. After that I lost touch. But that's not why I'm calling you now. Listen to this. Two days ago his wife was brought in with almost the same type of delusion that he had. I was just getting started in trying to treat her after a very preliminary examination when she signed herself out of the hospital and disappeared. I'm calling you to see if you want to take a few moments to talk with her and see whether as you say some demons may be involved that I need to know about."

"Well old buddy you know I have no problem in speaking with anyone who seems to be having a spiritual problem, but you said she disappeared."

"Yes that's right, but I have the police searching for her now and I'm confident she'll be picked-up soon and brought back here. I just wanted to know whether you were interested."

"Certainly, soon as you have her in your shop give me a call and I'll try to set up a session with her. Now what else is going on in your life?"

The two friends went on to start talking about old times, the golf tournament and a host of other things for about another hour until the doctor was called away.

Meanwhile Monica was having a difficult time accepting the fact that she had practically reached a dead end in her search for her mother. It seemed that every time she made an advance and got a lead on her mother's whereabouts that ended up being no more than another false positive. She finally came to the place where pursuing her quest was like living the impossible dream, so she ceased looking. As a result of her devoting so much time invested in researching her mother's location, her studies slipped and her grades showed it. As a rising Senior this was not the time for her to be slack in maintaining a high grade point average if she wanted to at least compete for scholarship funding. She realized this and began to refocus her attention on her goal.

The undercover relationship with Tony was blossoming and the not so secret love affair was well known by all the student body. Although he could not ask her out in the evening for a real date, they made the best of what they could by meeting at times when and where they could. The rest of the first semester seemed to fly by and now Tony was not so available as he had been because the basketball season started. But even then she didn't fail to show up at every home game and was the loudest single cheerleader, mostly for him, in the gym. Into the second semester for seniors graduation was becoming the highpoint of school life along with vying for whatever scholarship funding they could secure in getting into their favorite college. For Tony this was not so much of an issue like the others because the coach had already positioned him to get a number of offers from some top universities. The other major focus for them was the major event of the year – the Senior Prom.

There was no question about who Tony was going to escort to the affair, but the question remained about would she be permitted to go. The situation at home had not improved and at every turn when Harold suspected that she was seeing some boy after school, his efforts to inquire about her after school activities became more like the FBI than the real FBI. It had gotten to the point, as the time approached when she knew she had to let her father know about the prom and hope he would realize how much this meant to her. Well before committing to Tony that she would be able to go she started dropping little hints around the house about a major event coming up. Her mother picked up on them, but Harold remained clueless. For once in that house Laura came to her rescue, because she remembered how important it was to her when she was in school so she talked openly about what Monica was hoping for. After it was explained, Laura said she would lobby for her and convince her father to let her go. This was the best news she could have received from her, even though it did not completely make up for all of the other injustices that she had done.

When Monica came to school the next day she almost ran to find Tony before the school day began to tell him the news. What she forgot however was that the team not only practiced after school, but they were involved early in the morning in what was called strength and conditioning drills. When it finally occurred to her why she couldn't find him she stopped looking and went to her homeroom. There the three musketeers, along with the rest of the class, were all abuzz about who was taking who to the dance. For the other two of the trio going to the prom was not an issue as far as being allowed to go, but they were concerned that their friend may have a problem.

"Did Tony ask you yet?" said Soun.

"Ask me what Monica replied playfully?"

"You know what I'm talking about. Did he ask you to go to the prom with him?"

Then Monica got down off of her high horse and answered.

"Of course he did. Who else was he going to ask?"

"That's great chimed in Reilly, but what about your step dad, did he agree to let you go?"

"You two won't believe this, but it was my step mother who persuaded him. That's probably the only righteous thing she did for me since I came into that house. Anyway I do owe her a kind of debt of gratitude because she came through. Okay now what about you, who is taking you?"

Each of the other two revealed their dates and the plan on how to celebrate at and after the affair. Of course it was the strategist, coach Reilly leading the pack.

The days seemed to move faster in the second semester than they did in the first. Preparation for the prom had reached the level where the whole school was excited about it even those who were not going. The place that it was to be held was The Rainbow Garden Resort Hotel, one of the swankiest sites in the immediate area. The cost for the students and their parents would have been very high, but when Mr. O'Donell stepped in and negotiated, the price suddenly became reasonable. The place was set, the time was set all that had yet to be done now was for the girls finding the right prom dress and for the boys the most elegant tuxedo. To Reilly and Soun this was not a big issue, it was just a matter of going shopping. But to Monica it became almost embarrassing when she thought about how was she going to get a suitable dress. Getting Harold or even Laura to chip in was unthinkable so what to do now was the question. Her only other option was to possibly go to Trish for help. Since she had been discovered Monica frequently called Trish to try and keep abreast of what may be happening with the search for her mother. Although Trish was retired and not well off, she often would send Monica small monetary gifts because she knew about her situation.

When Monica started shopping for the right dress, she was astonished by the prices. Each store she visited seemed to try and out price the one she visited previously. Exasperated and disillusioned by what it was going to cost to get a decent dress, she knew she couldn't ask Trish to sponsor her. What to do now was the question? As she pondered her dilemma, a thought that had been dormant in her mind for at least two years resurfaced. This was the dark side in her persona that had been suppressed for good so she thought. But now, being in a no viable solution situation the idea of shopping without money came back to the forefront of her thinking. She had seen the ideal dress in one of the department stores and now she was hell-bent on adding it to her wardrobe regardless of te cost.

It was Nords High Fashion Emporium in the heart of the downtown area where she set her sights on retrieving the garment. Developing a fool proof theft plan, after all these years of inactivity, was going to take some heavy consideration. Aiding in her planning was the idea she had heard her mother say years ago that where there's a will there's a way, she started her scheme. The first thing she had to do was to go back to the store and make sure that dress in her size was still there. Secondly she had to reconnoiter the whole store to determine where the security posts were and the best escape route for a quick exit undetected. Having formulated her plan it was time to carry it out so she went. Inside the store she first confirmed what the booty was and it's disposition then she walked around pretending to shop but in reality surveilling the target. Satisfied the plan was workable she left.

Three days later in mid day just after school let out, she chose one of the busiest shopping days when she knew the store would be crowded to execute her plan. Removing the dress from the rack she then took it to the dressing room where she cleverly took the dress still on the hanger and hooked on to the back of her dress and smoothed it out. She had worn an extra large overcoat so that no unusual bulges would be noticeable. Looking in the mirror before leaving, she believed that her plan was working. Boldly walking out her preplanned escape route was the height of her brilliance. Outside the store she wasted no time in getting to the nearest corner and rounding it. Breathing a sigh of relief she slowed her pace and casually walked to the bus stop.

Once she got home and passed the usual family scrutiny she went directly to her room and took off the overcoat. Only slightly wrinkled she spread it out on the bed and smoothed it out. Only now did her conscious start to bother her and she wrestled for just a moment on what she had done. Looking at the beautiful dress and considering that she never could have been able to afford it under a normal circumstance, her conscious lost the battle between good and evil. Quickly she hung it up in her closet and concealed it behind some of her other dresses just in case Laura should happen to come in unannounced. The prom was only a few days away now and she was more excited now than ever knowing she had a dress that would dazzle everyone there, ,especially the one she wanted to impress. With the low cut cleavage that would tantalize anyone looking and the rest of the garment short enough to show off her very shapely sturdy legs, she was certain to be the bell of the ball. The problem now was to make sure she could get out of the house without Harold or Laura being able to see what she was wearing. She also had a plan for that.

At school **the next morning** when the trio were together again in homeroom, it was time to compare dresses. Reilly boasted that she had garnered the only Gaby Hearst original in the whole city. Soun Li, much less bombastic than Reilly, was happy to report that she was able not get one not by some high fashion designer, but one that would make her the highlight of the show. Next it was Monica's turn to weigh in.

"I know that I can't compete with you two in that area, but I did manage to find something I think will impress."

"Where did you get yours?" Reilly said talking to Monica.

"I got it from Nords."

"Nords? You went shopping at Nords?"

"Yes I did and found just what I wanted in my size."

"Where did you get the money for that?" asked Soun Li.

"Oh I have a secret wealthy admirer."

"You mean a sugar daddy don't you? Where's he been hiding?"

They all laughed as the bell rang for them to break up and go to class. Although Monica knew she was lying, it was becoming more of a habit with her than she wanted to admit. The thing she feared the most was that one day she might get caught lying and then have to explain the truth. But for now it was all working out fine.

The search for Elena was now into the second week and there was no sign of her location. It was not as if she had so many places to hide, but it was a matter of when a person does not wish to be found then they won't be. One day she would be squatting inside a vacant building then the next day she would be sleeping in some alley way. As the days continued to pass the search for her was becoming less and less of a priority. Sometimes she would even go to a shelter to at least get a hot meal for the day, but it wa never her intention to remain at any one of them for any length of time. Most of the facility's social workers had become accustomed to her transient life style and would provide for her food and shelter as she desired it. None of them ever reported to the police, even though most of them knew they were looking for her, that she had visited their place because it was felt that since she was not harming or threatening anybody, leave her alone. Whether the thinking consensus was that they were protecting her rights or that she did not deserve to be incarcerated by law enforcement, the behavior was generally agreed upon.

It was not until the winter season was approaching and the night time temperatures dropped to near freezing that her survival odds were dipping. The lack of proper warm clothing, especially heavy socks, gloves and a hat made moving around in the streets hard to manage. As much as she told herself she could survive, no matter what, the imminent outcome was just a breath and a heartbeat away. One night when the temperature had dropped below freezing she was found bundled up in some old rags and newspapers and barely breathing. It so happened that the alley was just behind a restaurant and when a worker inside opened the back door to take out the trash he spotted her and called the police.

Again she was taken to Trinity Memorial in such poor condition the medical professionals listed her as critical. In addition to suffering from hypothermia and malnutrition she was showing signs of pneumonia. There was nothing she had with her that could provide any identification for the doctors so the question of who to call for notification remained a mystery. At this point it was just fate that stepped in when one of the night nurses recognized her from being admitted not too long ago to this hospital. It took a few minutes for the nurse to recall her name, but when she did she went to the files and retrieved her history. Elena Miller again now had an identity other than Jane Doe and the only name on her emergency call list was Patricia Ramey.

It was 1:30 am when the phone rang and Trish was awakened and startled by the sound.

"Who in the world is crazy enough to be calling me this hour of the morning?"

She looked at the caller ID and saw that it was the hospital so she answered.

"Hello."

"Hello is this Patricia Ramey?"

"Yes, yes it is. What's wrong?"

"This is nurse Squire at Trinity Memorial and we have someone here who lists you as her emergency contact."

"Her name is Elena Miller do you know her?"

"Yes I do. Is she alright?"

"Well no not exactly. Are you able to come down here now we may need your authority in making a decision."

"Decision about what?"

"Please time is of the essence. If you can please come now and I will explain when you get here."

"Okay I'll be there soon. What did you say your name was?"

"Nurse Squire. You can ask for me at the emergency entrance and they will direct you to where I'll be."

"Thank you. I'm on my way."

Trish started to call Monica before she left, but then thought about the time and didn't want to wake her up before she got to the hospital and had more information. She could not have known that Monica was already awake still shaken by the latest visitation from the image earlier. This time the image of the spirit was vividly clear, still dressed in a long white robe and holding the Holy Bible. The words that issued forth from her mouth were no longer inaudible, but loud and clear.

"Monica, Monica, Monica do not be alarmed nor afraid for I have come to help you and to warn you of things that are about to happen and those that will take place soon. I am your grandmother Lois, your mother's mother. You have never met me, but I have watched you from the time you were born. It is unfortunate that you were never brought before me so that I could bless you, but it was your father who prevented it. Now that he is out of the way, I have come to guide you on your next phase of life.

You have been going through many trials and tribulations since childhood because this is the cross you must bear. Soon your mother will complete the circle of life that represents the infinite nature of energy, if something dies it gives new life to another. As her offspring you will continue that legacy. She is yet still alive now, but teetering on the brink of eternity. Soon you will receive a telephone call and it will tell you of her whereabouts. Do not go to school, but go to her for she will have much to say in a short period time.

I will continue to visit you as you need, but know this the blessings that are in store for you will not happen if you do not believe."

Monica was visibly shaken by the image and warning message, but she was also elated inside to know that her mother had been found. While she didn't completely understand the part about the circle of life, she felt that it had something to do with her mother's condition. Anxiously she waited for the phone to ring without trying to go back to sleep.

Trish arrived at the hospital about 30 minutes after her call from the nurse. After getting directions from the reservationist at the emergency entrance she was directed to a ward where Elena was. She found nurse Squire and was then shown to the room where Elena was. Although her condition was still listed as critical she seemed to be clinging to life for some reason. The nurse explained to Trish that her vital signs were fluctuating between stable and erratic and even though they were giving her various medications intravenously and a feeding her through a tube, it was just her will to live that was keeping her alive at this point.

Watching her good friend lying there hovering between life and death was traumatic for her, but then she realized that this was something she should no longer keep from Monica. Regardless of the time a call should be made now.

Ring, ring, ring, ring.

"Hello."

"Hello Monica this is Trish are you up?"

"Yes and no. I'm awake, but not up yet. I had the strangest dream last night. It was about my mother. Did you find her? Did something happen to her?"

"Yes and that's why I'm calling so early. You need to get dressed and come down to Trinity Memorial Hospital right away. Don't ask me a lot of questions now, but just dress quickly and get here. I can come and get you if you want."

"Yes, yes if you want me to get there right away then that's the only way I can. I'll be ready when you get here."

Trish left the hospital immediately. Twenty minutes later she arrived at the house. It was still very early and the Evans family was not up yet. Monica quietly slipped out the front door and got in the ear.

"Is she alright?"

"I don't want to alarm you unnecessarily, but soon you shall see for yourself. She is being treated with all that they can so there is still hope. We'll be there shortly so just hang in there, but be prepared for what you will see."

Moments later they arrived at the hospital and were permitted to go up to the room. When Monica saw her mother lying there her first thought was she was dead because she was so still. But all of the tubes and monitoring machines were still indicating that there was life in the body. She allayed her fear and moved toward the bed taking her mother's hand and holding it. Although the hand was just lukewarm it was a sign of the presence of life. Gently rubbing it for a few minutes stimulated a reaction that even the nurse, who was still in the room, was not expecting, Elena's eyes opened and after a brief effort to focus she looked at Monica and smiled. Monica felt so relieved she smiled back and started to talk to her.

"Mama I missed you so much, so much I don't know what to say now."

As Elena lay there attempting to form words of her own, the difficulty of speaking was evident by the nurse so she raised the bed slightly making it a bit easier.

"It's so good to see you my daughter I wasn't sure I would ever see you again. There is so much I need to tell you, I don't know where to begin.

The words were coming out, but it was a struggle to keep talking. The nurse tried to intervene and told her she must rest, but Elena waived her hand as if to silence her and kept on talking.

Baby I know I don't have much time left in this world so let me finish what I have to say before I go.

"Oh mama please don't say that."

Again Elena waived her hand and kept talking.

"When you were just a baby your father didn't want you at first, but he came to love you just as I did. Before his father died and he went to the funeral something happened to him there and he was never the same. He tried to tell me, but I never completely understood. After he got sick it was just you and me and I tried to do the best I could to raise you, but times got hard so I had to give you up, but I never stopped loving you. I searched for you for years, but did not find you. Now you are here and I want to say again I'll always love you. Though times may get hard for you in this life, remember who you are and that you are a good girl with a good future. I know we never took you to church like I wanted to because your father was against it, but I know now that that was wrong. Stay close to Trish she will lead the way there. Know and remember this before I close my eyes for the last time, you must find salvation for yourself. No one can get it for you, be strong and believe there is a God."

As she uttered her last words, she closed her eyes and departed this world.

"Mama, mama no, no, no" Monica cried out as she continued to squeeze her mother's hand.

The nurse wrapped her arms around Monica's shoulders and escorted her out of the room with Trish close behind.

"We did all that we could to keep her alive, but it was just too late" the nurse said.

"There are some things now that we have to take care of."

The nurse went over the procedures that had to be followed and the papers that needed to be signed. Monica was still distraught, but she realized what had to be done so she complied. Still ringing in her ears were her mother's last words and she vowed to never forget them.

Trish took her home and by now the Evans family were all up and eating breakfast. As she walked in the door with the evidence of tears still on her face, they just looked at her and kept on eating. She hurried past and went to her room to continue to grieve alone. Since Monica had turned seventeen Harold and Laura had ceased trying to be parents to her and permitted her more freedom than she ever had before. As long as she didn't do anything to embarrass the family as Harold put it, and as long as the checks still came in, their mutual existence was at arm's length. This was fine with Monica because it gave her more time to plot her escape from their capitivity.

The day that her mother passed was a Thursday and she contemplated not going to school that Friday. It was just one week prior to the prom event, so she decided to attend school just to keep abreast of what was happening regarding the ball. Soun Li and Reilly were concerned about her and asked about her health. She reluctantly confided in them about finding her mother and about her death. The two friends sympathized with her and asked whether she needed anything from them. Since the funeral had not been planned yet, she told them there was nothing they could now, but she would like for them to attend with her when it was scheduled. Assurances were given that they would so the subject was dropped.

Later that day when she ran into Tony she told him what had happened and he was the most supportive of all her friends. He told her though he was going to be leaving for a few days with the team to participate in a basketball tournament in Columbia, South Carolina and he should be back on Wednesday. He hoped that the funeral would not be held before then, becaue he wanted to go with her. Monica said that she was not planning it, but a good friend of her mothers was. She didn't think though that it would be held before he got back and had already talked to Trish, her mother's friend, about the upcoming prom so if she could she would not have it too close. Tony acknowledged it and said he hoped so too.

Trish had taken on the responsibility of planning the funeral, but she was having a difficult time in making it happen. Her first big challenge was who was going to eulogize her since she was not a member of any church that she knew of. The second hurdle was Elena had no insurance of any kind and the meager allowance the city would provide for people like her was insufficient for even getting a decent casket. So she turned to the Missionary Guild for help. When she talked with the same woman who had taken the picture to circulate among the group, she was told that they would be glad to help her, but the timing was bad. The church was already inundated with services for members in the very near future that placing a non-member on the schedule would be difficult any time soon. Trish was a little disappointed becaue she didn't know where else to turn, especially without any significant funds to bargain with.

The member did offer one caveat and that was to speak to the pastor and maybe he could arrange a possible double ceremony in one day. She said it was rare that they did this, but not unprecedented. Trish saw this as a glimmer of hope so she called the pastor's office immediately and tried to speak with him directly, but to no avail he was in meetings. Later that afternoon when he finally was able to speak with her she told him about her plight and asked whether there was something he could do. He began to explain that the church was booked solidly for the next few weeks with funerals, but when she mentioned the deceased name he stopped for a minute and asked her again. After she repeated it he asked her a little bit more about this person. Convinced now that she was the same woman his friend had called him about, he reconsidered the schedule and looked at a possible date to do a double ceremony. He also told her that it would not be before two weeks because he had to consult would the other family who is already scheduled for the date he had in mind. Trish said she understood, but at least now she had some option. He then asked who was holding the body and would that be a problem for that length of time. Trish responded that it was still at the hospital morgue and she wasn't sure about the answer, but she would check. The conversation ended with both of them needing to confirm their part and get back to each other.

The hospital was cooperative and told Trish it would not be a problem, but she needed to keep them apprised of what date they need to release the body and who would have the authority to remove it. She gladly agreed and told them she would definitely keep them informed.

Pastor Dumas after talking with Mrs. Ramey called his friend the same day.

Ring, ring, ring.

"Hello Doctor Danforth's office may I help you ?"

"Hello this is Reverend Dumas is the doctor available?"

"I'm sorry he's with a patient right now do you seek an appointment?"

"No he's a friend of mine. Please tell him when you can that I have some information about the woman we talked about and I think he may be interested in hearing what I have to say."

"Does he have your number I'll ask him to return your call?"

"Yes he does. Thank you."

He hung up and went about the rest of the business of the day.

When Trish got back to Monica and told her about where they stood with making the funeral happen, she was glad to hear that it was not going to be before her prom. Trish acknowledged her joy but added that as of yet even that proposed date was not a lock and could change. Monica responded that she didn't care, she was just happy to know that some arrangements were definitely being made to bury her mother properly. She then asked Trish where she was going to be buried. Trish responded that the church had a private burial ground just outside the city and she would be placed in a special section for those who were indigent. Monica was also glad to hear that and told Trish she would be forever thankful for all her help and felt her mother, wherever she is now is also thanking her. Trish laughed and commented that she wasn't so sure about that because she wasn't so sure where she went to.

When the receptionist told Dr. Danforth about his friend calling and what the message was that he left, it left a curious feeing in the doctor's mind. Was he calling about setting up a consultation session with Mrs. Miller because he was aware that she was still not at his hospital?" Perhaps he heard something on the radio or television that he may have missed about her being found. The only way for him to know was to place the call and find out.

Ring, ring, ring.

"Hello, Holy Trinity Church how can I help you?"

"Hello, this is Dr. Danforth I'm returning a call pastor made to me earlier today. Is he available now?"

"Hold on please let me check. He is available – I'm transferring your call now."

"Hey Milton how you doing? You're not going to believe what I found out today about that Mrs. Miller we talked about a few days ago."

"Oh yeah what about her, did you hear something good?"

"Well not really what I heard is something I'm sure you were not expecting."

"Okay man don't keep me in suspense. What did you hear?"

"She's dead."

"Dead, you heard that today?"

"Yes one of my church members came in earlier today wanting some help in getting a friend of hers buried. Her friend had no insurance, she was short of funds and there was no one to give her a proper burial. So naturally she came to the church as she should for help. When she brought up the friend's name it immediately jogged my memory so I questioned her a little more and sure enough this was the woman we had talked about."

"What happened to her?"

"From what I understand she was living on the streets and you remember that really cold night we had recently, well she was out there and in addition to suffering from exposure she caught a severe case of pneumonia. I'm not sure what finally killed her, but I guess it must have been a combination of things."

"Are you going to do the funeral service?"

"Yes I agreed to try and help her. I'm working on getting a firm date now, but you know lately we have been swamped with requests for services and it's been a real challenge to schedule without over extending our own resources. I am confident though that we'll be able to work something out in the next two weeks. Are you interested in coming?"

"Yes I would like to just because I had examined her not too long before she left here and I guess returned to the streets so I guess I do have a kind of vested interest in what happened. My attendance all depends on your scheduling. Like you I have been inundated with new cases needing my service. Let me know as soon as you can when the service will be held and I will definitely try to attend."

"I will have one of my people get back to you as soon as the date is firm. I'm sorry to bring you the bad news about your patient, but you know the devil is extremely busy for both of us and it seems like he's stepping up his game here lately."

"You got that right. I'm not exactly sure about the cause, that's your area, but I certainly can attest to the rise in cases coming through here. Okay I look forward to hearing from you about the arrangements. Take care."

"Right and you do the same as well."

The doctors ended their conversation and continued on about the business of the day.

At Kimberly Clark High School, just as with most schools on a Friday afternoon, there was a mad rush to exit the building and start the weekend. When Monica got to her locker and opened it she intended to only spend the least amount of time putting away what she would not need over the break and retrieving what she would, she saw a carefully folded note that had been slipped through the openings and fell on the books that were already there. She carefully picked it up, unfolded it and started reading.

"Monica you are one of the prettiest and gifted girls in this school. I have admired you since I came to school and wanted to talk privately with you but never had the courage to do so. I am in your class and have sat behind or near you on several occasions. Last year when we had swimming and gym classes together, I was the one who looked at you with such envy and longing to be like you that it may have given you the wrong impression about my intention. You see where you have it all I have the least, where you have been endowed with everything the boys pant after, I can't even begin to know how that would feel if it happened to me. Since I am very underdeveloped in some areas and have been all of my life it has caused me to be very shy and withdrawn except in class. The only thing I believe I have in common with you is our desire for academic excellence and there I think I compete fairly.

> I've written this note, and believe me it took all that I have to encourage myself to deliver it, to seek your friendship and perhaps guidance. The big prom is next week and I'm willing to wager that I'm the only one who has not been invited by any senior to go. I don't want you to feel sorry for me, that's not my intent here, but I would like to know if you would be willing to help me attract a senior to take me. My telephone number is (291) 735------. Please call me whenever you can I really would like to talk with you

> Your Sincerely,

> Stephanie Landolin

When Monica finishing reading the note she was almost brought to tears by the plea that was coming from this girl. She vividly recalled the incidents, on more than one occasion, when the girl just stared at her getting dressed or undressed in swimming or gym class. At first she was embarrassed and didn't know what to do, but later began to taunt the girl with some maliciously thought out moves.

Now she felt badly for that and after consulting with her posse, at that time who had given her the wrong idea about this girl, it made her feel even worse. As much as she was feeling compassion for this girl right now, she said to herself "Do I really want to get involved trying to get this girl a prom date? What are my girls going to think about that?" She took the note placed it in a pocket and ran outside to catch her bus before it left her as it sometimes did.

That night at home, after enduring another boring conversation at the dinner table and listening to her brother talk about how he had been able to eat ten hot dogs at lunch and his parents thinking that was funny, she excused herself and got up. The oldest son had joined the Army to get away from them too and was now out of her hair. Life seemed to be getting better for her in some ways because the pressure to bow to them at every turn was gone. She didn't have to report especially to Harold her every waking move was liberating. When she got to her room before she got on her laptop to relax for the evening, she pulled out the girl's note again and re-read it. It was even more touching the second time around and she was now seriously considering calling her. Then she thought about what exactly was she going to do for her? Was she going to really get her a date and with whom? This challenge she decided not to take on and dismissed the whole idea.

That week the few days before the big occasion not only was the student body all excited, but those in the city who were big fans of the basketball team had reason to celebrate. The team had gone down to South Carolina and brought back the biggest trophy the school had ever gotten. The principal was hard pressed to make room in the trophy case without breaking glass. They had won coming in first place over-all and everyone was proud of their accomplishment, especially Monica who was just so happy to see her guy come back home.

While everyone seemed to be enjoying the time preparing for the dance, for some reason the thought of Stephanie and her note haunted her. She brought it up with Tony and asked him what he thought about helping her. At first he laughed and asked her was she now playing Cupid, but when she said she was serious he stopped. As captain of the team he could kind of lean on one of the younger players to ask her out, but he said it's awfully late for that. They may not b able to even get a tux at this point. Monica responded saying everyone doesn't really have to wear a tuxedo do they. He said he guessed not, but they would be in the minority.. Monica kept pushing until he finally gave in and said he would try.

That very same afternoon Monica had her answer. Tony had kind of cajoled one of the new kids to escort the girl out and he would pick-up the tab. Tony could always go to the booster club and get the money. So it was done and Monica was ready to finish the deal by finding Stephanie and telling her the news. Not sure of what her schedule was searched around several places without success. Finally she gave up and said she would call tonight. However, before the day ended Stephanie appeared coming toward her as if she had been summoned. When Monica told her the news, she was so thankful she almost cried right on the spot. Then the question came up about where was she going to get a prom dress now. Monica politely and diplomatically bowed out of that issue and told her she was on her own. She had done what was asked of her.

One of Reverend Dumas staff had contacted Trish and advised her that the date had been set for the funeral of Mrs. Miller. Trish then called Monica and told her the news. The date was set for next Saturday,one week after the prom and it was going to take place in the late afternoon sometime after another service took place in the morning. In addition the repast was going to be held immediately after the service so that both families could enjoy the fellowship together. It all seemed to be working just as she hoped and she couldn't thank Trish enough for what she did. Trish graciously accepted her gratitude and told her she was happy to be able to do it for her dear friend. Even while she was so happy about the arrangements being made to bury her mother she asked Trish again about her father.

"Aunt Trish I know I asked you this before, but what about my father. Is there any way we can find out whether he's dead too?"

"I guess we can call that institution that he's in and find out? Would you like for me to do that too?' she said playfully.

"You do such a great job at it I'd be embarrassed trying to do it myself."

They both enjoyed the moment and the conversation ended. Trish was taking it upon herself to start the new research.

Saturday was finally here. Monica woke up that morning bright and early trying to calm her emotions. She must have looked at her dress and the rest of her outfit a hundred times making sure everything was in order. Satisfied with the last view she spent the rest of the day just anticipating the time when Tony was to come by and pick her up. To make sure there was not going to be any upsetting issues with her step parents she asked tem if they would like to go to a movie that she woud pay for. This was the plan she had been hashing for some time and saved up enough money to pull.it off. Always hungry for a freebee how could they resist? So now that part was set in order the only other possible hurdle was what to do with the other wrinkle. Fate must have been watching, because on his own he announced before his parents left that he was going to a professional basketball game with his friends and he would be back late.

They all left before the time when her knight in whatever armor he had would be showing up. The time was set for 7:00 O'clock. Right on time the car pulled up and he got out corsage in hand ready to go. When she opened the door to invite him in, he stood still for a moment not even moving. What he saw in front of him was not permitting his feet to move any further. She was standing there in her low cut gown exposing a good bit of what she was endowed with and the eye candy was making him salivate over the taste. She had to grab his arm and pull him in he was so mesmerized at what he saw. He recovered quickly and fumbled a bit trying to put the corsage on without sticking her with the pin.

She put on her coat and they were off to the ball. Within minutes they arrived at the resort and it was the beginning of a most exciting affair for both of them. The valet came and offered to park the car which Tony cautioned him to take good care of his baby. With that said he danced around and escorted her out of the car and they went inside. The setting was as fabulous as they could have imagined and the tables were decorated with the school colors and roses at each one. The band had already started playing as each couple walked in. Tony and Monica were directed to their table where they were joined by two other Seniors from the basketball team and their dates and two other couples who they only knew casually. High fives were passed all around as the night of celebration got under way.

The music was superb, the food was excellent and even the wine which had been served secretly was tasty. It was not known by the owner that wine was being served, but the manager was well aware of it and he made sure that not too many people knew. Monica took a few sips of the wine and thought it was delicious and so did Tony. Later on well into the night when all of the couples were feeling rather mellow one of the waiters came over to Tony and told him that the manager wanted to see him. At first Tony thought he might be in trouble for drinking under age, but when he got to the manager he pulled him aside and told him how much of a big fan he was of him and the team, especially him because he was the star. Then he offered him a room free for the night if he wanted it. Surprised at the offer he had to think for a minute, but then the wine convinced him this was a great idea so he said "great". The manager stepped away for a short time then came back and handed him a key and told where the room was. Tony still having a hard time believing what just happened was not quite sure how he ws going to tell Monica. As the night went on and the music slowed down the dancers got closer and closer to each other. As Tony embraced her and continued to stare down at those lovely breasts the idea of what could be ahead grew larger and larger in his head. Monica was feeling the grand emotions of romance also and she was swept up in the ambience of the setting so much so that she had already lost her heart to this handsome young man.

As the night grew old and it was finally time to say goodnight, the band played their final song and ended it with the song Goodnight My Love.

As they walked out Tony whispered to Monica;

"Do you want to go home?"

"No do you?"

"Well I have a place we can go to all by ourselves if you want to go there."

"Okay let's go."

She said that while caught up in the emotions of the moment and not really knowing where she was going. He grabbed her arm and they walked around to the hotel side of the resort. There were so many guests in the lobby it was hardly noticeable that the couple walked right through the crowd and caught the elevator to the 7th floor. When he looked at the key and got the room number she started to giggle.

"Are we going to be naughty?" she said.

"You bet we are."

Once inside the room and the door was locked he went to her held and kissed her so passionately there was no denying what was to come next. He undressed first and then she reluctantly did the same. As he watched her his desire was mounting with each strip of clothing that was removed. When all was gone and she stood there bare for a moment she said to him:

"You know I've never done this before, so please don't hurt me."

She got in the bed and for a long time he kissed, fondled and suckled her until he thought she was ready then with great care it was done.

CHAPTER 6
The funeral

I t was 3:00 O'clock Sunday morning when the two lovers awoke after their second round of mating. Tony looked at his watch and said: we got to get out of here." Neither one of them realized how much time had passed since they were too in love to notice. They both got up, scrambled to put clothes on and hurried out the door. Tony left the key on the night table. Once outside, there was hardly anyone moving around so he wondered how he was going to get his car. Fortunately the night security was making his rounds so Tony asked him. The guard directed him to where the valet cars were sheltered and that the keys were usually inside. Tony had told Monica to wait at the hotel entrance while he went to get his car. The valet parking area was not too far from where the ballroom was so it didn't take long for him to get there find his vehicle and return. When he picked Monica up and got in, she was shaking, not because of the cold, but because she was afraid of what was going to happen when she got to the house if her step parents were up. He tried to calm her down by telling her he would take the blame and go in with her if she wanted.

Fortunately when they arrived at her house there was not a single light on. Quietly she got out of the car and entered softly. He waited for several minutes to see if any lights came on, but nothing happened so he left. She tiptoed up the stairs and entered her room without any problem, then quickly undressed and jumped in bed. Then she uttered a sigh of relief and smiled as she felt the joy and pain of her introduction into womanhood. Then she went into a deep sleep.

Later that morning after sleeping until about 11:00 O'clock she finally showered, dressed and came down to find the Evans remaining family firmly ensconced in their favorite Sunday morning activities. Harold was in the living room reading the paper, Laura was in the kitchen cooking and

Ricky was playing a video game on the main TV. When Monica walked in the kitchen Laura just looked at her for a minute or two viewing her up and down as if giving her a physical examination with her eyes, then she said "Good morning how was your prom?" There was no snideness in her question, so Monica wondered was there something different about how she looked that may have indicated her new life status.

"Oh it was really great. I had a wonderful time."

"We didn't hear you come in was it very late?"

Feeling that she might be getting set up for a trap, she paused before answering.

"No it wasn't that late" she replied without actually giving a time. Then she quickly and cleverly changed the subject before Laura could try to pinpoint the time.

"Do you remember your prom?"

The question caught Laura off guard and since she loved to talk about the old days she started rambling on about it. This gave Monica time to fix herself a sandwich. When Laura finished reminiscing about her prom and her date, Monica just said: "that must have been fun" then grabbed the sandwich and took it to her room. When she got there the first thing she did was go to her full length mirror and look at herself to see if there were tell tale signs of her recent activity. The balance of that Sunday was without any inquiry from any of the Evans about the dance so it was a beautiful day.

At school Monday morning when she walked in to her homeroom and met with her trio that's when the real questioning began.

"What happened to you after the dance was over? We looked for you and couldn't find you?" asked Reilly.

"Yeah, we were all going to this after hour joint and wanted you to come along. What happened?" Soun Li added.

"Oh Tony and I just decided to drive around for awhile talking about the affair, then he took me home."

Both girls looked at her suspiciously with a smirk at first then out right laughter.

"Okay so that's what you told your parents, but we know better. Did you give it up?" said Reilly

Monica almost embarrassed tried not to show it when she responded.

"No I didn't give up anything and if I did it's not your business."

'Okay so you gave it up we won't tell" Reilly went on.

Then they all started laughing and changed the subject.

By the time their common lunch period came the girls had heard all kinds of talk circulating about Stephanie. Monica's ears perked up when Reilly and Soun Li were talking about it. It seems that the boy Monica had set up a date for her with, had raped her after the dance. The trio didn't have all of the details, but no one had seen Stephanie at school today. Monica was shocked and couldn't wait to find Tony to ask him what he knew about it. The trio kept trying to put together a scenario where they had seen the couple leave the dance, but no one could remember exactly how that scenario went. They continued talking until the bell rang to end the period.

When classes ended for that day Monica went in search of Tony. She caught up with him at his locker as he was apparently in a real hurry to deposit his books.

"Where are you running to?" she asked.

"The team has a meeting with coach right now, can't talk to you."

"Before you run away I have just one question."

"Okay make it quick."

"I'm sure you heard about what happened to the girl I asked you to find a date for. Did you hear that he raped her?"

"Yeah I heard that this morning, but I also talked to him and he said he didn't rape her. It was her idea, she wanted it. Look I really have to go now, that's probably what this meeting is all about. I'll call you later and we can talk."

Tony moved away almost running to get to the gym. Monica stood there speechless trying to absorb what he just told her. She wanted it? Is that really the way whatever happened, happen? Although Monica didn't really know Stephanie hardly at all, she still was finding it difficult to believe she would be the one to advance any kind of sex act.

From the time she received that note until the time when she gave Stephanie the news about her date, she had talked to her no more than three or four times. Always whenever they met Stephanie was dressed in the most unflattering outfits imaginable. Everything she had on would try to downplay any semblance of a figure. It was very clear to even any casual observer that the girl had a thin frame and was embarrassed by having very small breasts that she tried to hide. Although she saw her at the dance, Monica couldn't remember what she was wearing, but she would almost be willing to wager a bet it was nothing provocative or daring like hers. For this reason she was having a hard time believing the story that the boy raped her.

Most of the stories circulating about the biggest event of the school year were very positive and it was a shame that something like this would tend to mar the celebration of the affair. The school newspaper editor was going to have a very difficult time trying to put a positive spin on the ball without mentioning what happened after. The school principal did not suspend the accused boy because the offense happened away from school grounds and until some kind of police report came to his attention there were no solid grounds for him to act. The coach assembled his players and with the boy there in the meeting, without pointing fingers, reminded them of the responsibility they all had wherever they go of how they are viewed as representatives of Kimberly Clark and ambassadors for fair play. He ended his speech by telling them their season was not over and a state championship was on the line. All of the team after the coach dismissed them and left, huddled around the boy and asked him did he do what they're hearing. When he responded with his side of the story, they accepted it and that was the end of it for them.

That night when Monica got home after she finished eating dinner and was getting started on her study schedule, the phone rang.

Ring, ring, ring ring.

"Hello."

"Hi Monica, Trish are you busy?"

"Not really just getting started on my homework."

"I Just wanted to confirm with you that everything is set for Saturdays' funeral service for your mother. It will be at 3:00 pm. Will you be needing a ride from me?"

"No my boyfried is going to take me there?"

"Boyfriend, boyfriend how did you manage to pull that one off?"

"Well it wasn't easy given my situation here, but he's also a student so we are able to meet in school and after whenever we can. He's a really great guy and I think you will like him when you meet."

"If you picked him, I'm sure he must meet your high standards. Okay looking forward to seeing you and him Saturday. Goodnight."

"Goodnight."

At Holy Trinity Baptist Church Mondays were usually a day when, after preaching two services on Sunday, pastor Dumas would take a day to recuperate. However, given the daunting number of funerals that are scheduled to take place over the next few weeks, he decided to come to his office late that afternoon and review them. He certainly was not going to try to eulogize all that were on the list because he had enough qualified associate clergy to handle the overload, but he was curious about several of the deceased. One of the names that stood out in his mind was that of Elena Miller. His memory kept going back to the case with Norman Miller, her husband. It was years ago now, but for some reason the final outcome of how he had been shuffled off to a facility in another state without him being able to complete his work bothered him.

When Milton, Dr. Danforth, had invited him to the hospital to interview Mr. Miller the circumstance under which he had been brought to the hospital was very strange. It appeared to the doctor that Mr. Miller was suffering from some type of possible demon possession that had been foisted upon him by his father at his death so he was told. Since this area was more in the purview of Reverend Dumas, he called his friend. Reverend Dumas was only able to have three sessions with Mr. Miller and was still in the process of building a profile for him, when he was transferred out of the hospital. Milton and David had discussed the need to continue his examination at Trinity Memorial, however Milton was unable to persuade his superiors to continue footing the bill since he was not now the primary care giver in the case.

Reverend Dumas was disappointed because he believed that there was something to a possible spiritual possession, but he needed more time to substantiate just how manifest was the entity within the subject. Even though Mr. Miller exhibited several signs of the condition, at no time was there enough of a consistent display of abnormal behavior to warrant a positive diagnosis. Too often he just rambled on about how his father had put a spell on him. Reverend Dumas realized he would probably never be able to revisit examining Mr. Miller. But now that his wife had come to his attention he wanted to know more about her and her cause of death prior to it actually happening. Therefore, he decided to perform her eulogy and needed to do some research about her before doing so.

Patricia Ramey, now a member of Holy Trinity Church was the one who brought Mrs. Miller to his attention, so it was logical that she would be the best place to begin his investigation. He asked his staff to try and set an appointment for tomorrow afternoon to have her come in to his office. The plan was set in motion and by the end of the day the task had been carried out and the meeting was scheduled for 2:00 O'clock the next afternoon.

"Good afternoon sister Ramey, it's good to see you. Thank you for coming in on such short notice, but I've decide to give the eulogy for Mrs. Miller myself and I need to know more about her. I believe you knew her for some years, is that right?

"Pastor it's good to see you as well. I am so grateful that you were able to schedule the service for her so I knew I had to come here to do whatever I could to help. To answer your question yes we lived next door to each other for about ten years and got to know each other pretty well. The apartment building we lived in was part of the Fairview Gardens complex over there on Main Street. I'm sure you are familiar with that site.

"Yes, yes I am. Quite a few of our members come from there. Please go on."

"I believe we met when she and her husband were moving in. I had only been there just a few months ahead of her and was still learning how to get around myself, but she knocked on my door while they were getting settled and asked me where the nearest supermarket was. It so happened I needed to go there myself, so I told her if she liked I would take her there. I drove and on the way we started talking about a lot of different things, you know just making small talk and feeling each other out.

She said that she and her husband had only been married for about three years and as of yet had no children, but she was thinking about it. She also said they both worked for that big telephone service company and this was their first nice apartment together. They had been living in a rundown, third floor, one bedroom place in a house over on Avon Street. Later that day she invited me over to meet him. Right from the start to me it seemed like there was something strange about him, but I didn't pay much attention to it. They were still unpacking a lot of boxes so I didn't want to over stay my welcome, but I noticed he didn't seem too happy about me coming in at that time.

From that first day she started coming to me for a number of different things. Since I was a little older, I guess she thought I knew it all. Her personality was really very pleasant, almost the opposite of his and we got along fine. It didn't appear that they were a religious couple, because I never saw or heard them going out to church on Sunday. But then again, at that time, I wasn't exactly going myself. She never mentioned her family, but did say that she was from Brooklyn and he was from one of the Carolinas, I forgot which one. Anyway as time passed and we became real good friends it looked like they were a happy couple and enjoying the best of life. Then she got pregnant and everything changed in a minute.

He became increasingly hostile toward her and I could hear them arguing constantly. You know the walls in those apartments are almost paper thin so I could hear much of what they were saying. He blamed her for getting pregnant and not telling him that's what she was planning to do. He lambasted her practically every night and I believe I heard him one night telling her to get an abortion. She told him she wasn't doing that and I don't know whether he hit her or not, but I heard something heavy hit the floor and then the door slammed so he must have walked out. After that it was a constant battle between them. Often she would come to my place when he wasn't home and we would sit and talk. I don't know how she was managing, but I do know that she tried everything she knew how to do to make him love her and want the baby. It was not working.

Then one day after they had been arguing and he had been out for a long time, he came home like a changed man. I don't know where he had been or what happened, but it was like he received an epiphany. He started acting better treating her with respect and he said he with accept the baby. He had never failed to be a provider even during the troubled times. The rent ws always paid, food on the table and they were starting to get little things for the baby. Things seemed to be moving along fine with hardly any loud arguments. After the baby arrived, although at first he didn't take to her like a loving father should, over time he started to love her.

It was not until the death of his father, a few years later and he went to attend the funeral that there was a profound change in him. Per the request of one of his sisters he had been summoned to spend some time with his dad while he was still in hospice care. It was then just before his father passed that according to what Elena told me his father cursed him and put some kind of spell on him.

Of course she didn't believe him at first, but then he started acting strangely, doing little crazy things. They began to get progressively worse and then one night Elena caught him holding the baby high up in the air as if to hurt her. That's when she knew there was something definitely wrong with him and she tried to get him some professional help. She was not yet fully convinced about the being cursed story, but his behavior was beginning to point in that direction. Not too long after that incident he was caught in the nursery where the baby was trying to get the teachers to release the baby to him. That's when he was arrested and taken to the hospital for a psychiatric evaluation. As a result of that he was admitted and eventually ended up at a facility in New Jersey which is where I believe he is to this day. I'm not sure about that.

Anyway after that things really started to get rough for Elena. She lost her job and eventually the apartment and moved in with me for a little while. The biggest loss she felt though was having to give up her baby Monica to adoption. Living with me didn't work because my place was just too small for the both of us so she moved out. Then she went from one shelter to another until she finally ended up living on the streets. That life was what eventually caused her death. One thing good happened though out of all that. While she was on her deathbed in the hospital she was reunited briefly with her now grown and beautiful daughter. She was able to tell her how much she always loved her, blessed her with some words of wisdom in her own way then said goodbye. That's about it that's her story."

"Thank you so much for that. It gives me more than enough to prepare her eulogy. That's a very interesting tale about the husband's role in her downfall. I'm sorry I did not get the opportunity to continue examining him perhaps I may have discovered exactly what his spiritual issues were. You said you didn't know whether he is living or deceased right?"

"No. I stopped going with her to visit him when he failed to recognize her anymore."

"I understand. It is something though I would like to look into further sometime. Well again thank you for sharing with me and I hope all goes smoothly for all on Saturday. Have a blessed day."

"Thank you. Once again I am glad to help in any way that I can for her. Good afternoon."

After meeting with sister Ramey, Pastor Dumas felt better about being able to deliver a suitable eulogy for Mrs. Miller. To him her story was quite interesting and the connection to Norman Miller her husband, still intrigued him. Now he had to decide how much he wanted to go into that part of the story as far as her life being affected by powers that can be detrimental to our well being if we are not protected by the Divine Spirit. He sat there for several minutes contemplating what should be the appropriate scripture (s) to deliver his message about this, he spent the rest of the afternoon pondering the thought. No final resolution came so finally he decided to leave for the day and let his inner spirit come up with the right decision when it was ready.

Saturday morning the day of the multiple funeral services turned out to be a gorgeous day. It was somewhat brisk because of the oncoming winter breezes, but it was not bitterly cold. The sun was shining brightly and the clear blue sky displayed a sense of peace and serenity as if to bless the upcoming day's activities. Ministers, deacons, choir and other service personnel began entering Holy Trinity about 7:00 O'clock to begin preparing for the first service at 8:00. Flowers had already been brought in and set up and the musicians were there waiting for some directions.

The associate minister assigned to oversee this service took charge and proceeded to put all things in order as some early mourners also started to trickle in.

By the time the clock reached the 8:00 O'clock hour the sanctuary was filled almost to capacity because the first funeral service was for a well known community service counselor who had been an attorney for many of the worshippers in attendance who could not afford his legal advice so he often provided it to them without cost. The ushers directed the incoming crowd to seats in the front first, then filling up the rear as appropriate. At 8:10 the choir director instructed the musicians to begin playing the opening hymn. This was followed by a rendition of Total Praise sung by the choir that set the stage for a very emotional service.

The rest of the service followed the traditional opening ceremony until it was time for the pastor to deliver the eulogy. Reverend Dumas stood up and approached the sacred desk, dressed in his elegant black and red robe and began to speak. He had decided to do both funerals since he knew the first deceased very well.

"Brothers and sisters isn't it good to be in the House of the Lord one more time. Although the circumstances for this occasion are not what we would have desired it to be, it is not our will, but His will that shall be done. We gather here this morning not to despair over the death of our dear loyal congregant, but to celebrate his life and acknowledge all the good and noble accomplishments he achieved while he was with us in life. No one knows the day nor the hour when each and every one of us will be called to stand before the judgment seat and account for all of our deeds, whether they be good or evil. We mourn the loss of our dear faithful servant, but we do not mourn as if we have no hope and know that one day we shall meet him again in a different sphere of living.

Reverend Dumas continued to deliver a fiery sermon and there was practically no dry eye in the house. The family was obviously moved by the send off their loved was being given and they were grateful. At the conclusion of the service, it was announced that today's service would end slightly differently because there was another service scheduled to be held at 3:00. Instead of going directly to the cemetery it was asked that the mourners stay for the second funeral and then they would all go to the cemetery together and afterward there would be a collective repast for both families in the recreation center. There was some obvious muttering initially when the announcement was made but, as the recession was conducted and the casket brought out, no one seemed to be unhappy about the service they just attended.

It was now only about 11:45 when the first service ended and it was then announced that for those who decided to stay for the second service they would be directed downstairs to the large fellowship hall where they would be fed a light lunch enough to hold them until the repast later. This was received most graciously by those who decided to stay. Reverend Dumas staff had done a marvelous job in anticipating and preparing for what to do with the congregants who would be willing to stay after the first service. It worked out well.

Once those who remained were seated in the hall and starting to be fed, the clean-up crew immediately began to remove the flowers from the first funeral, and started preparing for the second one. Again the coordination effort by the staff for their meticulous attention to the details required for a successful smooth transition was to be applauded. Everything went as planned and by the time the clock showed 2:30 and the late afternoon mourners started coming in the house was ready for the second service.

Tony picked-up Monica right on time and without any hassle from the Evans, who had been told about the funeral, the couple were on their way to the church. Arriving almost simultaneously, but in separate cars Trish and Monica were able to enter the church together. When Monica introduced Tony, it was obvious when Trish greeted him that she was impressed by the young man's looks and dress. After entering the sanctuary they were ushered right to the front and seated in the pew reserved for the immediate family. To Monica's surprise a man then walked in and sat down with them. He then introduced himself as Elena's brother and had read the obituary in the newspaper so he decided to come. Monica was pleased to see and meet him after all of the years she had wondered about where her mother's remaining family might be.

The service began just like the earlier one with the playing of an old favorite hymn, Rock Of Ages, then followed by the reading of an invitational scripture by a deacon. The choir then starting singing the popular song titled Leaning On The Ever Lasting Arm joined by the whole congregation. This was followed by a reading of a very brief bio of Elena's life given by one of the associate pastors who had received it from Trish. Next another minister opened the floor to anyone wanting to give remarks about the deceased. No one stood up immediately then Elena's brother casually walked to the front and stood before the microphone.

"My name is Howard, Howard Watson which is Elena's maiden name some of you may not know that. I'm Elena's older brother. Usually I'm not the one in the family who stands before an audience and delivers a speech. Whenever that kind of occasion happened when we were kids she was the one to do the talking, because she liked to talk."

At that point there was a muffled laugh from the congregation.

"We grew up in Brooklyn and I remember there were many times when I had to protect her in school from some of the other students because she was so smart and wasn't afraid to show it. After her graduation my parents moved down south and she got a job. I had already left to go to college to play football. I'm so sorry to say I never came back to this area until recently and we didn't keep in touch while I stayed in Chicago playing professional football. I was invited to her wedding, but could not come because at the time the team was in Europe playing a game. I never did get to meet the guy and unfortunately, it was a long time before I found out I had a niece who I just met today. Time goes by so quickly and I never realized how much of my life had passed without even seeing my only sister. The other day when I read her obituary all of the promises I had made to myself to go and see her made my heart break. Now I don't know what to say except that I loved her and I'm here to say goodbye."

When he finished he gingerly walked back to his seat and was hugged by Monica. After him it was Patricia who took the mike next.

"Hi, many of you here already know me, but anyway my name is Patricia Ramey and I am perhaps the only close friend that Elena had. For many years she and I lived next door to each other and shared many memories living life. Especially when she had her daughter and the memories really increased. Elena was a genuinely loving and giving person who was just exposed to a series of undeserved hardships that I wouldn't want placed on anybody. She struggled with the vicissitudes of life and did the best she could. There were times that when I started coming to this church I tried to get her to come with me, but her husband was not having it. I'm not here to place or judge him or anybody, but I just wish she had come and things may have turned out differently. Goodbye my friend, rest in peace."

Trish sat down and there was a hush over the whole sanctuary for a few minutes before the next speaker got up. It was another associate pastor who read a Psalm and then introduced Pastor Dumas who gave the eulogy.

"Let us pray-Father God as I stand before these your people who have come to hear a word from You and say goodbye to the one you called home, hide me behind the cross for I have nothing to say, but let the words of my mouth be Your words and the meditation of my heart be acceptable in Your sight. Brothers and sisters I give you greetings in the blessed name of the Lord. I stand before you now with a heavy heart after hearing the remarks by sister Ramey who I had a chance to meet with a few days earlier this week. I listened closely to what she told me then and was reminded by some of the things she said just now. You know life has a way of presenting hurdles in all of our situations that we must learn how to jump over. When one is burdened by events or trials and tribulations as the Bible says we must discover that there is one who can carry us when we falter.

I'm not going to keep you much longer, but I do want to talk for just a few minutes about the life of the one we are saying goodbye to here today. Mrs, Miller came to us when her child, whom you see here today, was just a baby and she had the wise idea to let us be the first life guide. I met her then, but I didn't get to know her because she never came to church then except to drop off and pick up her child. I'm not here to judge or condemn either, for that role is left to the one who has the right to do so. I am here to remind all of us that the time will come when we all must lay down our wicked ways and stand in the judgment.

I want to talk to you from the words in the gospel of St. John beginning at Chapter 14 verse 1.

'Do not let your hearts be troubled. Trust in God, trust also in me.' As we go through life and are confronted by dangers both seen and unseen there are times when we don't know which way to turn. It was Jesus who said in this world you will have trouble, but take heart for I have overcome the world. No one can escape being challenged by the evil one who walks among us and whispers in our ears to do wrong. The weight that we carry can often be a burden we don't have to bear by ourselves, if we just learn to call on the name that is above every name and that has the power to lift you up when you fall.

To know Him is to know that everything is going to be alright. To know Him is to be able to see the path you must travel even when the lights are dim and darkness begins to cloud your way. The journey will be long and the way might be dark, but if you believe in Him and trust in Him then you will come to know how to navigate the road. Darkness is not eternal if you believe. My brothers and sisters the one that lies here before us, as far as I know, did not come to know Jesus and it is difficult to say or know how it will be for her when that day comes and we all must give an accounting of our lives. I do know this, that we serve a merciful God and it is in Him that we have our blessing and our grace, so it is not for me to say what her final disposition will be, but to pray now for her soul and trust Him to be merciful.

As we close the final chapter on her life let me say to you that if you have not already come to the one who can make things alright, the one who can save you from the evil one, the one who knows your burdens and offers you a way to place them on Him, don't let the opportunity go by when you can give your- self to Him and be saved. As I close this portion of the service I invite you to go with us to the cemetery where both the body from the earlier service and the one here now will be interred in their final resting place.

"Now unto Him who is able to keep you from falling and to present you faultless before the presence of His glory with exceeding joy, to the only wise God our Savior and power, both now and ever more. Amen." (Jude 1:24-25 KJV)

As the recession got underway and the casket containing Elena was wheeled out Monica lost it. She had composed herself fairly well up until that time, but when she saw that the tears fell like a gushing waterfall and it took Tony and Trish wrapping their arms around her for consolation to stem the tide. She sat back down and wept bitterly for the next few minutes before finally recomposing herself enough to get up and walk out. Near the rear exit she spotted her two closest friends Reilly and Soun Li and she nodded a greeting to them.

The number of cars that lined up for the procession to the cemetery exceeded the expectations of the few police that had been assigned to the duty. A call was made to get more help and it arrived just as the procession started to move out. As the line snaked along the streets having to make several turns to avoid the Saturday afternoon traffic the officers were having a hard time controlling the traffic and trying to kep the procession intact because of some unyielding motorists who do not respect funerals. After about a fifteen minute ride the families arrived at the cemetery and were separated to where each deceased body was to be laid to rest. Monica along with Trish, Tony and Howard rode in one limo followed by several cars of members who were not necessarily friends of Elena's but were so moved by Rev. Dumas sermon they decided to go to the burial.

The final interment ceremony took place with an assistant pastor rendering the service for Elena. Reverend Dumas had to be at the other plot for the dignitary. It was completed with all due respect and the act was completed. Monica held herself together there as she was supported by Trish and Tony. When they returned to the church and were directed to the recreation center for the repast Monica looked for her two friends, but did not see them. She wondered if they had gone home. it was not until they entered the rec center that she spotted both of them already seated at a table. Apparently they had not gone to the cemetery, but waited here. A special table had been set up for the grieving family members and Monica and her party were directed there. Monica wanted to invite her two friends to be seated with her, but was advised it was not tradition so she let it go.

The repast was a hardy occasion with all of the trimmings of a banquet, mainly because of the dignitary, not so much to honor Elena, but it was a pleasure for all anyway. At the end of the dinner as people were exiting many of them who had attended both service came over to Monica and wished her continued blessings. She was thankful and spoke to each one of them kindly. There was one man who when he held her hand and looked into her eyes held it longer than was necessary until she had look at him to see whether she knew him. She did not. He was just taken by her beauty. Even Tony noticed the act and was about to say something when Monica nudged him with her leg under the table. The man left and there was no incident.

That night after everyone said goodbye and returned to their homes Monica was feeling especially happy about the way everything went and how blessed she thought her mother had been. When she walked in her house even Harold and Laura inquired about the funeral because they had heard it being referenced on the local news channel. They wondered if her mother had become some kind of important person that they didn't know about, of course trying to see if there was a way they could exploit Monica's relationship for their own benefit. Monica sensed the selfishness of their probe and did not reveal to them that the accolades were for the prominent lawyer, but just casually mentioned that her mother was important and walked away.

That night as she was preparing to go to bed she had the strangest feeling that something was wrong. She felt fine and didn't notice anything strange about her appearance so she looked around the room to see if there was anything different. Not seeing anything out of the ordinary she dismissed the feeling and went to sleep.

Along about the midnight hour she woke up and again saw the image standing before her. By now she was accustomed to being awakened by this friendly spirit so she was not afraid. Lois, her grandmother started to speak to her.

Monica, now that you have witnessed the departure of your true mother and her spirit lies with me, there are some things that I must share with you that will affect your life in the very near future. For this reason I have come here tonight to warn you that........." Suddenly the sentence was cut off and the image was swept away. Monica tried hard to summon it back, but to no avail. It was a warning and not knowing what it was for caused her to fret about it for the rest of the night unable to go back to sleep.

CHAPTER 7
Guilty Or Guiltless

T he school year finished successfully for most students and all were looking forward to enjoying the summer break. Two of the Three Musketeers maintained their class ranking with Soun Li topping the list and Monica maintaining a close second. However, Reilly dropped out of the top five percent. Over the entire school year there were some good things that happened and some bad that would remain in the memories of every student who was in attendance. On the good side, the basketball team won the state championship, every student advanced to the next higher level. Tony graduated and was accepted with a full scholarship to the college of his choice –Nova University, the debate team also won their competition at the state level and Kimberly Clark Regional High School received another award for academic proficiency by the National Board Of Educators. On the other side there were some thngs the principal wished had never taken place. First was the oversight error in first semester enrollment, it appeared that the selection committee sent out letters of acceptance to more students than there was current seating capacity, secondly, a parent filed an ill conceived report that the school wasn't teaching any African-American history and finally the most egregious of all was the police report he received that one of his students had committed an assault on another student (Rape).

Regarding the enrollment mix up, as much as it pained him the principal had to send out letters of retraction, with a very lengthy explanation, to the parents telling them that there was just no room for additional students for this school year. He knew that once the parents received the letter there would be an avalanche of irate parents lambasting the school because they all wanted their child to get the best education available and Kimberly Clark was it. It took some doing, but the teaching staff and the school's alumni association were able to pacify parents by telling them that their child would receive top priority for next year. Concerning the subject of African American history a committee was formed to develop a new curriculum that would address the issue and by the time the second semester began a new course was ready. The third issue, the rape charge report, was rescinded because the city's medical examiner did not find sufficient evidence to support the charge

So all issues were addressed and resolutions were achieved that satisfied the school's administration. However what remained was the needed resolution for Stephanie and the boy she accused. Truth has a way of always coming to the forefront when given time to understand it. Stephanie had adopted Monica as her role model and near the end of the year came to her as a type of father confessor and told the real story. Monica was at her locker one day preparing to go home when Stephanie came up to her and said she needed to talk with her urgently. By now Monica was aware that this girl adored her and listened to anything she said.

"Can this wait until tomorrow? I'm going to miss my bus" Monica said.

"No, no no it can't wait any longer. I've been living with the lie for too long and I have to tell somebody before I have a breakdown and crack up.".

"What are you talking about?"

"That boy, the one you arranged for him to take me to the prom and I said he raped me, I lied. He didn't rape me. It was all my doing to have sex with him. I knew since he was younger than me and an underclassman he would jump at the chance to nail an upperclassman, even me. So I told him about the janitor's apartment in the basement of the hotel that I knew would be empty because I paid him to disappear for a little while after the dance and leave the door unlocked. Before you judge me listen you don't know what it's like to be me and never having boys give a second look to. I wanted him and I wanted to lose my virginity that night. It didn't take much to persuade him so we went to the apartment and that's where we did it. After it was done I had to lie and say he raped me because the janitor threatened to tell what he knew if I didn't give him more money which I didn't have. You know they say that confession is good for the soul, well now that I've told you the truth I do feel better. Are you going to expose me?"

"Stephanie, I'm certainly not the one to judge anybody and I agree telling the truth is always best even though I don't always do it. Still I can't believe you would do something like that. Do you realize what kind of trouble you put that boy through having to deal with the police and his own parents, much less yours? I'm glad you feel better, but you put the burden on me now. Do you think it's right for me to keep your secret? I don't know, I just don't know right now. Regardless of what I end up doing or saying, you are the one who has to make things right with that boy first and then the police so they can clear his name."

"Yeah I know you're right, but I'm too afraid to face telling the truth out in the open. I don't know how to even begin. Can you help me?"

"Not this time. I've got my own troubles to deal with and can't afford to take on yours too. I'm not going to say anything now, but if you don't before we break for the summer I will. I really don't want to get involve in your mess, but I will if I have to."

Monica walked away feeling like a lead weight had just been dropped on her from a ten story building. Although she had been suspicious from the start when the story about rape first came out, now that her suspicions were confirmed what should she do? The idea of telling the truth when it would mean justifying a wrong with a right she wasn't sure Stephanie had it in her to carry it out and then again she wasn't completely sure of herself either. All the way home after having to lean on Tony for a ride she kept thinking about what to do if Stephanie didn't confess.

The school year ended and Stephanie did not confess nor make any attempt to right the wrong committed against the boy. Monica knew this and yet she didn't do anything to help either. The issue was quietly suppressed simply by the passage of time, inaction and apathy so both girls went on with their lives. The boy who shall remain nameless transferred to another school.

Kimberly Clark High School had many programs for their students that were designed to provide experiences that would be beneficial to them after graduation. One of them was a work-study program which was conducted in cooperation with several city businesses. Monica was recommended for and received an offer to work at one of the program stores. Ironically it was Nords High Fashion Emporium that accepted her as an intern to be trained in the area of marketing and sales. When she received her notice that this is where her work assignment for the summer was going to be she chuckled. Inside she was thinking the first task she would perform would be to tighten up the security.

Now that she was working and had a small, but steady income Harold and Laura did not require any rent from her because they were still receiving assistance from the state, but Harold stopped buying her clothes and allowed her more freedom coming and going in the house. With the new freedom she spent more time with Tony and they frequented the free room at the hotel quite often. He had also received an assignment in the sporting goods outlet and was enjoying the luxury of being a kind of spokesperson for some of the big name brand sneakers they were selling. Between the two of them life seemed to be moving along fine and he was looking forward to going to college while she was just looking forward.

On the job the managers discovered that Monica had a real sense of business acumen and a gift for selling. By the end of the summer she had received a raise and was invited to continue working there after school started. She was excited by hearing that because the money was beginning to allow her to afford some of the things that Harold would never buy for her In addition one of the higher level managers told her that if she wanted to go a good business college he was in a position to make a strong recommendation for her. Although he didn't say it at that time, he was an adjunct professor at NYU teaching a business course at night. The thought set Monica to believing that she could go to college and she decided to intensify her study when school did reopen so that she would possibly get some kind of financial assistance.

In late August as the summer break was drawing to a close and Tony was preparing to leave. the couple got a scare from mother-nature. Monica had missed a period for the last two cycles and was worried she might be pregnant. She was afraid to tell Tony because she didn't want to spoil his excitement about going to play for a big time basketball program. But as the time was getting near when he would have to go and she was fearful of what she suspected might be true, she decided to let him know. Even though she had not been to a doctor to confirm what she believed, it was time to include him. One night when they were having their usual rendezvous and this one would be for the last time before he left, she told him.

"Tony do you love me?"

"What kind of a question is that? You know I do."

"Would you be willing to not go to school right now if you had to stay here with me?"

"Okay you're scaring me. What's up?"

"Well I'm not absolutely sure yet, but I may be pregnant."

The expression on his face went from a joyful inquiry into what she was saying to a sudden scowl as his mind immediately saw his future taking a turn in the wrong direction.

"What do you mean you're not sure? When and how will you know?"

"If nothing happens for me by the end of next week I'm going to the hospital clinic and get checked out."

"You know I have to report to the coach there the first week in September if I want to keep my scholarship."

" Yes I know and no matter what you go ahead and keep that appointment."

"I'm not going to just up and go and leave you by yourself if it's true, but let's wait until you know for sure before we start to panic."

"Okay."

The rest of that night until it was time to go home, at about 11:00 O'clock, they just lay there not engaging in anything other than holding each other.

It was the last week in August and the high school was scheduled to open the next week. Monica was contemplating her visit to the clinic after work and was preparing to go when she suddenly felt some slight discomfort then like a runaway river that had broken through the dam, it happened. She ran to the ladies room and sought the necessary items that could stem the tide. After a few minutes of attending to her hygiene she wasn't sure whether to laugh or cry because this was so irregular. Then she washed her face and strolled back to her station with a completely different look. When it was time to check out she said goodnight to her coworkers and walked to a place where she could call him with some privacy.

Ring, ring, ring.

"Hello."

"Tony it's me guess what just happened?"

"Oh no nothing bad I'm hoping."

"No, no this is all good. My friend just arrived and we're safe."

"What do you mean your friend? You mean your period?"

"Yes, yes ain't that good news?"

"Wow! You bet it is. Now I can stop worrying and finish packing. Where are you now?"

"I'm still at work why?"

"You want to go and get a bite to eat and celebrate?"

"Yeah that sounds good when do you get off?"

"I got another half hour. Why don't you come down here, it's not that far you can walk."

"Okay see you shortly."

The elated lovers were so jubilant about the latest status in their relationship that they couldn't wait to see each other and hug. He took her to a fast food restaurant and they laughed and joked about the scare for almost an hour until it was time to go.

.Now that the scare was past and she realized that things could have been very different had the opposite result occurred. She sat at her desk and thought about what they would have done if there was a baby on the way. Would he really have stayed with her and sacrifice his ambition to play professional basketball? She knew that she loved him very much, but would it be fair to ask him to do that for her? For a long time she pondered the thought until it became something of an afterthought so she went to bed. .

The first day of school was always an exciting time for returning students, but for the new students coming for the first time it was even more of a thrill. To have been accepted to this particular high school placed them in a category that was high above those forced to attend the other public and even private schools. As the doors were opened and the traditional marching in line was formed, the principal first then the teachers stood ready to welcome them. Of the returning students, especially seniors, many had already received acceptance letters from the college of their choice. For others it was hopefully just a matter of time.

As the Three Musketeers stood in line among the others waiting to greet and be greeted by some favorite and some less than popular instructors, they were together as usual. Even though they had seen each other over the summer at various occasions, birthday parties, backyard BBQs, concerts and the like it was not like seeing each other every day as it would be in school. They laughed and giggled about how quickly the summer had passed and wondered what kind of academic schedules would be handed out to them this year. When the principal saw the trio he commented on the fact that they were almost inseparable and wished them a good year. Following his welcome the teachers who knew them well because they had been there now almost four years also greeted them.

Next as usual was the handing out of the schedule of class assignments and also lockers then the traditional mass assembly in the auditorium to hear the general principal's academic challenge. It was especially good for the first time students, and then the general welcome was made again. Then off to their homerooms to start the day.

Again the trio were assigned the same homeroom and as they usually did they sat together. The difference this year however, was in their academic assignments. Since Reilly had fallen out of the top percentage in ranking she no longer was included in the accelerated honors classes and fell into the general academic program. Reilly was not disappointed or had any inferior feeling because she knew her grades had been slipping for some time so this was to be expected. The other two did not see her as any less than a musketeer and they remained close friends. For Soun Li and Monica they were placed in some classes that were equivalent to college courses which would look good on their academic resumes. Each also had the opportunity to select two elective classes of their choice. Soun Li chose Advanced Biology and Advanced Chemistry while Monica chose the newly added African American History course and Driver Education.

The academic week got underway without any major incidents or turmoil and most students settled comfortably into the routine. It was not until the second week that Monica ran into Stephanie who sought her out once again seeking her friendship. Monica tried as best she could to avoid her, but when she was cornered there was no way out.

"Hi Monica looks like you've been ducking me right?"

"Oh hi Steph. No I haven't been ducking you, but you know I have a pretty heavy work load this year and been kind of busy. How are you?"

"Well nothing much has changed for me and you already know that I did not confess my sin from last year regarding that boy. I understand he transferred anyway so that's over. I would still like to be your friend because I need your strength and companionship. You always seem like you have it all together, not like me."

"Well Stephanie thank you for seeing me like that and I would like to spend some time with you, but as I said I'm going to be very busy with my studies. I'll do what I can to help you when I can. Now I got to go."

"Okay Monica I understand. See you around."

Monica walked away from her as quickly as she could without running and did not look back. Stephanie stood watching her back for a few minutes then also left. As Monica rushed to get to her next class she wondered just what could she do to get this girl to adopt somebody else in stead of her. At times like this she would find Tony and talk to him, but now since he had graduated and was gone and she didn't want to burden her posse with it, she had to decide just what was going to be her escape strategy. She didn't want to hurt her feelings by outright telling her to get lost, but then she really did want her to just go away. It was beginning to weigh heavy on her mind and tried hard to dismiss the thought.

In the second week of the second month of the first semester, Monica had been doing a successful job of getting out of the way whenever she spotted Stephanie far enough in advance to avoid her. However, this day Stephanie had waited outside of one of Monica's classes so when she came out there was no running away.

"Monica I need to talk with you now."

"Steph I have one more class to day can't it wait until after."

"No I'm sorry it can't. I've come to a conclusion about a lot of things in my life and I just don't have the answers to. Won't you help me? It's been so hard for me lately and that incident with the boy has really been growing like a cancer inside of me. Can you skip that class and talk with me?"

"No Steph I can't not go to this class it's one of my most important subjects. You'll just have to wait until after school and I can see you then. Come find me."

"Oh okay, goodbye."

Late that afternoon when all classes were finished for the day and students were preparing to go home the halls became inundated with emergency personnel, EMTs, fireman, police and the like were scrambling to get to the girls gym locker room. Everyone students, faculty and staff were all abuzz trying to find out what happened. No one left the building.

After about an hour, those that were in the hallway close enough to see witnessed a body being carried out on a gurney. It was completely covered up so no one could tell whether it was a student or not. The emergency personnel had spent the last hour in the locker room trying to revive the victim until it was determined that that effort was not going to be successful. After the body was removed, the police advised everyone to go home. Questions were circulating rampantly and furiously searching for an answer. Finally, one of the teachers came out of the locker room and made the announcement.

"Students, fellow teachers and staff it is with the heaviest of heart I have to tell you that one of our own has passed. I don't have all of the details yet on how it happened, and I'm sure I'll have more tomorrow, but for now we must say goodbye to Stephanie Landolin one of our beloved seniors."

When Monica, who was still standing in the hall along with several others, heard this she feinted, Quickly those who were nearby turned their attention to her. The gym teacher who had just made the announcement came over and attended to her. The school nurse who was also still in the building was sent for and came back within minutes with a resuscitation kit. After she was revived they walked her to the nurse's office where she was questioned.

"What happened to you out there? Did that announcement about Stephanie shock you?"

Monica still a little groggy was slow to answer.

"I don't know. It's just that I was talking with her only a little while ago and she seemed a little distraught, but she usually has some kind of a problem when she comes to me so I didn't pay it much attention."

"Do you remember exactly what she said to you?"

"Well no not exactly, but she said she wanted me to go on being her friend and wanted me to help her. She didn't say specifically help her with what. I was in a hurry to get to my next class so I told her I would see her after school and we could talk. Then I left."

"Did she seem okay when you left her?"

"Yeah other than what I just told you she seemed fine to me."

"Okay I guess we have to wait until we get the police report tomorrow to know what happened. Are you feeling well enough to go home?"

"Yes I'm fine. I was just a little light headed for a while, but now - now I'm okay."

"Do you have a way to get home?"

"No I usually ride the bus."

"Okay no problem I'll take you."

When Monica got home it was well after seven and the family had already eaten dinner and gone to do what they normally did. Laura had left a plate in the refrigerator for her so she sat down and ate. All the while she was asking herself was she responsible for what happened to Stephanie? Doing her homework assignments was almost impossible because of the guilt feeling that was imbedded in her brain. She wrestled with the idea that if she had not turned her away when she did perhaps things would be different now. Not knowing exactly how she died didn't help her resolve in her mind whether she had anything to do with her death. She speculated for a minute that perhaps she fell and hit her head on something, or maybe she choked on something. She was looking for something, anything to turn the thought away that Stephanie may have taken her own life.

Sleep did not come easy that night and she was really hoping that Lois would make an appearance and maybe ease her trepidation, but this was not to be. Eventually however, she went to sleep simply because her temporary adrenalin boost had exhausted her.

The next day even after a fitful night's sleep Monica woke up and prepared to go back to school. She was anxious to find out anything that would confirm or dispel the thought she had last night about how Stephanie died. It was not long before an announcement came over the PA (public address) sysem that a brief assembly would take place during first period in the auditorium. Monica as well as the other students were sure that the questions about what happened yesterday were going to be answered and they were right. When the bell rang to start the period there was a rush to fill the auditorium. Normally the room was seated by class level, but not today it was first come first be seated. The trio were able to garner seats right near the front so they could hear everything being said. The principal didn't take much time in getting right to the point of his message, but he gave them all that they expected.

"Students, teachers, staff and administrators I'm confident all of you heard about what happened here on yesterday. Never before have I had to witness a tragedy like what occurred to one of our beloved seniors. I received the police report early this morning and I'm sad to say that apparently Stephanie committed suicide by slashing her wrists and bleeding to death in the shower before anyone discovered her. My message to all of you students, staff, faculty alike if you are experiencing some personal problems or issues and don't know what to do, do not hesitate to talk with someone. There are many talented people around here who I'm sure will be able to help you find a solution to whatever is bothering you, but you must take the first step and reach out. There will be grief counselors arriving here this afternoon around the sixth period. If you feel you need to talk with one of them do not hesitate to ask to be excused from class and go to where they will be. An announcement will be made when they arrive what room or rooms they will be in. That's all for now. Try to concentrate on the work you have to do and put this behind you as best you can. If we receive any more information I will be sure to advise you . Okay you are dismissed please go directly to your class for this period.

It was like a knife cutting into her heart when Monica listened to his words. It seemed he was talking directly to her. Knowing now that Stephanie killed herself just confirmed what she suspected, but didn't want to believe. The what if's started pouring through her mind like a hurricane through a desert, there was nothing to stop it. What If I had really listened to her pleading for help? What If I had just talked to her right when she asked me to? What if my action could have prevented her from taking her own life?" All of these thoughts were weighing in so deeply that the headache that followed was cause for her to seek help herself. She then went to the nurse's office.

"Monica please come in and sit down. Are you feeling okay?"

"No I suddenly have this giant headache and don't have any aspirins. Can you give me something?"

"Sure, but let's do a couple of other things first okay?"

The nurse then took her temperature and blood pressure and asked whether she was reacting to what she heard from the principal this morning?"

"Yes I guess so because I was the one she tried to reach out to yesterday and I turned her away."

"Well now. You think you are the one who caused her to do what she did. I'm not going to try and provide an answer to that for you, but I am going to recommend that you speak with one of the grief counselors when they get here this afternoon. I believe they can help you. But for now take these and lie down here for a spell. I'll wake you for the next class."

Monica took the aspirins and stretched out on the couch for a few minutes. When the bell rang for the next class the nurse awakened her and asked if she was okay. Monica said yes and left to go to her class. She did not seek the comfort of any of the assigned grief counselors, but managed to get through the rest of the day alright.

That night after she left work and got home she decided to call Trish who she had not spoken to for a while. She had to talk to someone about how she felt about contributing to Stephanie's decision to commit suicide.

Ring, ring ,ring, ring,

"Hello."

"Hello, Aunt Trish it's Monica are you busy?"

"Hello my dear haven't talked to you lately. You know I'm never too busy to talk to you are you alright?"

"Well yes and no."

"Now what does that mean you want to be a little more specific for me?"

"Okay. One of my friends, well she wasn't really a good friend, but let me say one of my fellow classmates killed herself right here at school yesterday and I think I'm to blame."

"Oh no how tragic. What do you mean you were to blame?"

"Well yesterday, the day she died, she came to me earlier and told me she needed my help. I had no idea she was even thinking about what she did then so I turned her away and told her I would talk to her later. Before I saw her again I heard that she was dead. I feel terrible and I know I had to talk with somebody."

"I'm so glad you called me. Now I want you to listen to me very carefully I'm going to tell you something that I want you to absorb in the essence of your very being. You are not responsible for her or for anybody else. What she did she did because she lacked the faith to confront or face whatever it was that was troubling her. The fact that you could not talk with her at the time she wanted to talk was not the problem. The problem was that she had already made up in her mind what she was gong to do and was using you just as a way to avoid the truth. Listen I want you to come to church with me this Sunday Pastor Dumas is going to begin a sermon series about Jesus over the next several weeks and I think you ought to hear what he has to say. I'm sure it will help you with whatever guilt you might be feeling. Will you come with me?'

"Yes sure Aunt Trish I'll go with you if you think it's going to help me. What time do I need to be ready?"

"I'm certain it will help you. I can pick you up for the morning service at 10:30, please be ready to go when I get there."

"Okay I will be. Have a good night."

"And you as well. Don't worry about anything it will be alright. Goodnight."

It was Wednesday afternoon when Stephanie took her own life and Thursday morning when the principal received the confirming report that it was a suicide incident. Since that time and now through today Friday, there has been an overhanging atmosphere of glum throughout the halls of the once renowned Kimberly Clark High School. There never was prior to now any type of situation that would mar the almost pristine reputation of the school. Even the news reports from the various media outlets were as gentle as could be without distorting what really happened. Students were struggling to dismiss any negative thoughts and continue to concentrate on their studies, but it was difficult. Faculty and staff were also challenged to lay aside the incident and perform to the best of their ability.

For Monica she was especially glad it was Friday because it would give her the weekend break to mull over her relationship with the deceased and to try and absolve herself of the guilt feeling. She was also happy that she had a chance to talk with her Aunt Trish, who always seemed to have good advice (just as Elena once believed) and was willing to offer it. Getting through the rest of the day without stumbling in pursuit of excellence in her course work, she made an extra effort to stay focused.

Saturday while she worked the four hours she was permitted to labor she spent much of that time with a change of thought. She had not heard from Tony in the last few days. When he first arrived at college he was texting her two to three times a day and periodically made a phone call. Now something was different. She accepted the fact that he had to get acclimated to a new routine quickly and she was being patient, but hearing nothing from him over the last few days when she needed to was beginning to bother her. After work she sent him a text asking if all was well and would he at least respond to it. She heard nothing the rest of the day and decided to call him. No answer so she left a voice mail message. On top of all that was happening in her life recently she knew adding this to her trouble was not good so she again tried to stay positive.

Sunday morning came and she arose almost at the crack of dawn feeling somewhat refreshed. She had a good night's sleep even though she heard nothing from Tony. Her excitement about going to church with her Aunt was mounting because Trish told her there might be something good coming out of this service and she was looking forward to something uplifting.

At 10:30, right on time as usual, Trish pulled up to the house. Monica who was looking out the window was dressed and ready to go. There was no questioning anymore about where she was going or when she would be coming back by the Evans, because she had turned eighteen years of age. So she just walked out and got into th car.

"Good morning you look lovely" said Trish.

"Thank you I feel good. Had a good night's sleep and I thank you for helping me do it."

"Oh how so?"

"Well after I talked with you and you said not to worry about feeling guilty about that girl's death and I would hear a good word today, I felt better."

"Good for you, that's a nice start."

A few minutes later they pulled up to the church and entered the parking lot. It was almost full, but Trish was able to find a spot not too far from the front entrance door. Once inside they were ushered right near the front not far from where they had been seated for the funeral. Monica was impressed by how many more people had gathered today then who were at the funeral. There were hardly any seats left unfilled. She looked around almost like a tourist from out of town trying to take in all the things she failed to notice when she was here before. The décor was a little different than what was shown at the funeral service, but it was an elegant presentation.

At a few minutes after 11:00 the choir director got up at the front of the altar and motioned for to musicians to start playing. They started playing Precious Memories and from the rear of the sanctuary a thunderous sound issued forth from a fifty plus voice choir as they began marching in. They moved with a pulsating rhythm as they walked up to the choir loft and filled it. Continuing to sing and sway back and forth to the rhythm of the song the congregation was invited to join in. When they finished an associate minister stood up and gave the prayer of invocation. A reading of a Psalm was then offered by another clergy member followed by a gospel rendition of You'll Never Walk Alone. Following that was a prayer offered by another minister praying for the sick and for the healing of the nation. Then the mass choir stood up and offered a rendition of Total Praise that set the house in order and prepared the way for a rousing sermon.

While this was going on Pastor Dumas entered and took his seat in the pulpit. There was such an overwhelming movement of the spirit throughout the sanctuary when the choir finished singing it begged a comment from the preacher.

"Brothers and sisters in the Lord I believe the Lord is in His Holy Temple and He's moving right now. If you believe it and you feel it I want you to holler Hallelujah."

The response was a resounding Hallelujah, Hallelujah that shook the rafters in intensity becasue of the size of the congregation.

"My, my, my I believe the Holy Spirit has arrived."

"Yes Lord, oh yes Lord" came a response.

"Isn't it good to be in the house of the Lord one more time? If God has done anything good for you this week please let Him know and say Amen."

Again the response was thunderous as the thank you Lord, hallelujahs and Praise God rang throughout the room.

"Brothers and sisters as we come here today seeking a word from God let me say that we are living in some precarious times right now. I know that there's somebody here who knows what I'm talking about. You are witnesses to the things that are going on right in our very neighborhoods and across the country. Well today I want to start on a series of talks that will address the need for someone who can not only address the wrongs, but fix them. His name is Jesus. I'm going to begin by giving a little history about how the world came to be and what was the original intention before man corrupted it and set a pattern of destruction underway.

Please pray with me now – Lord God of the heavens hide me behind the cross for my words are meaningless, but let your words fill my mouth that they may be spoken with conviction and clarity. Let the words of my mouth and the meditation of my heart be acceptable to you oh Lord my strength and my redeemer.

Brothers and sisters for the next few weeks I want to talk to you from several different sections of this holy writ called the Bible so that we may see how God is working now and has been from the very beginning working for our good. I invite you to turn with me now in your Bibles to Genesis Chapter 1 verses 1 and 2. For those of you who are still searching it's the first book in the Bible."

A slight laugh came from the crowd.

In the beginning God created the heavens and the earth. Now the earth was formless and empty, darkness was over the surface of the deep, and the Spirit of God was hovering over the waters. (NIV 1-2).

Many of you are familiar with this passage of scripture and your understanding is correct that indeed God did create the heavens and the earth in the beginning. But what I want to help you with your understanding today is that this reference was not the very beginning. For that let us turn now to the New Testament and the gospel of St. John Chapter 1 versus 1-5 (NIV).

In the beginning was the Word and the Word, was with God, and the Word was God. He was with God in the beginning. Through him all things were made; without him nothing was made that has been made. In him was life, and that life was the light of men. The light shines in the darkness, but the darkness has not understood it.

You see the true beginning and the creation of the earth was performed by the Word. Now who is the Word? The Word is Jesus and it is He that created the earth. It is He that we're going to be talking about for the next few weeks because He is the one that can fix the problems we are having now. Okay so now you're confused. The original creation by the Word was inhabited by angels under the direction of a high ranking angel called Lucifer. But Lucifer became disenchanted with his position and wanted to be God and take His place. He rebelled and convinced one third of the angels to follow him. He lost the battle and was banished to the earth where it became the formless void that the second in the beginning refers to. So you see it was actually Jesus as the Word who is earth's creator. Okay now we have established that let's move on. I'm sure you've heard the story about the Garden Of Eden and how after Jesus had made a man and a woman to inhabit it, they disobeyed His instructions and were tempted by Satan who was known before as Lucifer to do wrong by eating from the fruit of a tree that was forbidden. You know it as the apple from the tree – Knowledge Of Good And Evil. Once this was done it was the first test that was given to man and he failed miserably. "After that man was ejected from the garden and set on a path of destruction that we are the inheritors of today.

I'm not going to inundate you with too much information today, but I just wanted to establish the framework from which we will be working for a while. Let me close this section of the sermon series by telling you that the time is rapidly growing short when there will not be an opportunity to escape the coming disaster and receive salvation. Look around now and see the direction that the world is headed and you must know that it is not good. What we see now though pales in comparison to what has been foretold in the Book Of Revelations regarding what lies immediately ahead. There is a way however, to protect yourself receive your salvation and be spared that is by joining with God's army. Open you heart right now and receive the Holy Spirit as it move among you in this house. Do not let the time pass you by and be left out when He returns and finds you wanting.

The doors of the church are open. Give the deacons your hand, but give Jesus your heart. Won't you come?" He ended his sermon and there was an immediate stirring among the congregants as the Holy Spirit took hold of many of them. Monica felt the tugging at her heart strings, but right now her feet refused to take the next step so she watched as the parade of new believers passed her by. – .

CHAPTER 8

The Awakening

In a large metropolis an incident like what happened at Kimberly Clark Regional High School concerning the death of one of her students does not usually cause a widespread controversy. The news media had given proper coverage to the story and did not slant it in any direction that was not appropriate. However, the issues that arose as a result of what to do with the body were dividing much of the population on religious grounds. Stephanie Landolin came from an old school Catholic family who believed in the practice that one who commits suicide should not be allowed to be funeralized and buried in consecrated grounds. The modern Catholic church however, dispelled that tradition long ago and insisted that the child receive a proper burial and be placed in land belonging to and blessed by the church. Citizens from both contingencies lined up on either side wanting to uphold and support their traditional belief.

The funeral home that was gracious enough to remove the corpse from the school was now caught in a dilemma. Normally they would like to have a body interred no later than four days from the time they receive it, but now since there has been no agreement or resolution on the disposition of the deceased the funeral director was caught between the proverbial rock and a hard place. At one point, soon after he had been notified of her death and knowing that this situation could arise, Stephanie's father went to the legal authority seeking help. No one in the city's assortment of agencies nor in the state's likewise variety wanted to make any type of ruling in the case because it was considered a religious issue and should be handled by the church. The separation of church and state powers was clearly in the forefront of the debate.

While the two sides argued, Stephanie lay in a state of repose not being considered worthy by either side of receiving proper treatment. The matter was being bantered back and forth for so long without it looking like a resolution was forthcoming any time soon, until the owner of the funeral home went to Reverend Dumas, the prominent pastor of a large church for help. He called him and requested he be able to meet with him as soon as possible. The meeting was set for the day after the call was made.

"Reverend Dumas thank you for agreeing to meet with me on such short notice. My name is Arnold Harrington and I'm the owner-director of the Sleep In Peace funeral Home here in the city. I'm sure you've heard by now about the squabble between the family and the Catholic church of the girl who killed herself at school recently. I have the body and I've had it now longer than I should have and it causing me a problem. The city and the state refuse to make a decision and the church is divided. I don't know what to do. Can you help?"

"Mr. Harrington I understand your problem and I'm not sure that this is something I should be getting involved in. I am the pastor of a Baptist Church and our traditions are certainly different from the Catholic church and we are not at liberty to try and persuade the government either municipal or state to intervene because I asked. I don't just want to dismiss you arbitrarily though because the deceased regardless of who is arguing about her body, needs to have her soul attended to. No one who is a child of God and we all are should be held at the mercy of man who is an arbitrator of bodies, but not of souls. I can't make you any promises right now, because I have to consult with a higher authority in my tradition and see how I should act. Give me until this time tomorrow and I will call you with perhaps a way to find relief."

"Oh thank you so much pastor. I certainly look forward to hearing from you. Have a good day."

"Thank you and you be blessed on this day."

Reverend Dumas after meeting with Mr. Harrington was sincerely concerned about the fact that two supposed men of the God, the high priest and child's father would not be able to come to an agreement that would allow the dead child to receive a proper burial regardless of what each side considered to be proper. He sat at his desk in deep meditation and reflection for several minutes until the Spirit moved within him. He was drawn to the scripture where Jesus talked to the Pharisees and the Sadducees about keeping the traditions of men and not the laws of God.

He recalled the passages in the old testament where Jewish law required that a dead body be buried the same day before sundown, but he also noted that the reason then was not much a spiritual requirement ss it was a situational necessity. Back then no embalming processes existed or any other means to preserve the body for any extended length of time. Then he researched the new testament view and discovered that the reasonable time to return a body to the ground was between 3-4 days again not because of any spiritual dictate. So he was not able to make a positive decision based on this, but then the Spirit told him that in this case where a child lies in limbo, because of man's indecision, then he should confront both the priest and the father and tell them that they will be held accountable. The soul of the dead will be judged by God at the proper time and their reason for delaying a burial will be charged against them also at that time. Therefore let the priest who is the ordained representative of God bury the child in the church cemetery and let the father pray for forgiveness for keeping ancient traditions. When Pastor Dumas finished his meditation and felt he had a positive solution by the power of the Holy Spirit he was ready to talk with Mr. Harrington. He didn't wait until tomorrow, but called him right then.

After talking with Mr. Harrington the funeral director asked if pastor Dumas could stay on the line while he tried to set up a three-way call to the priest and the father to see if they could resolve the matter right now. Call it fate, Karma, Divine Intervention or whatever, all parties were able to attend the call and the matter was settled. The funeral was set for Friday morning at the Catholic church.

The funeral was held and the modern Catholic rituals were conducted. There was no great attendance except for the immediate family and a few friends. The high school students were not told in time to make arrangements to attend so they were not there, but Reverend Dumas and one of his ministers was there out of respect for the disputing parties realizing that the child's welfare should have always been first in their decision making. And so it was Stephanie was finally laid to rest.

After the funeral was over and word got back to the school principal he prepared an immediate announcement telling the student body that

Stephanie had finally been given a proper burial and was now at rest. Some of the students were at least sympathetic hearing the news because they had heard how long she had been delayed in being buried, others were not so appreciative of the situation mainly because they didn't know Stephanie that well anyway. With Monica, she had mixed emotions. On one hand she was glad that a proper burial had been given, but on the other she wondered why it took so long in the first place. She was aware of all the talk about the argument on both sides regarding the religious dispute over what was the right thing to do regarding someone who commits suicide. It bothered her that a church would argue with a family decision on how to bury their loved one. She didn't quite understand about the religious protocols concerning somebody who just needed to be buried and how could a tradition be the cause for preventing it to happen.

After having attended a service in the Baptist tradition and being moved by something so much so that she was almost ready to commit herself, she wondered just how the idea of religious beliefs affected people so differently when they were supposedly serving the same God. She said to herself this was something she was going to find out more about if and when she went back to the church. For now she was satisfied that Stephanie was at peace having witnessed personally the internal turmoil she was going through.

When she got home that night and still had not received any text messages or a phone call from Tony she was becoming concerned that something was wrong in their relationship. She called him again once and then an hour later called again with no response. Had he found someone new there and started a new relationship or was he just really so busy with his sports program and academic schedule he didn't have time to respond to her? Her heart was still his so the lack of communication was beginning to play a heavy role on her mind.

Several days past then over a week and still she received no word. Now her heart was near the point of thinking was this the end of her first real love affair and is this how a broken heart feels. Her studies were starting to slip thinking about her love situation until Mrs. Rabinawitz, her favorite teacher who had been her confidant all through her time at Kimberly asked her to come to her classroom after shool one day.

"Hi Monica come on in."

"Hi you wanted to see me?"

"Yes please sit down. I've been talking with some of the other teachers about you and they told me that your grades are beginning to decline. Is there something wrong at home?"

"Oh no everything is fine there it's just that I have such a heavy load this year that I'm finding it hard to keep up with all the homework. I'll do better."

"Monica let me say this. As a senior in great standing right now you are close to getting a scholarship offer from a few schools. But you can't let your guard down and lose your ranking before they even make you an offer. Remember there are only a few weeks left before they will be making decisions and I would hate to see you miss out just before the finish line when you're so close. Remember if something si bothering you, anything you can always talk to me. I'v been where you are and I know what I think you may be going through. So keep that in mind. Is there anything you'd like to talk about now?"

"Well there is one thing. I've been trying to handle it myself, but maybe I do need to talk with someone. Do you remember Anthony Underwood, he graduated last year?"

"Of course I do. He was the handsome jock on the basketball team right?"

"Yes. Well he took me to the senior prom and after that we have been dating for some time and got real close over the summer. He went off to college at the beginning of this year and I haven't heard anything from him for weeks now even though I've tried to contact him several times."

"Oh okay that's it. Now I understand. When you say you got real close you mean sexually?"

Monica paused for a few minutes looking at her then she answered.

"Yes, but I love him."

"Monica let me share with you something that I along with many other young girls have gone through since the dating game started. You are not the first victim of a guy like that and I'm sad to say you will not be the last. He has probably discovered a whole new opportunity on a different level with college girls who can offer him more than just sex. Take my advice and do not let him be the reason you squander your opportunity to go to college also. You can't change him nor what he may have done to you, but what you can change and you need to do it right now is forget about him and refocus on your studies. That's the most important thing for you right now, not him. Are you listening to what I'm saying? Please believe me I know I'm right - been there."

"Yes I'm listening. Thank you Mrs. Rabinawitz for sharing your story with me. I will refocus."

Monica left her classroom feeling good. She was so glad to have talked with someone she believed understood her. Now it was up to her to raise her grades and go after those scholarship offers.

It was late Friday afternoon when the letter was delivered to Dr. Danforth. He was still in his office at the hospital and just finishing up entering a report in the computer on his last patient. When the letter was handed to him he first casually glanced at it then laid it aside to look at again later. However, as he was typing he noticed, out of the corner of his eye, that the return address on the mail read – Saddle River Behavioral Health Center, 800 Meadowbrook Road, Wayne, NJ 07470. This caught his attention because he recalled that this is where Norman Miller had been transferred to. He stopped typing and opened it.

Dear Dr. Danforth my name is Kenneth Oniyuki, MD at the Behavioral Health Center here in Wayne. I am a resident psychiatrist that has been assigned to the treatment for a Mr. Norman Miller who I understand may have been a patient of yours some time ago. I have been working with this patient for a few years now and have not noticed any marked improvement in his mental health or stability until just a few days ago. At that time he showed a remarkable sign of recovery, albeit very temporary (a few hours), but during that short interval I was able to communicate with him in a manner that was not previously achieved. He mentioned that there was a woman named Elena who had visited him here recently and was wanting to ask him about what his father did to him? I checked the visitor log over the past two weeks and there was no such person, not even close that came to see him. As a matter of fact he had no visitors at all.

I am writing to you as the last doctor who treated him before he arrived here to see if you would be interested in consulting with me on his history and together possibly we may conclude a viable treatment going forward for him. Further, there was one other significant moment while he was fairly lucid for that short time, he said that he had a daughter by this woman and he wanted to see her. I'm not sure whether he was hallucinating or not, but he seemed very convinced of this. Again I have not been able yet to determine what caused this sudden and temporary return to a semblance of normalcy, but I'm sure you would agree that it could be a sign of a possible long tern recovery.

> At your earliest opportunity, if you are interested, please call me at (201) 525-6730. My regular office hours are 7-5 Monday through Friday, but you may leave a voice mail at any time on this number.

> Yours truly,
> Dr. Kenneth Oniyuki – (Psychiatrist)

When Milton finished reading the letter he could hardly believe the message. It was not too long ago that he had been discussing with his friend David Dumas the disposition of Mr. Miller when Elena came in to his hospital. Now here was an odd coincidence of a chance to revisit that conversation and perhaps gain a better perspective regarding the relationship spiritually between the Millers. He didn't hesitate in picking up the phone, not to call Dr. Oniyuki, but to call Dr. Dumas.

Ring, ring, ring.

"Good afternoon Holy Trinity Baptist Church how can I help you?" .

"Hello this is Dr. Danforth is Pastor Dumas available now?"

"No I'm sorry he's not. He's in conference with somebody. Would you like to leave a message on his voice mail?"

"Yes please I'll hold."

"Okay – transferring you now."

"You have reached the mail box of Reverend Dumas. I'm sorry I can't take your call right now, but your call is important to me so at the sound of the tone please leave your name, telephone number and a brief message and I will return your call as soon as I can. Please speak slowly and clearly."

"David – Milton here. I just received a letter from someone we both need to talk to ASAP. He is a shrink at that hospital in Jersey that Mr. Miller was sent to years ago. He has information we both need to hear about. Call me soon as you can so we can decide how we want to proceed. Okay 'bye."

Milton hung up hoping that his friend would call soon. He was getting excited just thinking about what this could mean in terms of coming up with a treatment that could help his patients if Dr. Oniyuki has really discovered something to restore mental health to someone who has been lost for a long time. As far as his friend would be concerned he would be interested in a possible spiritual visit from the deceased – Norman's wife.

Milton returned to finishing entering his report on the computer, but in the back of his mind he was already contemplating setting up not a consultation phone call, but going with his friend over to meet the doctor in person. Time seemed to stop while he was waiting for the return of his call so he began going through the old files on Mr. Norman Miller. Since it has been a number of years when the last entry was made the records had been moved to an archive storage area. Locating the records he needed became somewhat of a challenge because the file was now in a common storage area where all hospital personnel had access and not everyone was meticulous about placing records back where they retrieved them from. After spending almost an hour going through files he was able to retrieve the information he needed.

By the time he returned to his office and checked his messages he had indeed missed the very call he was waiting for. Feeling a bit embarrassed he picked up his phone and dialed right away.

Ring, ring, ring.

"Good afternoon Holy Trinity Baptist Church how can I help you?"

"Hi this is Dr. Danforth again I called earlier is Pastor Dumas available now?"

"Please hold let me check. Yes he is I'll transfer you to his line."

"Thank you."

"Milton how you doing? You called me saying you got something urgent then you don't answer when I call you back – you alright?"

"Yeah, yeah Dave sorry about that but I went to retrieve some files to look at when we talked and it took longer than I thought it would to find them."

"Well did you find what you were looking for?"

"Yes I did and I'm glad I did. You know why I was calling with the urgent message is because I received a letter this afternoon from a Dr. Oniyuki, a psychiatrist at that mental institution in New Jersey where Norman Miller was transferred after he left here. He said in the letter that apparently he had some kind of a breakthrough in Mr. Miller's treatment and for a short time he seemed almost normal. He wants to consult with me because there are some things that Norman said while he was in that lucid state of mind that the doc needs more information about. He referred to Norman getting a visit from Elena recently. Now we both know or at least I believe that's impossible, but that's why I want to bring you in. The doctor said he checked the visitor log and not only was there no visit from Elena, but he had no visitors at all. Remember now this was during his supposedly normal mental activity. All of this has peeked my curiosity. What do you think?"

"Well it sounds like something that needs further study. What are you proposing?"

"I want to call the doc and set up a meeting with him, maybe not a real consultation as such, but I think we both should talk and perhaps learn some things neither one of us knew before. While I was reviewing his file there are some notes I made in there about his father putting a spell on him that may have driven him to the point where he lost it. I didn't have enough time to finishing exploring that area before they transferred him. Maybe now we might be able to get a better handle on what happened there."

"I totally agree, so what's the plan?"

"I wanted to talk with you first before calling him to find out what's on your schedule and what would be a good time for us to go over there."

"Well let me see here. Give me a minute I need to step out and check with my assistant on a couple of things. Hold on I'll be right back. Okay it looks like the best I can do is next Tuesday morning around 10:00 would be good for me, but I need to get back here by 2:00."

"Okay that sounds good to me. I can rearrange my appointments for that day. Hopefully he can accommodate that day and time. I'm going to call him right now and see if it works for him. If I get through and it's good then I will call you right back, if I don't then you won't hear from me again until l do. Please keep the date open."

"Okay I'll wait for your call."

Milton hung with Rev. Dumas and immediately tried to get hold of Dr. Oniyuki. He called the number given in the letter, but a message came on from the telephone company saying it was not a working number. Suspecting that it may have been just a typographical error he researched the hospital data and found he was correct. One of the numbers in the letter had been transposed. So he wrote it down and tried calling again.

Ring, ring, ring, ring.

"Hello Saddle River Behavioral Health Center how may I direct your call?"

"Hello my name is doctor Danforth and I'm trying to contact Dr. Oniyuki is he available?"

"Please hold I will transfer you to his extension."

"Hello Dr. Oniyuki."

"Dr. Oniyuki this is Dr. Danforth I just received your letter regarding Norman Miler. Do you have a minute to talk now or are you busy?"

"Oh I'm so happy to hear from you. No I'm not busy now my next appointment is not for another hour. Did you read my letter and what do you think?"

"That's why I'm calling you now. I would like to set up a meeting with you and I have another person I would like to bring with me who may have some important information to contribute. We're hoping we can schedule next Tuesday morning at 10:00 if that's alright with you?"

"Yes, yes that would be fine. I look forward to meeting you and anybody else that you feel may be of help."

"Okay then we will see you on Tuesday at 10:00. Have a nice day."

"Thank you and you also. Goodbye"

"Goodbye."

Ring, ring, ring.

"Holy Trinity Baptist Church how can I help you?"

"Hi Dr. Danforth again is Pastor Dumas available?"

"Yes he's standing right here."

"Milton give me a minute to get back to my office then we can talk. Guess you have good news since you're calling back so quickly. Okay be right with you. Well now what do we have?"

"We are on for Tuesday at 10:00. You want me to come by there and pick you up or do you want to come by here?"

"Have you ever been to this hospital?"

"No but I have a fairly good idea about where it is."

"Okay then you drive. Come by here and get me at 9:00. You don't think it will take more than an hour to get there do you?"

"No that should give us enough time. One thing I wanted to ask you before we meet with the doc and it's about something you said in your euglogy for Mrs. Miller. You said that she was a child of God, does that mean she would have been protected from any evil spirits at her death?"

"Milton I'm surprised at you asking me that question. We are all children of God from the time we're born until the time we die. Now whether she was protected from evil spirits all depends on whether she was saved or not when she died. Why did you ask me that now?"

"Because I think when we talk with Dr. Oniyuki that's going to enter into the conversation at some point. Okay if I don't talk to you again before Tuesday have a nice weekend."

"Aren't you coming to my church Sunday?"

"You know I would be there, but this Sunday I have to cover for one of the residents who is on vacation."

"Okay then I guess I'll see you on Tuesday. Be blessed."

"Thank you goodbye."

"Goodbye."

Milton continued going over the files he had just retrieved from the archives and the more he read the more he became engrossed in what happened in the period that he was examining Norman Miller. His reference to South Carolina and the Gullah/Geechee religious practices and possible voodoo curses his father believed in was peeking his curiosity. Could this possibly have anything to do now with his sudden temporary recovery? Had the curse been lifted and if so by who - Elena?"

He left his office that day not having any answers to the questions he was pondering and he was having trouble getting them out of his mind. There was not much else he could do prior to the meeting so he called his special lady to see if she was available tonight for dinner. He just wanted someone to talk to about anything else, but this subject. She was available so he made a date.

That night when Monica got home after work she reflected on the advice Mrs. Rabinawitz had given her earlier. She knew she was still in love with Tony, but from what the teacher said could he really be having a good time with someone new while she was waiting around for the telephone to ring. The words sunk in and she made up her mind to forget about him and concentrate on her studies. After eating dinner with the remaining Evans family which was now just Harold and Laura she decided before tackling her homework assignments for the night she would call Reilly who she hadn't talked to after school for a while.

Ring, ring, ring.

"Hello."

"Hey girl Monica here whatcha doin?"

"I just walked in the door. You know working for my father is becoming more demanding than I anticipated and I see now why he is always tired when he comes home. I'll be okay though. Don't know how I'm going to finish all this crap these teachers have been loading up on us though. Are you okay?"

"Yeah I'm fine. Had a long talk with Mrs. Rabinawitz today though and she really schooled me about some things I hadn't even thought about. You know I told you that I haven't heard from Tony for some time now and it was starting to get me down. She opened my eyes and painted a very vivid picture about good looking sports jocks and college girls that made a good impression."

"I remember you saying something about him abandoning you. Wow I thought he was really into you. Guess they're all alike when they leave home. Anyway so what are you going to do now?"

"Clear my head and refocus on my studies so I can qualify for some type of scholarship. I've decided after talking with some of the managers at work that I may have a good shot at going to college. There's this one manager who says he can help me get into NYU's Business School if I want to go there. That would be fantastic, but there's no way I could afford that without a lot of help."

"I agree with that guy you have the smarts and certainly you deserve to go. You and Soun Li should go. I don't think I'm going to go, at least not right away because the more I look at my dad lately and see him getting older I think he's about ready to retire and I'm all he's got. I don't know I haven't decided yet. One way or the other finance would not be one of my problems. I truly wish you and Soun Li well though. Well let me get started on this stuff before I really get out of the mood. See you tomorrow."

"Yeah right. Later."

The girls said goodnight in their own special way and Monica started in on her assignments. She had just gotten started in tackling the advanced economics work when her phone rang. She first got a little excited thinking it might be Tony, but when she looked at the caller ID that thought quickly vanished. It was Trish.

"Hello Aunt Trish."

"Hi Monica I know it's kind of late to be calling you, but I was just thinking about you and realized we haven't talked since we buried your mother. How are you feeling are you alright?"

"Oh I'm fine. I sure appreciated all you did to make that a wonderful send off for her and I couldn't be happier how things turned out."

"That's so good to hear, especially since you had been looking for her for so long and not being able to find and talk with her it was good that at least for a little while she could bless you."

"Yes that was nice. That sermon at the church was really good also, it almost got me to get up and go down that aisle and join up."

"I really wish you had. But if it's not your time yet, I believe the day will come when you will sincerely feel the urge to do so, I'm not going to keep you up any longer because I know you still have school work to do, but if you want to I can pick you up again this Sunday for church."

"You know as much as I liked the things he was saying I didn't hear anything that directly answered my questions."

"Well you know that was just the beginning of the sermon series and there are more weeks to come. You need to keep coming because I know that in one of those you will hear the answer to to whatever you're questioning. Okay I going to say goodnight now."

"Okay. I'll call you tomorrow after I get off from work and let you know if I want to go."

"Okay. Goodnight."

"Goodnight."

After that phone call as pleasant as it was talking to her aunt it took a few more minutes for her to get refocused on the task at hand-her economics homework. The thought about not getting her questions answered however lingered in her mind. For the next two hours she went hard at the books until her eyes were beginning to water and her brain was having difficulty absorbing what she was reading on a page. She got up stretched then went downstairs to get some refreshment and possibly recharge. When she got to the kitchen Harold was there apparently for the same reason, getting some refreshment.

"How are you doing in that high class school of yours?" he made the snide remark.

"I'm doing fine, no thanks to you."

"You're just about finished there now right? You're supposed to graduate this summer aren't you?"

"Yes I believe I'm on the right track for that. Why are you asking?"

"I just wanted to know whether you think you're going to college 'cause we sure can't send you.?"

"Yes I know that and I wouldn't think of asking you to."

"Good at least we got that straight. Okay I'm going back to bed goodnight."

"Yeah you do that goodnight."

Harold left the kitchen first then Monica grabbed a snack and some orange juice then went back to her studies. She always got so frustrated whenever she talked with him that she couldn't ever remember a time when his conversation made any sense to her. Now that she was on the edge of getting out of that house away from him and his wife the anticipation was a joyful and uplifting feeling. After another hour and half when she completed the final piece of her assignments her body had reached the state where it wa crying for some resting sleep.

She got ready for bed and as was her usual custom now for a long time she went and made sure her bedroom door was locked. Along about 2:00 AM she heard the sound of what seemed to be leaves rustling in her room. Half awake she opened her eyes and rubbed them once and then again trying to focus on what she thought she was seeing. It had been a long time since her grandmother Lois had come to her and since she was not now under any unusual stress she wondered why this visit. Then she recalled that the last time Lois was there she had left something unfinished. Maybe now she was coming to continue. She sat up in the bed and became wide awake.

"Monica, Monica, Monica my dear grandchild I have left you alone for too long. This is because your future is still being determined and I wanted to wait until I had more clarity. Now I can continue my warning with more certainty then I had before. You are very soon about to enter the maze of life called destiny. There are going to be many twists and turns you will run into many of which will have high walls and blocks that will challenge you to make the right turn. In the center of this maze of life the ultimate love, peace and understanding that you seek resides. You must learn how to get there. Disappointments and false witnesses will rise against you and lovers will use you for their own joy. There will be times when you will think you are lost in the maze, but are not. I will always be with you if you just reach out and call to me, but most importantly you must accept the power that will be made available to you and you must learn to open your eyes, open your mind and open your........"

She never finished the sentence and just like before she disappeared.

CHAPTER 9
The Session

On Monday afternoon the day before the meeting was scheduled to take place with Dr. Oniyuki, Dr. Danforth called Reverend Dumas to make sure everything was still set.

Ring, ring, ring.

"Holy Trinity Baptist Church how may I help you?"

"Hello this is Dr. Danforth is the pastor available now?"

"Yes he is please hold while I transfer your call."

"Hello."

"Hello Dave, Milton how are you?"

"I'm fine feeling blessed everyday I get up. What about you?"

"Yeah I'm good too. I just wanted to follow up and make sure we're still on for tomorrow's meeting with that doctor at the mental hospital. You good?"

"Yes. I think we agreed you're picking me up at 9:00 right?"

"That's right I will be there then and hope we won't hit any major traffic issues on our way. I think I know generally where it might be, but I have no idea how the traffic pattern will be in that area. Guess we'll just have to play it by ear."

"Yes. I think though by the time we should be getting there the morning rush will have finished."

'Yeah I agree, but you never know. Okay I'll see you tomorrow. Goodbye."

"Right goodbye."

They hung up and the scheduled meeting was confirmed.

That Tuesday morning after picking Reverend Dumas up right on time the two men found themselves snarled in a traffic jam on Rt. 46 coming off of Rt.3. Traffic had come to a complete standstill. Unable to see what was ahead of them Dr. Danforth turned the radio on and tuned it to a local channel. It turned out that a tractor trailer had overturned just beyond where they were and it was tying up everything on all lanes. Apparently it had just happened because the police and emergency apparatus were still arriving. It was now close to 9:30 and he believed they were less than twenty minutes away. Dr. Danforth picked up his phone and called Dr. Oniyuki on his private cell.

Buzz, buzz.

"Hello."

"Dr. Oniyuki this is Dr. Danforth I'm on my way with a friend I told you about, but we are stuck here on Rt. 46 I suspect we may be here awhile from the looks of the traffic and I haven't seen any kind of towing truck come by. How much time can you give us because I'm sure we will be late?"

"Oh I'm so sorry to hear that. Let me talk to my receptionist and see if we can reschedule my next two out patients. The number that came up on my screen is that where you're calling from?"

"Yes you can get back to me on that line."

"Okay give me a few minutes and I will call you."

"Well were you able to hear that?" Milton said to David.

"Yes I heard. Now remember I need to be at my church by 2:00. You still want to try and meet with him today?"

"I would, just to get a feel for what he was able to do with Mr. Miller even if we have to schedule another time to come back and get deeper into it."

"Okay but hopefully this traffic mess will be cleared up soon."

Before he finished his statement a police car with lights flashing and siren blaring sped by with a heavy duty tow truck following close behind.

"Well that's encouraging" Dr. Danforth said.

Within the next fifteen minutes traffic was starting to move again, but they had not heard back from Dr. Oniyuki. Milton wondered should he call him again, but Rev. Dumas said to give him a few more minutes since they were on their way there anyway.. Fve minutes later the phone rang.

Hello."

"Dr. Danforth this is Dr. Oniyuki sorry it took so long, but we had difficulty getting in touch with one of my patients to reschedule. However,

I was able to clear my schedule for the rest of the day so when you get here we can have as much time as needed."

"That's great. Thank you so much for doing that we'll see you shortly, hopefully. Goodbye."

"Okay see you soon."

The traffic was moving but at a snail's pace and Dr. Danforth was considering using his MD plate to get some possible help. When they got near the place where the truck had overturned he flagged down one of the policeman and explained his situation to him. The officer looked at his plate, asked him for his ID then got in his car, radioed his dispatcher then provided an escort right to the hospital. It took less than fifteen minutes. The two men thanked the officer and hurried inside. At the front entrance they stood before the receptionist and asked for Dr. Oniyuki. The time it took for them to get there was much less than what they had told Dr. Oniyuki so it was good that he was still in his office when they arrived.

When they got to the fifth floor and were directed to his office he was so glad to see them.

"Gentleman, gentleman it's good to see you. Sorry about your delay, but that route has problems all the time. Please, please come in and sit down."

Both Dr. Danforth and Reverend Dumas walked in. Before sitting down Milton introduced Rev. Dumas and they shook hands.

"Dr. Oniyuki this is Reverend Doctor Dumas who is not only a friend of mine, but he has had some professional contact with the subject we are talking about here today..

"Oh is that right? What was your relationship with him please?"

Reverend began explaning how he was introduced to Norman by Dr Danforth and he was just beginning to creatr a profile for him when he was removed from the hospital in New York and brought here, so there wasn't much that he was able to establish.

"Okay so now Dr. Danforth where would you like to begin?"

Before answering Milton looked at his watch then at David. Then he asked Dr. Oniyuki if he would excuse them for just a minute as they stepped outside the office.

"David is there any way you can reschedule your 2:00? Remember this man just cleared his whole schedule for today for us."

"Yes I realize that and I'm sorry, but my meeting is with the Mayor over some key church issues and I've been trying to get a sit down with him for weeks. So no I can't reschedule."

The two men walked back inside and Milton was embarrassed to have to speak.

"Dr. Oniyuki I feel so embarrassed with what I have to say next because it's certainly not what we planned. However, that accident threw off our whole agenda time wise. You see my friend has to be back at his church this afternoon for another meeting and I'm sorry to say that one cannot be rescheduled."

"Oh I see. So what would you like to do? It's now 1:15 and I guess you would like to get on the road by at least 1:30 right?"

"Again I feel so embarrassed I don't know what else to say. Perhaps we can reschedule another time quickly and get a fresh start."

."Don't feel badly these things happen. What I would like to suggest however is maybe we can meet over the weekend. I don't schedule appointments then. I don't know about you. What do you think?"

Milton looked again at Rev. Dumas before answering. David nodded his head in agreement and Milton responded.

"I think that's a great idea and I really appreciate you being so gracious. What time Saturday would be good for you?"

"So that we don't tie up the whole day can we start at 9:30 in the morning?"

"That works for me David are you okay with that time?"

"Yes I guess it will have to do."

"Okay so we are set for Saturday at 9:30 am" Milton said.

The meeting ended, another apology and a thank you offered for being so accommodating was made then the two men hurried to the car to get back to New York hoping there would not be any more traffic incidents to snarl things going that way.

That Saturday morning Dr. Danforth went to the church at 8:00 O'clock and Reverend Dumas was there ready and waiting. The two men drove through the tunnel got on Rt. 3 then Rt. 46 and arrived at the center in less than forty-five minutes. What a difference a hurdle like an accident can make when you're trying to get somewhere to meet a schedule. They walked in as before and informed the receptionist of their purpose. Again they were directed to the office on the fifth floor. The big difference today was that there was minimal activity and few people in the halls and corridors. When they got to Dr. Oniyuki's office he was already there and welcomed them in.

"Good morning, good morning good to see you again. I trust you had no difficulty getting here this time."

"No this time it was smooth sailing" offered Milton.

"Would you like some coffee or orange juice or a bagel I have them all?"

"No thank you we're fine." Reverend Dumas said.

"Okay then shall we start? I believe where we left off the other day was that I was asking you Dr. Danforth how you wanted to proceed. Shall we begin there?"

"Yes that would be good. What I would like to start with is in your letter you mentioned that you had some kind of break through with Mr. Miller in which he appeared to be rational and lucid for a short period of time Can you elucidate on that session please?"

"Sure. I had been treating Mr. Miller for several years since I got here and in every session prior to that day his responses were irrational and incoherent. Medically he was just being given the usual Prozac, Celexa and Benzodiazephines in the standard dosages along with various vitamins you know mainly to keep him calm and out of any deeply depressed state. His anxiety level when I first began treating him was sporadic and he would go into and out of unpredictable bursts of laughter then crying. This was not an exhibition of the usual manic–depressive syndrome, but was more like there was actually something driving him to behave that way.

One day, it was on a Monday, I can give you the exact date if you like, I came in to do my regular examination and something was different. Normally he would be sitting in the chair that we usually use to consult, waiting for me, but that day he was standing with his arms open wide as if he was inviting me to hug him. I asked him if that's what he wanted me to do and he responded that it's what his wife thought he should do. Then I asked him about his wife and he told me that she had been there over the weekend and removed his curse. I obliged him and hugged him then suggested he sit down and talk to me more about his visitor.

At that point his responses were like that of any normal rational person and I wondered what caused this so I asked him and again he said his wife removed his curse. Then I asked him how she did it and he said she touched him. This normal and very pleasant conversation went on for about an hour then he dropped his head and seemed to become another person, the person he usually was, Incoherent, irrational, exhibiting a pre-panic state, restless and highly emotional. That's when I ended that session and had him brought back to his room Other than what he told me about his wife I have no explanation for what caused the brief normal state of his mind and behavior. That's when I wrote to you."

"That's very interesting. I don't know whether you know this or not, but he did have a wife and her name was Elena as you mentioned in your letter, but she's dead so she couldn't have visited him at any time. You said you checked the visitor log and confirmed there were no visitors anyway isn't that right?"

"Yes that is correct."

"Then that brings us back to how did he reach that lucid state even for the short time he did. Is it possible that something did touch him?"

"Dr. Danforth do you believe in spirits?"

"Yes, Jack Daniels, Tanqueray, Bacardi Gold they're my favorites."

All three men had to laugh for a minute and it lightened up the room.

"No seriously I'm not referring to those kinds of spirits. The ones I mean are the ones my grandparents use to tell me about when I was a little boy. You see I am originally from Ghana in West Africa and there even now the practice of ancestor worship is still very prevalent. They truly believe that the spirit of one's forefather can manifest itself at any given time and even dwell in a person. I don't believe this myself since I came to this country as a little boy and have been educated in nothing but American schools, but I never dismissed the ideas of my grandparents because I have witnessed some healing when I was still there that did not come from any kind of modern medicine, but from supposedly an ancestor's spirit touching a body. So I'm not quick to dismiss the notion arbitrarily."

"Okay now you're getting into an area that is why I invited my friend, the reverend here to come along. David what do you think about that?"

"Well let me begin by saying that God is a Spirit and if you are to worship Him correctly the Bible tells us that we are to worship Him in Spirit and in truth. Now whether this applies to the case we're dealing with here it remains to be tested, but like you Dr. Oniyuki I wouldn't rule it out that some type of spirit did indeed visit our subject and touch him."

"Let me ask you this Dr. Danforth how long ago did Elena pass away months, years or recently?"

"Now that's a great question because I think I know where you're heading. We just had her funeral about two weeks ago and she died earlier that week. When was your session where he claimed to be touched occur?"

"Yes it was right around that time. So you're thinking that after we laid her to rest her spirit came here and removed the curse from her husband. Is that right?"

"I can't honestly say it's not possible, but then again how can we prove it?"

"David is there some kind of a spiritual test we can conduct to prove what we're thinking?"

"Whoa, whoa wait a minute doctors there are some things I don't think we want to get into regarding that realm. However, there is a passage of scripture in the gospel; according to St. John, I believe it's around chapter 4 that says beloved believe not every spirit, but test the spirits to see whether they are of God because many false prophets are gone out into the world. So with regard to testing the spirits I believe if we do do this it must be done with a sincerely holy intention and not to just satisfy your scientific curiosity."

"I totally agree with that premise Dr. Danforth what about you?"

"One hundred percent I agree. So what now we set up some kind of test?"

"Yes. I think we can conduct a session with Mr. Miller in which all three of us are in the room visible to him and ask him again how he was healed. We have to bear in mind though that he's not completely healed and has his moments of relapse more often than normal behavior. So we just have to hope we can catch him when he's displaying some normal sensibilities. Okay when do you want to try this?"

"Next Friday or Saturday would be good for me what about you reverend?

"Friday would be better for me if we can do it again early in the morning."

"Yes Friday would be better for me also, but we can't do it too early because we don't wake the patients before 9:30 here. We find it is disturbing for most of them to be awakened before that time. So it would have to be at least 9:30 or perhaps later."

"9:30 works for me."

"Okay 9:30 it is. I will have everything ready so we can begin promptly at that hour. Thank you gentlemen I think we may be on to something here so let's hope we can find a way to completely heal Mr. Miller and possibly some others."

"Amen to that."

The group broke up and the New Yorkers headed back home.

The next few days after their first meeting passed Dr. Danforth was still going over the file he had retrieved from the archives concerning Norman Miller. Then he got hold of the records regarding Elena Miller while she was at the hospital. He wanted to be able to, prior to meeting with Dr. Oniyuki again this Friday, if possible, establish any kind of relationship, other than normal marital, that could help him interview Mr Miller and make sense of what was told to Dr. Oniyuki about his wife visiting him. He was specifically looking for any reports or notes from the nurses, doctors or anyone else who had contact with her during her stay. The focus would be on anything she may have said indicating a spiritual connection to Norman or some other entity. The statement by Mr. Miller that Elena had touched him and removed his curse had really peeked Milton's curious scientific mind and he was seeking to dig deep into the possibility that this could be a way to provide healing for some of his current patients. When Dr. Oniyuki said that as a child living in Ghana he had witnessed a healing process that was effective even without the provision of any modern medicine, it compounded his interest in the subject of spiritual healing.

The more he read and researched the files and records there was nothing he could find which gave him any indication that she had any special powers or was in contact with any ethereal entity that did. As far as he could tell she was just a very unfortunate woman who had suffered many discouraging and negative situations which drove her to try and run away from life to avoid the pain. Sinking in the pit of despair and being lost in the tragic maze of an unfulfilled life she sought relief in the only way that she thought was left for her – street life. If something happened with or to her after her soul was released from the burdens of this life and the limitations of her earthly body, perhaps she was given the ability to heal others and prevent them from suffering as she did. Dr. Danforth unable to find anything in the records or files that could corroborate his theory closed them all and returned to dealing with the issues of his current patients. His final thought before he closed the books was that maybe at the session on Friday there could be some kind of revelation that would enlighten all of them in the room about the existence of a benevolent spiritual world.

The next few days passed by quickly and Friday was here. Dr. Danforth made it a point to go and pick up Reverend Dumas as early as 8:00 so that if they encountered anything like what happened the first time they made the trip they would at least have some time to spare. He called his friend the day before and proposed the new time and it was agreed to. He arrived at the church and as expected the reverend was ready and waiting for him.

They arrived at the hospital well before the scheduled start hour so they, remembering what Dr. Oniyuki said about not waking patients up too early, sat in the car. Ten minutes before the hour they went in and again informed the receptionist about their appointment. When they reached the fifth floor and walked into his office Norman Miller was not there, only Dr. Oniyuki.

"Good morning once again gentlemen it's always good to see you" he said.

"Good morning to you also it's good for us to be here. Are we too early to begin with Mr. Miller."

"Oh no I just wanted to wait until you actually arrived before I have him brought in. I didn't want to ignore the possibility of another mishap in your coming."

He then dialed his intercom and asked the attendant to get Norman Miller and bring him to his office. Moments later Norman walked in looking somewhat confused and nervous. Dr. Oniyuki began talking to him.

"Norman how are you feeling today?"

Norman did not immediately respond, but looked at the two men whom he had not seen before and began shaking his head violently from side to side.

"Norman, Norman it's all right these are my friends and they are not going to hurt you in any way. Please sit down and calm yourself."

Norman looked at the doctor then slowly walked to his favorite chair grabbed it and sat down holding tightly to the arm rests. Dr. Oniyuki got back on his intercom and quietly out of the hearing of Norman asked the attendant whether Mr. Miller had his usual medication this morning. After receiving a confirming answer he turned to his guests and told them he just wanted to make sure that this session would be as close to the breakthrough one as he remembered. Then he continued talking to Norman.

"Norman I want you to feel very relaxed and comfortable with me and don't be afraid. Norman I want you to relax and let go of the armrest. Please let go of the armrest and fold your hands in your lap. You can hold your hands together if you want them to help you relax."

Slowly Norman let go of the armrest and folded his hands in his lap.

"Now Norman I'm going to introduce you to my two friends who are here to help me help you. Is that okay?"

Slowly Norman did not answer, but nodded his head.

"This is Dr. Danforth he is a doctor like me and this is Reverend Dumas who is a preacher.

When the word preacher was said Norman looked up and straight at Reverend Dumas with a scowl on his face.

"Norman he is not going to hurt you remember he's here to help you so please stay calm and relaxed."

Norman changed his scowl to a slight smile and relaxed his tight grip on his hands.

"Now we are going to ask you some questions like I always do so please answer them like you always answer me okay?'

Again Norman did not answer, but nodded his head.

Dr, Oniyuki then looked at Dr. Danforth and said he was going to begin with reviewing the breakthrough session. Dr. Danforth nodded in agreement.

"Norman do you remember when we talked the last time and you told me that you believed Elena, your wife had come here and removed your curse?'

Again he nodded his head without speaking.

"Norman from here on I want you to speak, talk and don't nod your head okay?"

"Yes."

"Do you remember when you told me that about Elena?"

Then a sudden change came over him and he started talking in gibberish.

"Montoloki ekay abba donner su. Nany, nanny nikiwayu abba abba diu."

"Norman what language are you speaking?"

Again Norman repeated it.

""Montoloki ekay abba donner su. Nany, nanny nikiwayu abba abba diu."

Reverend Dumas eyes opened wide and he leaned in trying to decipher if Norman was perhaps speaking in tongue.

"Norman can you say that in English please?"

Then a third time he repeated it.

"Montoloki ekay abba donner su. Nany, nanny nikiwayu abba abba diu."

Then again suddenly he dropped his head and held it down for a couple of minutes before raising it again.

"Norman are you okay now, do you feel better?"

"Yes doctor I'm perfectly fine now. You may continue with your questions."

Both the reverend and Dr. Danforth were amazed by this sudden transition and Dr. Danforth burst in with his question.

"Mr. Miller did something just happen to you?"

"Yes Dr. Danforth it did and you may call me Norman. My wife, Elena just came in and she touched me again."

Dr. Danforth continued.

"Norman you said she just came in is she still here?"

"Yes she was standing behind me, but now she's standing in that corner over there smiling at you."

All the doctors and the reverend turned to the corner to see if there was anything that indicated a presence in the room. They saw nothing. Dr. Danforth went on.

"Norman why is she smiling at me?"

"Because you want to believe yet your mind is not open to receiving spiritual things that you do not understand."

"How can I fix that ?"

"You must learn to open your mind and your heart and listen to your friend when he preaches."

Dr. Oniyuki questioned Norman again.

"Norman how often does Elena come to visit you?"

"Whenever she can get through. There is a force that my father put on me that is still around that keeps me here in this place. He won't let me go for long."

"But you said that she had removed the curse is that right?"

"Yes, but even she can't make it permanent only another power, another Spirit can do that." Even now she has to go because he is coming in."

Norman dropped his head again and kept it there longer than before. All of the men looked at him anxiously waiting for him to raise it again so they could see who he is now. When he raised his head he was back to the nervous and afraid man who first came in. Dr. Oniyuki decided to end the session then so he could consult with his guests.

"Norman I'm going to let you go back to your room now and rest. Do you remember anything about what just happened and what you said?

"Nnnn no what happened?"

Okay Norman you go back to your room and rest. I will see you again soon."

The attendant was called for and walked Norman back to his room. Then Dr. Oniyuki turned to his guests.

"Well now that you've seen the breakthrough what do you think?"

Dr. Danforth was first to respond.

"I have never seen anything like that and I'm at a loss just how to bottle it."

Then Reverend Dumas chimed in.

"What I saw here today was truly a miracle and a stark indication that there are truly spiritual powers for both good and evil that we do not comprehend nor are we capable of completely understanding the height nor the depth of the power. When he talked about another spirit being able to make the change permanent, I don't know about you, but I'm confident I know who he was referring to. Milton this is not something you can bottle, contain or harness in any way, but as Norman said you must open your mind and your heart and learn how to use what we do have at our disposal, and that is the Spirit of God to help him and others like him."

Then both doctors agreed, but didn't know what steps to take next. The meeting ended with the doctors saying they were each going to write up their summary analysis about what they just witnessed and some time during next week consult over the phone about how to treat Norman and others going forward. Reverend Dumas just said he now has some new evidence he can add to his sermon for Sunday. They broke up and the New Yorkers went home.

Trish had not been feeling too well lately so she called Monica on that Friday afternoon just around the time when she thought school would be out. Monica had just left school and was walking toward the bus stop when her phone rang. It was Aunt Trish asking her if she could come by tonight. Monica said she was on her way to work, but then inquired about her health. When Trish told her she was not well, Monica did not hesitate one minute, but said she would take the night off and be there as soon as she could. She then called for a taxi which was slow in responding, but was able to get to Trish's apartment within the hour. She rang the vestibule bell and waited for the intercom to come on.

"Who is it?"

"Hi Aunt Trish it's me Monica."

"Wait a minute."

The buzzer sounded and the entrance door unlocked so she went upstairs. At the apartment door she rang the doorbell. The chimes sounded and then the door opened.

"Hi come on in."

"I got here as soon as I could. What's the matter?"

"Oh I guess it's just old age catching up with me. I've been feeling kind of poorly here lately and I believe I may be headed to join with your mother."

"Oh don't say that please. You're all I have I can depend on. Have you been to a doctor?"

"Yes two or three times, but they keep telling me what I already know. Between the Arthritis pains and my sinus issues I can hardly walk or breath right sometimes. I guess I'll last a little while longer though so don't you be worrying about me now. I called you to come here tonight because I wanted to tell you something. You know I have this car sitting out there that I'm not driving too much anymore because of my bad knees and it's hurts to bend them a lot. So I drive now only when I have to go to the store or need something else urgently. Other than that it just sits there gathering dust. So I want you to have it when you graduate. Did you get your license yet?"

"No not yet, but I'm practicing driving with my Driver Education teacher now so it shouldn't be too long before I can take the driving test. I wasn't expecting you to give me that car it's only a few years old isn't it?"

"Yes five to be exact and it has hardly any miles on it since your mother moved out of here I don't go a lot of places. Anyway it's paid for and I would rather see you get it then for me to try and sell it or give it to some charity. You know it's one of the better ones Ford made in that model and it has served me well. It hardly gave me any trouble at all so you shouldn't have much either if you keep it up. I'm going to show you now where I keep the keys and the title which I will sign over to you the day you graduate."

"Aunt Trish I don't know what to say other than thank you so much. Guess I have to graduate now huh?"

"I never thought you would do anything else. Now how is everything going, I know you're working hard and making all that money, but don't overdo it."

"So far most things are going okay, but I'm not sure whether I've told you this before, but I keep getting these nighttime spiritual visits. At first I thought it was mama trying to tell me something then one night it told me that she was my grandmother. Do you know what my grandmother's name was?"

"Yes, yes I do. I remember your mother saying many times that her mother's name was Lois."

"Right and that's exactly what she said.

"You mean this spiritual visitor came to you and said she was Lois?"

"Yes that's right.The first time I was scared almost to death, but then I realized she wasn't going to hurt me or anything so I calmed down. Each time she would come it would be when I was having some kind of stress or problem and she would try to encourage me. This last time though she gave me a warning and it really sent a chill down my back. She told me about some things that might be happening to me in the future and told me I needed to open my eyes and mind. There was something else too, but she never finished. I don't think she was wishing me any ill will, but her warning was scary."

"Monica I don't know what all that means, but I do know if it is your grandmother Lois she is looking out for you along with your mother. Now I want you to go to church with me this Sunday. I know you said that you didn't hear what you wanted to the last time you went, but you need to keep going especially now since your grandmother has given you a warning."

"You know I took off today to come here you think I ought to take off Sunday too?"

"Monica that's not your full time job, you're still a student. You need to do something to protect your personal well being not become indebted to any job especially that one."

"Okay Aunt Trish I'll go. Are you going to be able to drive and pick me up?"

"Yes I can still drive I haven't given it up totally yet and besides I can't afford a chauffeur."

"Okay I'll see you Sunday. I hate to ask this, but can you drive me home?"

The both laughed as Trish got ready to do so.

Reverend Dumas sat in his home office reviewing his sermon for Sunday. His thoughts however, kept going back to the session he witnessed with his friend Dr. Danforth at the mental institution. What he saw was not totally surprising to him because as a preacher for many years he was well aware of the power of spiritual healing, but he had never seen a display like that. It was clear that Norman Miller had been exposed to a possession by some entity that refused to release him even when confronted by another spirit. It was an interesting conundrum and the reverend postulated whether a mass prayer session conducted by several of his church prayer warriors and himself would be what was needed to drive out permanently that entity from Mr. Miller. As he pondered the idea he had to recover himself, dismiss the thought for now and return to the task at hand – Sunday's sermon.

Last week he laid the foundation for the introduction of Jesus by reviewing the story about the real beginning of creation. This week he was going to expand on that beginning and then continue to set the stage for the eventual need to have a Savior like Jesus. He needed to make it perfectly clear that it was from the beginning when the first man disobeyed God's instructions and warranted the death penalty that a blood sacrifice was the only way for atonement to be made. His challenge now was to get that point across in the time allotted without inundating the congregation with too much information at once nor confusing them by skipping over much needed passages of scripture.

Experience over many years of preaching and pastoring taught him that if he would just get started and then let the power of the Holy Spirit take over at the right time, then the sermon would be effective and his delivery would be fine. Believing in that premise for all those years had served him well and he was determined to continue along that line. He made some final adjustments to his notes then closed the tablet and took a nap.

On Sunday morning it was a day that weathermen would hope could be the setting for all days. The sun was up, the sky was a pale blue with just a hint of a few clouds and the temperature hovered around the low seventy's. For a fall day it was unusually warm, but the chill in the air foretold an imminent change was coming. Trish got up early and set out to pick up Monica early enough so that they would be able to find a parking space near the church front entrance. At 10:30 she pulled up to the house and just as before Monica had been looking out the window so she was ready and came outside.

At the church several other patrons were arriving about the same time so jockeying for a parking space became a weekly ritual. Fortunately there were church volunteers responsible for traffic control who were able to direct cars into open space without any mishaps. Once inside, just as before, Monica and Trish were ushered to the seats near the front pews. Monica now had gotten over the tendency to appear like an out of town tourist looking around to see what was there and settled in to wait for the service to begin.

A few minutes after the 11:00 hour the choir director stood up in front of the altar and started the music playing. Again from the rear of the sanctuary the thunderous sound of the mass choir issued forth at his direction and the service was underway. The choir procession began with the members walking down all three aisles singing What A Fellowship as the congregants inside tended to join in the singing. Once the choir loft was filled and the house was ready the singing stopped and a minister stood before the lectern. He asked the people to stand as he gave the prayer of invocation. Following that another minister offered the reading of a Psalm of uplift then a welcome message was given to all visitors inviting them to participate in the service and receive the blessings of the Lord. Next church announcements were made advising the body of activities scheduled to take place in the upcoming week and beyond. Then the mass choir stood up again and offered a rousing rendition of the song Stand that set the stage for the pastor's message. When the choir finished there was hardly anyone in the house who was not ready for a word from the Lord. Reverend Dumas then stood up approached the sacred desk and began speaking in a booming baritone voice.

"Blessed be the name of the Lord, blessed be the name of the Lord, blessed be the name of the Lord."

Three times he said it with each time having more volume than the one before and the congregation responded to it.

"Amen, amen and amen came from them with a passion.

"My brothers and sisters in the Lord I greet you once again in His holy name. We serve a mighty good God and He is worthy to be praised on this day and all days going forward. Aren't you glad He woke you up this morning and started you on your way? This morning beloved I want to continue in the sermon series teaching about Jesus. If you were not here last week, I hope you will get the tape so that you will not be lost as I move forward in the series. Just for a quick review, I'm not going to go back and cover all that was said then, but for a quick review let me just mention a few things.

You recall I said that the real beginning of the world took place not as it is given in the book of Genesis, but rather in the book of the gospel of St. John in the very first chapter and the first verse where it is said that in the beginning was the Word. Now the Word is actually Jesus who was at that time yet to be born as such. Do not be confused by this I will explain more in the series to come. For now just accept that it was the Word who created the earth and formed all the things that went into it including man and woman. This is the foundation from which I want to begin here today and examine what happened after the earth was formed and man became a living soul.

We are going to be looking at several different books both in the Old Testament and the New Testament to study how the need for Jesus even came to be. First while we are still in Genesis chapter 3 the first test of man's willingness to obey God took place when he ate the apple from the tree of the knowledge of good and evil which he was instructed not to do. When he failed this test the death penalty was issued, which he had been pre warned was going to happen. Now of course Adam who is the man and Eve his wife did not die instantly or at that time, but that's when death entered the picture and man began to die. It was from that time that the curse of death was pronounced and man has not recovered since then.

Moving forward the first family procreated, that is they had children, even as God had instructed them to do and the family of generation after generation was started. Also while we are still in Genesis the first murder was committed by the first murderer when Cain slew Abel his brother and man's curse continued. From that first generation man continued to increase in number and filled the earth. Even as he increased in number so did his disobedience to God so much so that by the time we read in the late chapters of Genesis God had had enough of man's unwillingness to obey Him so He decided he would destroy the earth and all of His creation and start over again. This is the time that we know of as the great flood which covered the whole earth for forty days and nights.

There was one saving grace at this point in history however. One man who God had observed was a devout man, obeying God with his family and doing what was right in the eyes of God. So the Lord instructed him to build an ark at a time when there was no rain. He was ridiculed and laughed at by the people of his time who continued to disobey, but when the rains came and flooded the earth I guess he had the last laugh. From that time on when the flood waters finally receded and from that one remaining family a new generation was conceived and the new world order was begun. The man's name was Noah and he had three sons, Shem Ham and Japheth and from them all the nations of the earth were started. Man continued to increase and nations began to grow and just as before the flood disobedience ran rampant. God had already declared that He would not destroy the earth again with water, but He started sending prophets and wise men to provide warnings about what would happen for not obeying the Word. From the offspring of the three sons of Noah came another man who found favor with God and his name was Abraham who became the father of Isaac who became the father of Jacob and through him the twelve tribes of Israel were born.

All this may sound like a lot of irrelevant information saints, but please stay with me because we're going somewhere and you need to know this background. As the nations grew and dissension grew among them war and strife broke out. What had been one nation of Israel became two - Judah and Israel. The Israelites from the beginning had been God's chosen people. Not because they were better than any of the other nations, but because He wanted to have a nation that would be a role model for the other nations on how to live Over the next several hundred years and under the leadership of many kings, some good and some bad, the nations continued to sin and defy God's rules. Finally God allowed, as a punishment for disobedience, the people of both Israel first and then Judah to be captured and taken to foreign countries where they would be enslaved. After this for the next four hundred years God was silent. There was no prophetic utterance to redeem the people.

But a promise had been made to Abraham that through him and his descendants there would not fail to be a ruler to sit on the throne and rule over the kingdom of God. Through his line of descendants down through forty-two generations there was finally an event that spawned the beginning of the age called the New Testament.

I'm sure at this point you should be able to guess what that event was and next we will begin to explore the things that happened as a result of that advent. If you are having a problem and have to guess what event, then I want to encourage you come to our Bible classes."

At that point there was some laughter, which was his intent to lighten the heaviness of the subject.

"Brothers and sisters I'm going to close this message here and as I said we will begin to focus on the life of the one who came to save us - Jesus. Even though I was jesting about some of you not knowing what the event was, it will be no laughing matter when He returns to claim His own and if you are not among those who will be in that number then I dare to say it will not go well for you at the judgment. Look around you today and see all of the calamities and strife that man is committing against his fellow man. It's not as if we know how to live together in peace, it is because we have failed to understand the commandments that were given to us in days of old. We have not learned how to love one another as He loved us and surely we have not been practicing obeying His commandments. It's not too late now to come to Jesus and commit your heart and soul to Him for He can save you from the coming tribulation that is going to fall on us. Do not be afraid to commit yourself, but do be afraid of being left behind when the rapture happens.

Won't you come now? Give the deacons your hand, but give God your heart. Time is growing short when the choice will no longer be available so do it now. Brothers and sister the doors of the church are open. Take advantage of this opportunity and become one with the Onc who loves you."

Trish and Monica sat there watching the parade of willing new converts walking up to the altar to stand with the deacons. Trish turned toward her and looked to see if there was possibly a stirring in her heart to move her in that direction. Monica sensing the look and knowing what it was for turned her head to Trish.

I know what you're hoping for, but I'm just not feeling it. That was a great sermon, very informative and all that, but I just don't know. On top of that he still hasn't answered my question."

"Monica you keep saying that can you tell me--what is your question?"

CHAPTER 10
The Transition

The brisk chill in the air served notice that the fall season was ending and old man winter was getting off the train to stay for a while. The first school semester was ending and final examinations were to be conducted next week. Guidance counselors had met with most of the seniors and aided with college application preparation. Monica had been encouraged to submit applications to NYU (with a commendation letter from her work-study supervisor), Rutgers and the University of Pennsylvania. With each of these APs a request for financial aid was included. Soun Li applied to Harvard University Medical School, Johns Hopkins and the University of Pennsylvania Medical Schools. For her financial aid was not needed. Reilly did not submit any applications because she decided to work full time for her father after graduation. Monica completed her classroom portion of Driver Training and was now ready to begin on street driving practice.

The Three Musketeers along with the other seniors were excited about finishing their exams and then enjoying the long Christmas break. When it came, it was on the last day that each student hurried out the door ready to begin enjoying the holiday. For Monica working at one of the busiest stores in the city was a blessing and a curse. She had been promoted to assistant supervisor and with that came more responsibility. The extra money was the blessing part, but having to direct the work of others she felt was a curse. Soun Li was able to get assigned to aiding resident doctors at the hospital and learning much about the profession. Reilly was also taking on more responsibility as she was being groomed to take over the business. Overall it appeared to be a happy time for all.

Then Tony came home for the college Christmas break and called Monica. Although unlike the rest of the students, he only had a few days because of the basketball team's tournament schedule. He was anxious to see her. He called her home number first around 4:00 O'clock and got no answer because she was at work then he called her cell and got the same result. When Monica looked at her cell and saw who was trying to reach her she had to sit down for a minute. For the last several weeks she thought she had gotten over thinking about him, but now her heart told her something different. She thought for a minute did she really want to talk to him after what he did to her? Not much time was given for deliberation because she saw him walking in the door and there was nowhere to run away.

"Hi. I thought you might be working so I thought I'd drop by. Can you take a break or something now?"

She just looked at him for several minutes before answering, because she really wasn't sure what she wanted to say. Then she finally answered.

"No I can't take a break now and even if I could I don't think I want to. You know you have a lot of nerve coming in here like this after I haven't heard from you in weeks. Do you think I'm supposed to welcome you with open arms. Please just go and don't bother me again you're interrupting my work here."

Tony was shocked at her vehemence and now he wasn't sure what to say or do so he just turned around and walked out. Monica smiled as she watched him leave and knew then that it was really over.

Working later than usual because of the holiday hours when she got home she was even too tired to eat dinner. She went upstairs and lay down on the bed for almost an hour before getting up again. It was now about 11: O'clock and the hunger pangs tugged at her stomach. She tiptoed down the stairs hoping not to encounter Harold and made her way to the kitchen. There was a dinner plate left in the fridge, but she was too tired to eat a heavy meal so she made herself a sandwich and sat down and ate. All the while she was eating she kept thinking about how Tony brazenly walked into her store and thought everything between them was okay. Again she smiled at how she resolved that matter. Next she said to herself in reference to a possible next boyfriend.

That weekend she was asked by her supervisor to work Saturday and Sunday. She agreed knowing it was going to place a strain on her downtime. She had been working long hours between covering the holiday store schedule and preparing for her final exams. Fortunately she was able to do well on the exams and still make extra money. Now she was preparing to take her driving test right after the holiday anticipating getting her aunt's car at graduation. Saturday night after a long day she had to call Trish and say she would not be going to church with her because she was going to be working Sunday. Trish said she understood and cautioned her about over working is not good for her health.

The next week was the week just before Christmas and the two Evans boys were able to be home together for the holiday. Monica couldn't honestly say that she was happy to see them because it had been rather peaceful in the house with their absence, but she pretended to be glad just to keep them out of her business. Deciding what to get as presents for them and their parents was not going to be easy because her heart would certainly not be in any choice she made. However, since it was expected she would again honor the tradition just as she did last year and come up with something.

The Christmas holiday came and passed without any major or unusual awkward moments and the exchange of gifts followed the usual pattern. No one was really excited about what they actually received , but the pretend smiles were pasted on to keep the peace and let the day go on.

The day after Christmas for most of the stores it was always a mad house with customers returning unwanted gifts for a refund or exchange. In Nords it was no different and Monica now as an assistant supervisor was deep in the heart of the mess. She managed to survive the day and return home once again exhausted. The rest of the holiday went quickly and smoothly and even the New Year's celebration found the Three Musketeers together with dates for the night.

The new-year began and the start of a new semester got underway. Seniors were getting excited knowing this was the last leg of their journey at Kimberly. Monica received some good news early on in the second week. She was given a letter announcing that she not only was accepted to NYU's business school, but she was receiving a full scholarship. This couldn't have come at a better time for her because she was worried about first getting in and then how she would pay if she did. Three days later Soun Li received her acceptance letter to Johns Hopkins Medical School and she was totally elated because that's where her father had gone. Not that she needed it, but she was also given a Presidential scholarship for being the number one ranking student at the school and also the president of the local chapter of the National Honor Society. Reilly learned of the acceptance letters and congratulated both of her buddies, but it was obvious even when she tried to conceal it, she was a bit disappointed that she was left out of the musketeer celebration. Soun Li and Monica saw this and they promised after school today they were all going to go out and celebrate each other for all the good times they had together.

The rest of the semester passed by fast and graduation day was just ahead. All three of the musketeers had earned driver licenses, but only one was now the owner of a brand new car. When Reilly got the keys to the car the week before they were to graduate she took them out for a joy ride throughout the countryside. It was a wild ride and the girls were letting off some long held in energy. Even though Reilly took some unnecessary risks along the way, fortunately nothing serious happened and they all returned safely.

Graduation day was here. All Kimberely Clark seniors had passed their finals and were ready to receive diplomas. Most parents were very excited about the achievement of their offspring, but the one couple who attended were just thinking about what's going to happen when the checks stop coming in. The Evans Harold and Laura attended the graduation ceremony because they were expected to. They were not excited about her accomplishment, especially the part about her receiving a full scholarship to a prestigious top ranking college. After the ceremony concluded and the students came from the stage to hugs and congratulatory compliments, it was almost embarrassing for Monica when she just received the words from both of them saying "Okay now what?" No hug, no kiss on the cheek not even a cordial handshake. What appeared to be uppermost on their minds, especially Harold was when are you leaving and when will the checks stop. Monica shook her head and walked in front of them to the car to go home and get on the telephone to call her Aunt Trish who could not be there because of illness.

The rest of that summer she counted the days until she would finally leave that awful house and start a new phase in her life. Then she went shopping for clothing that she considered to be a killer college wardrobe. Harold and Laura contributed nothing to help her and just stood by watching the happy young lady live her life. They realized now that in a matter of days she would be gone and so would the checks.

Ring, ring, ring, ring.

"Hello."

"Aunt Trish - Monica well I did it. I graduated today just a little while ago and now I got that diploma."

"Young lady I'm so proud of you and I know your mother is too. It's too bad she couldn't be there physically to see it, but I know she's watching you from wherever she is. Now remember what I told you about the car. When do you want to come and get it.? You did get your license didn't you?"

"Yes I did almost three months ago now. I just haven't used it because those ornery people that I live with wouldn't even think about letting me drive their car. I am so grateful to you for giving me that gift I just can't thank you enough. Right now though I don't know when I will be coming over to pick it up, but hopefully it won't be too long. For the rest of the summer until I have to get ready to go off to NYU I will be working full time in the store and putting in all the extra hours I can to stockpile some funds."

"All that's good, but remember what I told you about overworking yourself. All the money in the world can't help you if you get sick and can't spend it."

"Yes I remember that and I won't. You know now that I'm thinking about it why don't I come by tomorrow since I don't have to start full time work until Monday and I can skip my regular part time schedule for a day or so?"

"That would be so nice. I'm going to go out and try and get something nice here to celebrate your achievement."

"Oh no you don't have to do that, you've already done enough for me please don't burden yourself with trying to do more."

"Now you hush. This is something I want to do and I'm going to do it."

"Well I know once you've made up your mind nothing is going to stop you so I'll just say goodbye for now and see you tomorrow. Have a goodnight."

"Yes now that I've heard that good news I know I will sleep good tonight. Good night to you too."

Monica hung up feeling very happy that at least one person was proud of her achievement and appreciated her difficult journey. In addition she could hardly wait to get her own car and bring it to the house, park it in front and saunter in knowing the Evans would be looking out the window. In her mind she was preparing her speech to respond to the questions she knew would be forthcoming about the vehicle. Without giving away the whole set of details she would just reveal that it was a gift from someone who loves me and let their evil minds fill in the blanks however they wanted to.

As a graduation present her store supervisor gave her the night off with pay and congratulated her on a job well done not only in school but at the store. The manager, the adjunct professor at the business school, also congratulated her and said he was looking forward to seeing her there in September. He had been instrumental in getting the scholarship for her and though she was not aware of it yet, his intentions were not entirely magnanimous toward her. Since she didn't have to work she decided to go to the store anyway and begin, at least pricing the wardrobe, she would soon be shopping for. When she got there those who knew of her graduation greeted her and wished her well and inquired about when she would be leaving.

The next day as promised Monica called her aunt early Saturday morning and asked if it was too early for her to come over. It was now only about 8:00.

Ring, ring, ring

"Hello."

"Hi Aunt Trish - Monica did I wake you?"

"Oh no child I've been up since the sun got up. Why are you up so early?"

"Well I'd like to come over now if you don't mind and get the car."

"No, no not at all, but you didn't even give me a chance to go out and get you that special something to celebrate your gradaation. That's okay though we can go together when you get here, It will give me a chance to watch and see how you drive."

"Now you're not going to make me nervous like my instructor are you?"

"Child as long as you don't come close to hitting anything or anybody and make me nervous then we'll both be fine. Okay come on over."

They both laughed at her statement and Monica told her she was on her way.

Driving the car for the first time with her aunt sitting next to her watching made her a little nervous, but Aunt Trish sensed it and told her not to worry about anything so she calmed down then drove to the supermarket and both went in. Trish told her if she was a little older she would buy some champagne to celebrate, but now she didn't want to get her started on that stuff too early. There will be plenty of time for that when she got to college. Monica didn't know then how right she was. So Trish bought some apple cider and a medium sized cake which she had engraved. While waiting for the cake they continued to grocery shop and Trish picked up some things so she could make a special meal for her only niece. Monica as she tagged along was paying attention to the cost of several items, especially those staples that she knew she would have to be getting on her own very soon. The Evans never allowed her to do any of the grocery shopping so she was a bit surprised at how much even the necessities cost. Her scholarship included her tuition, books, room and an allowance for board, but she knew that she was going to be living in a dormitory apartment building with roommates, so she wanted to be in a position to be able to pay her fair share.

When they got back to Trish's apartment Trish told her to make herself comfortable while she whipped up something very special and they would eat and drink cider until they felt enough celebration. While Trish was cooking Monica looked around the apartment casually and noticed some pictures of her mother with her father and her as a baby and it started her thinking again about the whereabouts of her dad. About an hour or so later Trish called her in to the kitchen table and they sat down to eat. Trish had prepared a wonderful quick recipe fish dinner with all the appropriate trimmings. Monica was again so thankful for all this and as she sipped the cider started talking about her father.

"Aunt Trish you know you never got back to me about what happened to my father. Were you ever able to find out anything?"

'Yes my dear and I'm sorry to say that the last time I was in touch with that hospital where he's at they only would tell me that he was still alive, but in his condition he would not be able to recognize you or anybody else. And I didn't want you to go and see him like that so I didn't tell you. This was way before your mother passed and I haven't talked to anybody there since she left us."

You know before I go off to school I really would like to see him even if he doesn't know me. I have such vague memories that if he walked by me on the street I wouldn't know who he was. I don't want to leave without at least knowing what he looks like. Can we go there one day before I go?"

"I understand what you're saying and I believe you have the right to do that. Let me know what day and time is good for you to go with me over there and I will try to set up a visit for us. Remember though when you see him, be prepared for a rejection."

"I won't care. I just want to know that he's at least alive and I want to leave my address as soon as I know it for them to contact me should something happen to him."

"That's a loving thought and you will be blessed for that. You are such a beautiful girl both inside and out I just hope that school doesn't do anything to change you."

They finished the meal and Monica promised to let her know when a good time would be for them to go see him. Then she left driving her own first car which she felt it was like a brand new Rolls Royce. Driving very carefully she arrived at the house and parked right in the front as she planned. However, her speech would have to be postponed, because the Evans were not at home when she walked in.

The rest of the summer was generally uneventful. She spent some time with the musketeers at various outings, had her opportunity to flaunt the car before the Evans eyes and gave her speech, visited her aunt often, bought her killer wardrobe and now was ready to go. She also got the chance to visit with her father along with Trish. Even though he obviously did not know who she was his blank stare at her and the expression on his face seemed to indicate that somewhere in the deepest recesses of his mind there was some recollection. Monica was glad to see him and to know that he was still alive even if the frail man sitting before her did not rekindle any memories of the stout, whole and hearty person she once knew. She left her dormitory address and left the hospital satisfied she received what she came for.

About the middle of August she received a letter from the residence hall director advising her about the rules for moving in and an assortment of other regulations. She was also advised it would be beneficial for her to visit the area and become familiar with the surroundings. This got her real excited and she wanted to go right away. Rather than go by herself she invited her other two cronies to come along. A day and time was picked when they were all available and they went. Monica drove her car.

"Wow this is really happening." Monica said. "I can hardly believe it."

"Yeah girl we're excited with and for you. Too bad I can't go and explore my surroundings at Johns Hopkins, it's just too far." Said soun Li.

"I'm glad it finally happened for you two. Maybe once you get settled I'll come visit both you guys and maybe we can hang out for a minute." Reilly offered.

"Reilly you know we love you and wish you were going somewhere too. Have you thought about even going part time to a local college?" Monica said.

"Well right now it would be hard. The number of big jobs that my dad has lined up and he's put me in charge of a lot I don't see how that would be possible. I'm getting my college education in on the job training and believe me it's not easy especially when your main professor is your father."

They all laughed and enjoyed the rest of the ride. When they arrived at the residence where Monica would be living she was surprised at how congested the area was. Finding a place to park on the street was practically impossible and when she looked at what it cost to use a parking garage, all together they rejected that idea. So they continued to ride around through the narrow streets of the east village and observe the frantic pace of people moving around. Monica commented on what she thought was a great positive and that was the number of small restaurants and quaint shops. The other two quickly agreed and told her she must remember why she's going here and it's not to shop. Again they all laughed. After about an hour or so of just riding around exploring the greater college area she decided it was time to go home.

Once back on their home turf they made a commitment to keep in touch and try to communicate as often as they could. Monica dropped each one off at her place and then went home. This was the last time they were all together before Soun Li and her left the area.

The day finally came when she was ready to pack up all of her things load them into the car and get on her way. There was no great farewell or goodbye well wishes. The Evans family just watched her depart and said "Please leave the keys." She acknowledged it left her keys on the foyer table made a hasty exit after everything was packed and never turned around. When she arrived at the residence hall it was gratifying to see that provisions had been made for ample reserved parking space in front of the building. Also there were volunteer upper class students available to assist in getting each new arrival moved in and settled. She had already received her instructions so she was ready to go and register at the front desk to get her keys and welcome package. Once that was done she caught the elevator up to the third floor and found apartment 307. The door was already open so she walked in to find two other girls unpacking and claiming their space. Being she was the last to arrive her choice was what was left. This was not a problem because the apartment was very large and well appointed. The only drawback was that it had two bedrooms for three students.

Quick introductions were made and the girls decided together to draw lots to see which one would get the private room and the others would bunk together. As it turned out Monica would have to share a bedroom. The names of the other girls were Marjorie Hopkins from Hartford, Connecticut, Caroline Clinton from Philadelphia, Pennsylvania and of course Monica from Queens New York. It didn't take long for the girls to start assigning nicknames as they continued to unpack and put things away. Marjorie became Margie, Caroline became CC and Monica was Moni. When they got around to identifying their heritage it seems that Margie was the moneyed one because her father was a big time commercial real estate broker, but CC and Moni were closer together in rank. CC's dad was a long distance trailer driver who was hardly ever home and her mother was a high school social studies teacher. When it came to Moni's turn she explained that her real parents had passed away (only partially true) when she was very young and she was raised by a set of real evil foster parents.

Her step father worked in the post office and her mother in a factory. She did not elaborate on how they treated her, but did make it clear she wanted out of that house for as long as she could remember.

They continued to share stories as they kept on putting things away. When it appeared that all was in order and they were ready to relax Margie suggested they go out and see the area. She also made it clear that she was very familiar with this area because with her friends from home often came down to the village to hang out on week-ends. So with her as their guide they set out to do the town. To Moni it was like forming a new musketeer rat pact. Margie took them to a small jazz night club that she said was one of her favorites where they served anybody who came in, no questions asked. As they entered, the bar tender recognized her and nodded his head. She smiled back at him and the girls went to a small table in one of the open corners and sat down.. Soon a scantily clad waitress came over and asked if they would like to order. Moni was a little embarrassed inside, and tried not to show it because she had never been in this type of situation before, and didn't know what to order. Margie sensing her hesitation asked her if she would like to try what she was having. Quickly Moni said "sure."

Margie ordered a Tom Collins with a lime twist and told the waitress to make it two one for my friend here. CC, a little more sophisticated ordered a Jack Daniels and ginger ale. When the drinks arrived Margie proposed a toast to their new friendship and said when they are ready to graduate they must come back here and celebrate because this is where it all started. For Moni the taste of the gin found a new favor with her taste buds and she loved it. They spent the next few hours listening to the jazz band and enjoying a few rounds of drinks. Around 11:30 that night when all of them were feeling pretty mellow the waitress brought the check because she was getting off. For some reason it was handed to Moni. When she looked at the bill her eyes opened real wide wondering how she was going to pay even her share of this. Again Margie sensing the awkward moment took the bill from her hand.

"Okay gals I got this one. Next time we can draw straws to see who pays.

Having said that she called the waitress over and handed her a credit card. When Moni saw that she was relieved, but more than that she aspired to become more like her new friend.

"You have your own credit card?" she asked.

"Sure. Don't you haee one?"

"No. All I have is some cash and I don't know how long that's going to last."

"What about you CC do you have one?"

"Yes, but it has a very tight limit that my folks can monitor every time I use it."

"Well ladies we're going to have to figure out some things on how we're going to do it if we want to party around this place and go to school.. Don't worry I'll figure it out."

Monica was enamored by this new friend's confidence and bravado and was already feeling a new sense of adventure ahead. Unlike the old three musketeers this new group was on a higher level. When they got back to the residence hall and having to sign in for the first time the security officer asked to see their identification cards. Since they had not been issued one yet and would not be until they completed their class registration and schedules tomorrow, They each had to show some form of ID with a picture on it before he would admit them. Even though they had keys to an apartment and showed them to him, he would not let them catch the elevator. Fortunately all the girls had a driver license that satisfied the officer when he checked their ID's against their names on the apartment roster. Once they got in the elevator and out of his hearing the laughter was as loud as it could be.

"Suppose I didn't have a license was I going to sleep in the lobby? My father would have a fit if he found that out and believe me that guy would be gone tomorrow." Margie said.

"Yeah this process is kind of backward don't you think? Why would they issue us keys and not give us an ID card to come and go." Moni said.

"Yeah right that doesn't make a whole lot of sense now that you think about it. Well we're here now and that bed looks awfully comfortable. Don't talk to me anymore you guys 'cause I'm already sleeping." CC offered.

"Yeah me too. Don't forget though we have to get up early and get over to that administration building and get registered so we have everything we're going to need. I hope. Who's an early riser naturally or do I have to set this stupid loud alarm clock my father gave me." Margie said.

"Set the clock, set the clock." The other two roommates replied almost simultaneously.

"Their first full day at school and going through the registration process was a somewhat daunting task. It was nothing like the high school they each had left. There were several different lines for each discipline and then a line for a meal ticket, if you qualified and then a line for this and another line for that. By the time they had completed everything they were ready to call it a day. When they looked at their schedules the one good thing about them was that they were able to sign up for classes together since they were all business majors. From the admin building now that it was late afternoon and none of them had eaten lunch they decided to try out one of the local sit in delicatessens. Monica had to be very aware of the limited pocket money she had brought with her until she could get the stipend from her scholarship put into her account so she ordered the cheapest sandwich and a small soda on the menu. Margie order a little bit of everything and said she would share it with them. To the less fortunate two of the trio this seemingly was going to be a good deal.

For the next two weeks as they got accustomed to their schedules and college life routines everything seemed to be working out fine until one day Monica came to the dorm early and when she opened the front entrance door she was greeted with a heavy aroma. It was not familiar to her and at first she thought something had burned or spoiled. But when she opened Margie's door there she was sitting on the bed with an impish smile on her face and smoking a joint.

"Come on in little sister. Welcome to my world."

"What is that smell?"

"It's the aroma of happiness my friend. Have you never inhaled this before?"

"No is it a special kind of cigarette?"

"You bet it is. It will make you forget your troubles. It's called a joint or marijuana if you want to be technical. Cone on over sit here and try it. Just take a puff and inhale and let the smoke do the rest."

Monica took the joint inhaled a small amount then coughed violently for the next five minutes.

"Oh my God a real newbie – a saint. I'll bet you've never been laid either."

Margie started laughing loudly just as CC walked in. Now CC was accustomed to the smell and asked who had it?

"Well my good sister come on in and join the party."

Margie handed the joint to CC and she smoked it. Monica recovered from her coughing spell and looked at the two seemingly enjoying themselves and didn't want to feel like the odd ball in the room, asked if she could try it again. This time it was less troubling and after another puff she began to feel the thrill that the other two were experiencing. They sat around for another hour laughing and joking about Moni's sainthood until it was time for them to go and get something to eat because the hunger monster had arrived. They went back to Margie's favorite jazz club and this time ordered a meal besides their favorite beverages. Again Margie picked up the check.

The next day after spending a terrible night recovering from her indiscretion Monica was the only one who was having difficulty getting up and going to class. The other two laughed and told her to suck it up and keep on going then they all went to class.

For the next several weeks their routine included getting high and intoxicated. Moni by now had become one of the crowd that started as the trio, then grew to a quartet then to a host of others who were part of that world. Margie always seemed to have enough for everybody and she became the leader of the rat pack.

It was amazing while they were doing all this that they were all able to continue to go to class and maintain their good academic standing. This was especially true for Monica because she absolutely had to keep up or lose her scholarship. The frequent visits to the same nightclub did not go unnoticed by the band and one of the members developed a longing for Monica. During one of their breaks the piano player came over and introduced himself to the trio.

"Hi ladies are you enjoying the music?"

"Oh yeah we're having a good time." Margie said.

"That's great. My name is Roland and I'm the leader of this group. I noticed you guys come in here regularly are you students?"

At first they hesitated answering because it might give their ages away, but then when he assured them that it was none of his business about the law, they answered yes.

"Just to show you how much I don't care I'm going to buy you all a drink."

After they each introduced themselves Roland zeroed in on Moni.

"I know you must all travel together, but do you ever go out alone?

He said this while looking directly at Moni. The other two got the hint and backed off waiting for her to answer.

She said "yes" and that started the relationship. Though Margie and CC were far from being ignored by the rest of the band, it was Roland who began a serious affair with his target. Over the next few weeks they became a tight couple. When he wasn't playing at his club he would take her to other places where he knew the bands and they would get free drinks. As the relationship became more intimate and she started spending some nights at his place on enight after they had made love he asked her if she wanted to try something new that would make her feel even better. She questioned what it was and he showed her.

"If you take one of these when you want to get higher than that weed you're smoking it will do the trick."

He took out a handful of pills and gave her one.

"Try it."

She took the pill and just like he said it sent her into another world she had never experienced before. After that they made love again and that's when her addiction began. It became more and more difficult for her to continue her studies without having to go to him for more of the pills. After a while he stopped giving them to her and told her they were not free, but she could earn her way to a regular supply. By now she was caught in the trap and did not know where to turn. Margie and CC knew what was happening and even though they had cautioned her she thought she was in love and ignored them.

When it got to the point that she realized he was just using her to get his own supply of cocaine by pimping her out. She knew she had to stop somewhere. She decided then one Saturday she was going to go back to see about her car which she had taken back to her aunt because there was no place to park at the residence hall and the garages were too expensive. She knew she lost some weight from the stress and not eating properly, but when she looked in the mirror before making the trip, she almost decided not to go. Something inside however, told her she needed to talk to Aunt

Trish so she caught the train and was on her way. When she got there she rang the bell and waited for the usual intercom response

"Hello."

"Hi Aunt Trish it's Monica, can I come up?"

"Monica, Monica of course you can come up. Wait a minute."

The buzzer sounded and the entrance door unlocked. When she arrived at the apartment door she hesitated not sure she really wanted to go in. Then she rang the bell. The door opened and Trish looked at her.

"Monica, Monica, Monica baby what's happened to you?"

CHAPTER 11

Learning To Live

S addle River Behavioral Health Center was one of the leading mental health institutions in the country, if not around the world. Some of the most influential and prominent psychiatrists were on staff there, if not permanently assigned they were on call. It's administration was highly organized and efficient and had a reputation for being very well run. What happened last night within the walls of this highly touted institution was so out of character that most doctors who were not part of the medical community there would not believe it. One of the resident patients had an episode within his room that was so frightening that it intimidated even the stalwart long serving nurses who worked there.

It was late on a Wednesday night about 11:30 well after the patient had been fed dinner and given his medication that a violent sound was heard coming from the room of Norman Miller. The night nurse assigned to that sector went to the room and had to stop immediately at the door. What she witnessed prevented her from going in any further. Mr. Miller was there suspended in mid-air gasping for breath. There was nothing visible holding him there and the nurse could hear sounds of voices arguing over his possession. She turned around and sought help first from some of the other nurses and then from the doctor who was on call. The nurses rushed to the room and then the doctor arrived and they all saw and heard the same thing. Mr. Miller was in the air with his arms out to either side as if being pulled apart by some invisible force. The audible voices were saying "He's mine, you can't have him. I was here first he belongs to me." The doctor approached Norman and tried to pull him down when the force knocked him back to the door.

Not knowing what to do next he yelled at the nurses telling them to help grab Mr. Miller and try to get him down. When they responded the same thing happened to all of them. For the next ten to fifteen minutes while the staff stood there helplessly watching the tug of war over the body it continued without a winner. Then as quickly as it started he fell to the floor and his breathing returned to normal. The doctor quickly examined him determined the episode had ceased and put him in his bed. Then he went back to his office to document in laborious detail all that he and the nurses saw. The rest of the night was without any further incidents, but when he came in very early in the morning just prior to him ending his shift to re-examine him–Norman Miller was dead.

When Dr. Oniyuki came in later that morning, but very early as he usually did, the buzzing at the nurse station was unusual. None of them knew whether he had been contacted about what happened last night and now the condition of Mr. Miller. He sensed the difference in their normal greeting and asked if something was wrong.

"Guess you haven't heard yet?" said the head nurse.

"Hear what?"

"Your patient Norman Miller is dead. He expired overnight."

"What are you talking about? When I left here yesterday he was fine, well he was his normal abnormal self. What happened?"

"According to the log that was left by the overnight doctor there was some kind of struggle by some strange things I don't understand. You have to look at his notes maybe you can understand what he's talking about beause as I said I can't."

"Okay, okay let me take a look and see."

Dr. Oniyuki went to the doctor's office and retrieved his notes. His detailed description about the struggle between two opposing spirits and the audible voices claiming him as theirs was not surprising. However, the fact that the doctor claimed to have heard the voices along with some nurses was. Dr. Oniyuki immediately called to verify what he was reading was actually true After several rings the doctor answered.

"Hello."

"Hi Dr. Harris?"

"Yes this is Dr. Harris who's calling?"

"Hi this is Dr. Oniyuki sorry to wake you I know you worked the late shift, but I need to get some clarification on the notes you left concerning Norman Miller."

"Yes I can understand how you would be baffled, but the things I logged really happened just as I described them. I can't explain it any further then that. There were two spirits in that room fighting over possession of him. Apparently when I examined him this morning that struggle must have been too much for his heart and he had a massive coronary thrombosis that led to him passing some time during the wee hours. That's all I can tell you. There's one more thing though, when I found him he had an expression on his face that indicated he suffered from severe fright and his eyes were wide open."

"Okay Dr. Harris thank you for that information, I'll take it from here."

Dr. Oniyuki went to his office and sat down to try and piece together in his head how the overnight incident played out. He read the notes again and again and still found it hard to believe it actually happened the way that Dr. Harris described it. He was certainly aware of the spiritual entities that hovered around Mr. Miller because of the session he conducted with Dr. Danforth and Reverend Dumas, but he never anticipated that it could come to a spiritual fight over Norman's body. This was something he definitely had to share with them before the body was disposed of.

Ring, ring, ring.

"Hello Dr. Danforth."

"Hello Milton Kenny here from Saddle River Hospital did I catch you at a bad time?"

"Dr. Oniyuki how are you? No, no any time you call it would not be a bad time. How's our favorite subject?"

"Well that's why I'm calling you now. He passed last night or more accurately very early this morning."

"What, what happened?"

"Well the medical report says he had a massive heart attack. As strange as that was, because the last time I gave him a complete physical which was not too long ago, his heart was strong as could be for his age, the cause of his death was brought on by fright. Something apparently scared the life out of him, if you will. When I reviewed the notes from the overnight doctor he described a struggle between two opposing spirits trying to claim Norman's body. What's even more strange is that he says he along with some nurses actually heard the voices arguing. That's really why I'm calling you. Perhaps you can get hold of your friend the reverend and we can have a conference call to talk about this. Now I only have a short time before I will have to do something with the body so we need to do this right away."

"Wow that really sounds interesting. Yes I know Dave will be anxious to hear your story once I alert him to what happened. Let me try and contact him right now and see when he will be available to do a conference call. If I get him I'll call you right back, if not I'll call you later after I do talk with him and then we can set a time. Okay?"

"Yes that sounds great. I look forward to hearing from you soon. Goodbye."

"Right. Goodbye."

Milton hung up with Dr. Oniyuki and immediately called the church. Ring, ring, ring.

"Hello Holy Trinity Baptist Church how can I help you?"

"Hello this is Dr. Danforth is the pastor available now?"

"No I'm sorry he's in a meeting and won't be available until later this afternoon. Would you like to leave a message on his voice mail?"

"Yes please."

"David Milton here I just got a phone call from Dr. Oniyuki. Norman Miller died last night under strange circumstances possibly having to do with the spirits that haunt him. Call me soon as you can."

It was around 4:00 that afternoon when Milton received the return phone call from his friend.

"Milton did I understand your message correctly? Mr. Miller is dead."

"Yes Dave that's right. He died last night and how he did is what we need to talk about."

"Okay fill me in. What's the story?"

"From what I understand he died from a massive heart attack as a result of him being stretched and frightened by the two spirits we witnessed during our session. Dr. Oniyuki believes that he succumbed to the pressure that each one of them was putting on him and neither of them had the power to prevail. He wants me to ask you when a good time would be for all three of us to have a conference call to discuss the incident. He also made it clear that his time was limited before he would have to dispose of the body so we need to do it soon."

"I understand. There is one thing we have to consider before he does anything with that body. Remember we now know that Mr. Miller really does have a daughter and we know how to reach her through one of my members. So while we're talking about what happened we need to advise him of that fact and ask him to let us contact her. I can't imagine he would have a problem with that. As a matter of fact he may even welcome the thought knowing that it would relieve him of having to deal with the disposition of the corpse. I'm available most of the day tomorrow, unless something comes up unexpectedly, so why don't we schedule a time now. For me 10:00 in the morning is good. Does that work for you?"

For this situation and what we need to do I will make it work. Alright I will call him now and ask him to reserve tomorrow at 10:00 for a call. You wsnt me to set it up or do you want to do it?"

"You go ahead just let me know the particulars to call in on or if you're going to call me."

"Will do. Once it's confirmed with him I'll call you again and give you the conference call information."

Dr. Danforth was able to confirm the details with Dr. Oniyuki then he called Reverend Dumas back and told him he would come to his office to make the call and put it on speaker. That way it would eliminate the need to do a conference call and risk the possibility of interruptions or bad multiple connections. So it was all set for tomorrow.

"Monica, my child what have they done to you?"

When Monica saw the look of such disappointment and astonishment on Trish's face, the tears immediately began welling up in her eyes. Seconds later they overflowed their lids and ran down her cheeks.

"Sorry, sorry Aunt Trish. I'm so sorry I don't know what's gotten into me. I've become everything you warned me about."

Trish wrapped her arms around her and walked Monica over to the couch and sat her down.

"Alright, alright hush now it's going to be okay. You lie down here for a minute. I'm going to fix you something good to eat. You look llke you haven't eaten in a month."

While Monica was still sobbing, Trish got up and went to the kitchen to fix a meal. Before long she called for Monica t come in and sit down. After they both ate the meal Trish asked her to tell what went wrong. Monica through her reddening tear laden eyes began to pour out her heart.

"I guess I started running with the wrong crowd starting with my roommates in the dorm. They introduced me to some things I know I shouldn't have been doing, but it felt so good being one of the gang. I've been drinking and smoking drugs and giving myself up to almost anybody looking for love in all the wrong places. I can't go on like that. I came here to see about my car, but I guess I really came to talk with you. Please help me."

"The car is fine just needs to be driven every once in a while and I'll do that while you're away, but look at you you're a mess."

Monica kind of laughed at that and said "Yeah I know."

"Tonight you're going to stay here with me and tomorrow you and I are going to church."

"But I don't have anything to wear to go to church."

"Don't you worry about that you rest for a little while then we'll go shopping. You definitely need to go with me tomorrow there may be a blessing waiting there for you. Lord knows you certainly need one."

Later that day Trish took Monica to a modest clothing store and they bought something appropriate for her to wear to church. After she put on the new wardrobe she said she felt better already and thanked her aunt again for being her savior. Trish immediately corrected her and said she's not the one to save her, but there is one who can. It was left at that.

That night while Trish was sleeping in her bedroom and Monica on the couch she was awakened again by her grandmother.

"Monica, Monica, Monica you have not heeded my warnings and are now falling into the pit of despair and drowning in darkness. You have allowed your friends to steer you onto a path of self destruction. Heed these words: Blessed is the man who doesn't walk in the counsel of the wicked, or stand in the way of sinners or sit in the seat of mockers, but his delight is in the law of the Lord, and on his law he meditates day and night. He is like a tree planted by streams of water which yields its fruit in season and whose leaf does not wither. Whatever he does prospers. Not so the wicked they are like chaff that the wind blows away. Therefore the wicked will not stand in the judgment, nor sinners in the assembly of the righteous. For the Lord watches over the way of the righteous, but the way of the wicked will perish. (Psalm 1 NIV) It is not too late for you to learn from your mistakes and seek to find the right way to negotiate the maze of life. I told you once before there are some things you need to do and now you realize you must do them. Tomorrow when you go to church remember my words and you must open your eyes, open your mind, but most of all you must open your heart. I will be with you whenever you need me, but there is one who also is available at your call, but you must discover this for yourself."

Just as she always does Lois said what she had to say and then disappeared without a trace. Monica still in a half awake and half sleep state heard the words and tried to absorb them, but her mindwas still being resistant to the wisdom coming from her grandmother. Even though she knew her most recent experiences had led her to a moment when she realized that the direction she was headed in was leading her down the wrong path, the answer to her problem was not entirely in what Lois and Trish were suggesting.

Monica rested comfortably for the rest of the night and when she awoke the next morning she recalled the visit. Trish had not awakened yet so she went into the kitchen and thought she would be helpful by making some coffee for the two of them. While she was still in there Trish came in.

"Well you're up early. Feeling better?"

"Yes I am, but so embarrassed to allow you to see me like this. However, I don't have anywhere else to go or anyone else to turn to. I'm going to do better."

"Please don't fret my child. You are not perfect and neither am I. No one is exempt from making mistakes or succumbing to some evil forces in life. It's how you deal with them after making the mistake that will make you a better person or a total failure. I'm not so old that I can't remember the number of times when I was about your age when I made some bad choices that led to an outcome that was not good for me. I remember falling in love once, so madly in love that I was blinded. I moved in with a man who for years used me like a wet sponge. Then when I couldn't absorb no more, he threw me aside like a hot potato, disappeared and left me to pay all of the bills. Somehow I survived and vowed never to let any man do that to me again. Sometimes the right choice is not easy to make when you are being influenced by evil. It is said that small is the gate and narrow is the road that leads to life, and only a few find it. So don't feel like you are the only one to have made some bad choices, but learn from your errors and try not to repeat them."

"You know you sound just like that preacher down there at the church."

"Well I don't mean to preach at you, but you will learn over time that if you go there often enough and really listen to what he's saying you will find there is much truth in his words and great learning can be gained from his preaching."

"I'll try to remember that and pay more attention."

Trish then started to make breakfast while Monica went back to the couch. Shortly she was called to the kitchen where they had their meal. As she sat enjoying her meal Monica wondered whether she should tell her aunt about the visit she had last night. She had told her once before and it led to the same advice about going to church that she was sure she would receive now, so she didn't mention it. In a little while it was time for them to get dressed and leave for Holy Trinity. On the way Monica kept thinking about what her grandmother said about opening her eyes, mind and heart so she kept them in the forefront of her thinking.

They arrived within the usual time it took to traverse the streets of the suburbs and drove into the parking lot. Monica drove while Trish played navigator and co-pilot. The number of cars pulling in at about the same time was not unusual and the volunteer traffic monitors were doing their job efficiently. After they were parked safely they entered through the front doors into the main sanctuary. Almost like a repeat of the last time she was there Monica thought it was just luck that they were seated in almost the same seats they had. For Trish this was normal because this is where she usually sat.

The service was started as usual about ten minutes after 11:00 am with the mass choir marching in and singing the opening hymn. The balance of the service followed the traditional sequence and then it came time for the pastor to deliver the message for the day. Reverend Dumas went to the sacred desk stood behind it and began.

"Good morning my brothers and sisters in the Lord. Once again I greet you in the Holy and matchless name of our Lord and Savior Jesus Christ. Isn't it good to be here in the His house one more time, walking, talking, smiling and most of all breathing the gift of the very air that is made available to us to sustain our lives? God is good and He's good all the time. Now some of you may question that statement because you have gone through some things that you don't understand and it made you wonder where is God now, but let me tell you saints it may seem like he's not answering your payer or even heard your petition, I'm here to tell you do not despair He will take care of you. Do not be discouraged, but wait on the Lord and he will answer at the right time.

Today saints I want to continue with the study of our Lord Jesus Christ. Last week we laid the foundation and began to trace the heritage of our Lord down through forty-two generations. As I said then the hereditary line began with a promise to Abraham that he would be a father of many nations and it was through his seed that the generations were begun. His son Isaac was the father of Jacob who was the father of the twelve tribes of Israel from which eventually came our Lord. Now we need to briefly review for a minute why there came a need for a Messiah as he came o be called. Originally the twelve tribes whom God had selected to be a model people turned away from obeying God and carried out worshipping other gods which was strictly forbidden. As a punishment over hundreds of years He gave them up to be enslaved by a number of different nations, but He would always spare a remnant. One of the nations that enslaved the people was Egypt, a mighty nation at that time. For four hundred years they were kept in bondage. During this time God heard the cries of the people and sent a man to lead them out of their misery. I'm sure you're familiar with this man because his name was Moses. You've probably all seen the movie."

At this point there was some laughter from the congregation.

"After convincing Pharaoah with the benefit of God's punishing miracles, Moses led the people out of Egypt with great riches and wealth. But even then not being satisfied with being brought out of bondage, the people started to murmur and complain about their predicament of having to traverse through the wilderness. God punished many of them by culling out the complaining generation and allowed only the young to enter into the land that had been promised to them. During their journey which lasted forty years God gave them a set of instructions and laws by which they should live by and obey Him. These laws are called the Ten Commandments, which I believe many of you are familiar with. When they entered the Promised Land and drove out the people who had possessed the land many of them chose to adopt the religious practices of the people who had been driven out. They disobeyed God's laws and statutes that had been given to Moses His chosen leader. This greatly angered the Lord and the chastisement began once again. Over the forty-two generations the people were led by many kings some of who were good and obeyed God others were just the opposite and disobeyed.

God knew the hearts of the people and each time there was a period of general disobedience He sent a prophet to proclaim the message of the coming kingdom and a savior. During the period of wandering through the wilderness God had Moses teach them about blood sacrifice and it was included in the books of Moses called the Pentateuch which is the first five books of the Bible. Now keep this in mind about the blood sacrifice because it will become very significant a little later in this sermon. It was only through the blood that the healing of the nations could take place. As the people continued to disobey and worship other gods, they were attacked by other nations who captured and scattered them throughout the then known world. This continued for many years and God had it in His heart to destroy the world again, but He had made a promise to Abraham that he would not flood the earth again.

Something had to be done to correct the disobedience of the people before the wrath of God came upon the entire earth. It was then that a savior, a Messiah had to be the answer. So after the four hundred years in which God was silent toward His people a search was made for the one who would bear a child whose name would be called Jesus. Before this blessed event took place, God had sent many prophets proclaiming the day that it would happen and they implored, begged and cajoled the people to return to faithful worship and heed the Word of god. There were some brief periods of time when this seemed to be a righteous practice among the people, but it didn't last long and they consistently returned to their evil ways and defied even the teachings of the prophets. One of the outstanding prophets who proclaimed the coming of the Messiah was Isaiah. He was a chosen man of God and a prophet who told the world that a savior was coming and His kingdom would last forever. It was in defiance of his leadership that the Jews took offense at his words and chose to punish him for proclaiming the things he said. After him there were many other prophets who also proclaimed the coming of the savior and to them the same punishment was delivered. But it was going to happen even without the blessing of the defiant Jews who did not want to lose their authority when and if what was being proclaimed were to come true. And so it happened even after the Savior was born that there was great dissention among the Jews. There were those who would follow the Messiah and those who would oppose Him.

When God in His search found who he considered as the right one to bear His seed he sent His angel Gabriel to announce to the young girl whose name was Mary that she would be the mother of the one who would be called Jesus and she would become the mother of the Savior of the world. She was astonished at first, but did not reject the words of the angel of the Lord, but said to him let it be unto her as he said. And thus the time was started when the arrival of the one who would come to save the world was begun.

I'm going to end this sermon here because what happens after Jesus is born is the subject, the final chapter in this sermon series. It will be what we talk about next week and explore His miracles, His teaching and what it means to us right now and what we should be doing to be sure to inherit our salvation and become a member of His little flock and receive the joys of heaven while still here on earth.

There are some among you who have heard the story up to now and yet still do not believe that this age is coming to an end rapidly and those who have not received tha hand of God nor accepted Jesus as their Savior will be caught up in a quandary to which there will be no answer. There will be no time for repentance at that point because the opportunity will have passed and you as they say will be left behind. The gates to heaven will be closed and the door will be opened to the lake of fire that will be forever burning. It will be too late. Hear the words of this preacher and realize that now is the time when you need to look at what's happening in the world around you and witness the beginning of the tribulation period that is coming upon you. There will be no time to run to and fro from one place to another trying to seek refuge because there will no place to hide and even the rocks will cry out that the Savior is Lord and only He can save you from the coming calamities that will be loosed upon this earth in such a manner that you will not be able to withstand it. So come now if you have not accepted Jesus as your Lord and Savior do it now before it's too late. Come forward and give the deacons you hand, but give God your heart. The doors of the church are open to all. Come as you are. Forget about what you have done in the past come now, accept the Lord Jesus and your sins will be forgiven as you confess them. You must be washed in the blood of Jesus in order to truly be cleansed of all your unrighteousness. Won't you come and be healed? Come, come. Give the deacons your hand and give God your heart.

As the parade of new believers walked up to the altar, Monica felt the stirring in her heart and started to get up when something inside of her told her to sit back down. She struggled for several minutes wrestling between the two spirits just as her father did, but she didn't know this yet. She sat down and Trish just looked at her wondering what was going on inside her mind, but she didn't say anything to her. The church service ended and Monica missed her opportunity once again. When Trish and Monica left and went home Trish wanted to ask her what she thought about the sermon, but she waited to see if Monica would start that conversation first. When they got to the apartment and walked inside nothing had been said during the ride home so Trish's curiosity was getting the best of her and she had to say something.

"So what did you think about today's sermon?"

Monica hesitated before answering then finally spoke up.

"You know I really felt something inside urging me to go up and do like that preacher was saying. Give the deacons my hand and give God my heart, but there was something else gnawing at my heart strings preventing me from doing it. It was a feeling like I didn't deserve to be healed because of the things I have done. It was stronger than the urge to go so I didn't. What does that mean?"

"It means you missed the most important part of today's message and the invitation to come to Jesus. That feeling telling you to sit down when an invitation to accept Christ was given was nothing short of the devil trying to keep his arms tightly held around you. I'm sorry you didn't say something while we were still in the sanctuary I would have held your hand myself and walked with you up to that altar because it was there that the feeling would have been cast aside. It's not too late even now if you are willing to accept Him and be forgiven."

"I don't know Aunt Trish I'm just not feeling it. Anyway I've got to get back to school and get ready for an early class tomorrow. I do feel much better though and once again I thank you for that. Also thanks for looking out for my car."

Monica said that with a smile knowing it was really still Trish's car while it was there.

"Monica baby the car is not the issue it will be alright wherever it is, but I worry about you. You're going back to that same situation you just left and without the spiritual protection I was hoping you would receive while you were here."

"Please don't worry about me I'll be fine. I've had my wakeup call and I think I can handle going back to the gang. Now let me check the train schedule I may have already missed the last one."

Monica checked the schedule and fortunately there was another one going into the city in the next twenty minutes. Trish volunteered to take her to the station, but made her last pitch before Monica got out.

"Can you come back next week and we can try it again?"

"I don' know Aunt Trish I really don't see where that would do any good. I'm just not ready yet. Well thanks again. I'll call you when I get back to my dorm and let you know I got there safely."

"Yes please do that. Okay have a goodnight."

"Yes and you too."

Monica got out and went into the station as Trish sat there watching her. She wondered what was going to become of the one she loved as if she were her own daughter.

At 9:30 the day of the planned call between Drs. Danforth, Oniyuki and Reverend Dumas, Milton arrived at the church. After checking in with the receptionist he was directed to the pastor's office.

"Good morning pastor."

"Good morning to you. Felling well are you?"

"Feeling great! I can't wait to get this call started so we can begin to try and analyze what really happened that caused Mr. Miller's death. I'm not sure that doctor Oniyuki is totally convinced with what was given to him from those notes."

I can't make heads nor tails out of what you told me either so I guess we have to wait and talk to him to at least get a better understanding. We have some time now before the call would you like something to eat or drink - coffee, tea, orange juicc, water? "

No I'm fine thank you."

"Okay suit yourself I think I'll have a glass of orange juice it always clears my mind and I think I'm going to need a clear head when we start talking about a war between two spirits."

"Yes I agree."

They continued the small talk until it was about five minutes before the hour. Milton waited another minute or two then started dialing Dr. Oniyuki's office number.

Ring, ring, ring.

"Hello Dr. Oniyuki."

"Dr. Oniyuki this is Milton Danforth and I have Reverend Dumas here with me. How are you this morning.?"

"I'm doing fine considering all that's going on around here as a result of the mysterious demise of our favorite patient. There are so many unanswered questions and the witnesses who were in the room that night when the so called spiritual tug of war occurred now want to recant their stories for fear of some reprisal from the administration. Other than that as I said I'm doing fine."

They all laughed for a minute.

"Well Dr. Danforth where would you like to start?"

"Why don't we go over it again with the notes that Dr. Harris left you. Please read to us exactly what he described happened that night."

Dr. Oniyuki read the notes aloud.

"Now I can understand why the nurses and even Dr. Harris might want to change their original version of what they said. It's hard to believe that the spirit's voices were audible to the human ear. David you want to weigh in on this. Is that possible?"

"Well remember we were witnesses ourselves in the room when two spirits demonstrated their interest in Norman and if I recall correctly it was the evil spirit that won that battle as stated by Norman."

"Yes I agree because it was right after that when Norman returned to his old self, but before he did he said that only another spirit had the power to permanently dispel the evil spirit from him." Dr. Oniyuki said.

"Yes I recall it that way also" offered Milton.

"Having said that my thought regarding the other power he must have been referring to had to be that of the Almighty God who I serve. As far as the voices of the spirits being audible to the human ear who can say where the limitations of the spiritual world begins or ends. I'm inclined to believe Dr. Harris and those nurses when they claim to have heard the voices. I wish they had the courage to stand by their convictions and not be intimidated by the administration. Anyway be that as it may where we are now is to accept the possibility that the same two spirits that we all experienced are the ones who caused Norman's death. But to me the next question should be why would they want him dead?"

"That's a good question because if the goal was to posses his body through their power then the winner would want to claim that soul alive I would think." Dr. Oniyuki said.

"In the notes it said that the end of the episode was when for no apparent reason Mr. Miller just fell to the floor. Can we speculate on what would have caused that? Did each spirit decide he wasn't worth fighting for or was some type of intervention made by some other means that caused each to withdraw?"Dr. Danforth asked.

"All we can do is speculate at this point because there is no way we can determine the cause without being able to reproduce the scene which is now impossible short of soliciting a medium to conduct a séance and contact Norman for further detail. I'm not inclined to take that route myself. It didn't go very well for King Saul and a few others" said the pastor.

Again they all laughed.

"So what we have is a possible draw between two spirits who for whatever reason left Norman alone that time, but came back again and scared him to death – is that right?" asked Milton.

"It appears that way." Dr. Oniyuki offered.

"Let me ask this gentlemen what is it that we want to try and conclude from this call? It's clear we can have no positive answer to whether the spirits actually caused his death and based on the notes from Dr. Harris and we have to believe he would not fabricate such a story so then what he said must be true" continued the pastor.

"For the record and to finish my assessment I'm simply going to enter his cause of death as a heart attack for the coroner and make no reference to any of the other portions of the report. As far as our conclusions in the matter it will have to be left as something of unknown origin. Do you agree?"

"I guess we have to accept that because there is nothing else we can determine by any scientific methodology or assumptions. Let me offer this however, I was contemplating calling you Dr. Oniyuki and suggesting that you allow me to come here with a team of my most accomplished prayer warriors from the church and set up another session with Mr. Miller and then through prayer let loose the power of that other Spirit that I believe Mr. Miller was referring to. It becomes a moot point now since the subject is not available to test my theory."

"That would have been an interesting session I agree, and I certainly would have welcomed it. Anyway let us now adjourn our call and let me make arrangements to dispose of the body."

"On that note Dr. Oniyuki you know one of the members of my church is in contact with the daughter that Mr. Miller claimed he had. She does actually exist. Why don't you let me contact her through my member and she can as the next of kin help with the disposition of her father."

"That would be fine with me. Please keep in mind I have only three days to decide what shall be done. So you need to let me know as soon as you can whether you were able to reach the daughter and what would she like to do?"

"Okay, as soon as we finish I will have someone from my staff try to contact her, then get back to you."

"Great! Well gentlemen unless you can think of anything else we need to talk about I guess that concludes this call. It's unfortunate we were not able to establish any further determination about what really happened to Mr. Miller. Be that as it may have a good day and I'll talk to you soon. Goodbye."

"You have a blessed day also. Goodbye."

The call was ended with no clear evaluation of what was accomplished other than now making contact with Monica to make arrangements for her father's burial. Pastor called one of his staff members and asked her to take care of getting in touch with sister Ramey and ask her to call me as soon as she can. After the task was assigned the two friends talked about the call.

"You know David I would love to have been a part of that idea you proposed where your prayer warriors would be pitted against that other spirit. I wonder who would win?"

"My friend and brother I have no doubt in my mind who would win, but it would be more than just a show of power it would be a test of faith for all of us. Okay now I have some other work to do so unless you need something else I will let you know also when I hear back from sister Ramey and the daughter."

"Okay I'm out of here I'll talk to you later."

Later on that afternoon pastor's intercom buzzed.

"Yes"

"Pastor I have sister Ramey on the line can you take her call now?"

"Yes please put her through."

"Hello."

"Hello Reverend Dumas this is Patricia Ramey you called me?"

"Yes sister I did, but first let me inquire about your health. How are you?"

"Oh thank you for asking, I'm doing fine."

"Very good! The reason why I called has to do with the husband of your friend we funeralized here a short time ago. I believe her name was Elena Miller is that right?"

"Yes and it was a truly blessed funeral."

"Thank you. Well we received word just a day or so ago that her husband Norman Miller has passed and if I recall correctly there was a daughter who attended Mrs. Miller's funeral. I thought it would be right for us to let her know about the passing of her father so that she can get in touch with the hospital and make arrangements for him to be buried. Now I don't know much about her or even where she is, but I'm guessing you do and that's why I made the call."

"Oh my God I'm so sorry to hear that. Yes I do know where she is and how to contact her. You know it's been some time since I saw him, but I also took her with me then. Her name is Monica and she had a chance to see him even though he didn't recognize her. But that was some time ago. I will call her and let her know. When did he pass and what would you like for us to do?"

"I've been advised it was two days ago and the only reason why I was privy to that information is because a friend of mine is a doctor who had treated Mr. Miller before he was transferred to that hospital and they called him. Please once you have made contact with her you can get back to me and let me know whether you want the church to conduct his funeral. As you know if that is her request we need to get it on the calendar as soon as we can."

"Yes I understand. I'm going to call her soon as we hang up and if I get her I'll call you back either today or early tomorrow."

"Okay. I look forward to hearing from you. Have a blessed day."

"Yes thank you and you too. Goodbye."

Trish called Monica right away, but since it was the middle of the day she was probably still in class, so she did not answer her phone. Then she left an urgent message asking her to call back as soon as she could. The rest of the afternoon Trish wondered about how he died because as she recalled the last time she visited him with Monica, even though he was rather frail it didn't appear that he was in any life threatening condition. There was no advisory from the doctors either about any pending negative health conditions that perhaps at least his daughter should know about. She also remembered that Monica left her school address with the nursing staff so why didn't they call her? But then again maybe they did.

It wasn't until around 6:00 O'clock when Trish received the return phone call.

"Hello."

"Hi Aunt Trish Monica you called me?"

"Yes dear how are you first of all?"

"Doing much better since I saw you last. I have tried to distance myself from the gang I was running with and even my roommates as much as possible. You said it was urgent that I get back to you right away. What's wrong?"

"Well I have sad news about your father. He passed two days ago and I wanted to let you know because you need to decide if you want my church to do his funeral."

"You know I was going to call you about that. I received a letter in overnight mail from the hospital yesterday informing me of his passing and advising me to come there as soon as I could to make arrangements to dispose of his body. Someone from there also called this morning and left an urgent message also. I've just been so busy I haven't had time to call either one of you back. But now that I have you what should I do?"

"Oh I was wondering whether they had contacted you because I remember you leaving your address with their staff. Well that's good. What we need, or more correctly what you need to do and of course I'll go with you is get over to that hospital and do what they said. Make arrangements for the removal of his body before the state does something without your knowledge or consent. When can you go? I suggest you come here first and we'll go up there together."

"Yes that's a good idea. I only have one class tomorrow and that's in the morning so I can catch the train and get to your house by 1 or 2:00 O'clock. Is that okay?"

"Yes that's good. Then we'll go and see what needs to be done there. Okay see you tomorrow. Goodbye."

"Right. Goodbye."

When they hung up Trish called Reverend Dumas back and left a message for him advising that she had made contact with Monica and they were going to the hospital tomorrow to try and make arrangements for the disposition of her father's body. Not too long after that she received a return call from pastor's staff person acknowledging receipt of her message and asking her to let him know as soon as she could about whether funeral arrangements need to be made here.

Back at school that same day Margie confronted her roommate and asked her why she had been avoiding her lately. She was in her room smoking one of her joints as usual and had invited Monica to partake when the confrontation started. Even though she had a kind of quasi smile on her face from the weed, Monica knew she was serious.

"You know you've been avoiding me and CC here lately like we got bad breath or something. What's up with you? You don't even want to share this good weed anymore. Are you trying to tell us something?"

"No girl I'm still with you guys, but you know I have to study harder than you two because it doesn't come as easy for me as you."

"So you're telling me you're spending all the time away from here in the library is that what your're saying? I think you've found a new sugar daddy that you don't want us to know about and that's where you spend your time. Who is he I won't tell?"

Monica thinking quickly as she has always been able to do responded.

"Wow you really peeped my hole card. You must be psychic or something, but I can't tell you who it is because he is a real straight no nonsense guy and if he knew I was doing what you do he'd out me in a minute."

"Okay friend that's your loss."

Monica started to tell her about her father's death but then decided not to because she would have to explain all about where he is and under what condition he was living. So she skipped over even the thought.

The next day after her morning class ended Monica caught the earliest train running and headed to her aunt's apartment. She rang the foyer intercom bell and received the usual question of who is it? The door buzzer sounded and she went upstairs. At the apartment door she rang the chimes and was allowed in.

"Hi you're early. I was just getting dressed. You're looking much better than the last time I saw you. Behaving yourself are you?"

"Yeah I guess you can say that, but it's not easy pretending you're still one of the crowd when you aren't."

"Well it will be better for you in the long run. Okay I'm ready let's go."

They got in the car with Monica driving and headed to Saddle River Hospital. At the front desk they asked for Dr. Oniyuki and was told he was in a conference session and could not be disturbed. Then the receptionist asked what they were there for and after hearing the reason he directed them to another staff member who asked that they follow her. They caught an elevator to a lower level then walked down a long corridor to a room where the bodies were kept. The attendant took over and asked who they were there for?

"Are you members of the family?"

"Yes, I'm his daughter."

"Would you like to see the body for confirmation."

"Yes please."

The attendant motioned both ladies to follow him to the cabinet where the bodies were stored then he pulled out a drawer. Is this your father?"

Monica and Trish looked at him and the expression on his face that had not been changed and they were shocked.

"What happened to him?" Monica asked.

"Far as I know he just had a major heart attack."

"Would a heart attack make his face like that?" Trish asked.

"I don't know, I guess it could. You need to ask the doctor that question. Now there are some papers you need to fill out before I can release him into your custody."

He took them back to his desk and handed Monica several documents that needed her signature as the next of kin. She read them carefully then handed them to Trish for her review. Neither of them saw anything suspicious about the wording so Monica signed. Next the attendant asked how and when they would be picking up the deceased. Neither one of the ladies could answer that because that part had not been worked out yet. Trish told the attendant to wait a minute while she made a phone call and then she would be able to answer his question. He acknowledged and stepped away. Trish got on the phone and called the church.

Ring, ring, ring.

"Hello Holy Trinity Baptist Church how may I help you?"

"Hello this is sister Ramey is pastor available I need to speak with him soon as possible."

"Yes he's standing right here hold on a minute."

"Sister Ramey are you alright?"

"Yes pastor, but I'm here at the hospital now with Monica and we're trying to make arrangements for Mr. Miller's body, but I don't know where to take him. Can you help?"

"Yes. How soon does he have to be moved?"

"Hold on a minute I have to ask."

She questioned the attendant.

"The attendant here said it should be taken out of here as soon as possible, but he could give them another two days."

"Okay that's fine. Take this information down and give it to him."

Reverend Dumas gave her the information and it was set for the body to be picked up by the Sleep In Peace funeral Home in two days. After that Trish and Monica left the hospital and went straight to the church to talk about the funeral service arrangements. At the church pastor Dumas was in his office and agreed to see them now.

"I didn't expect to see you this quickly."

"Well I thought since we were taking care of the hospital business we may as well do it all. You met this young lady before and I'm sure you remember her she's Mr. Miller's daughter."

"Yes I do. She's such a lovely young lady how are you?"

"Hi I guess I'll be okay once we take of all this stuff."

"Yes I'm sure you will be. I was sorry to hear about your father, but as you know this is the way we all will have to go at some point."

"Yes I know."

"Pastor do you have time to talk with us about funeral arrangements for him?"

"Certainly please sit down. Let me check the calendar and see what's open. Are you able to do something during the week he asked looking at Monica?"

"Yes if that's what has to be done I will do it. What date are you looking at?"

"Next Wednesday is open and we can have a brief ceremony that morning and then bury him beside or near your mother if you like?"

"Yes that would be wonderful. How much will it cost?"

"Don't you worry about that I understand in talking with sister Ramey you are a college student and he didn't have any insurance is that right?"

"Yes."

"Alright we will take care of everything including the funeral parlor."

"Once again I am so thankful I don't know what to say."

"Just thank God for His blessings."

Now that the arrangements had been made for the disposition of the body and the funeral the two ladies left the church and went back to Trish's apartment. After they left Reverend Dumas called his friend Dr. Danforth.

"Hello"

"Hey Milton are you busy?"

"No pastor just finishing up some paper work. How are you doing?"

"Just fine thank you. Mr. Miller's wife's special friend and his daughter just left here. We are going to have the funeral here next Wednesday morning. Are you going to be able to attend?"

"Let me check my calendar. Yes that looks okay. You know there was something that still bothered me after we had that conference call."

"Really what was that?'

"I just wondered how the funeral home is going to fix that expression on his face."

CHAPTER 12

Friend Or Foe

P rovidence is an unsearchable truth and cannot be truly defined according to the limited vocabulary of man. What determines one man receiving an abundance of fame and fortune while another sinks to abject poverty has often been said lies in the realm of Providence. They both begin at birth being exposed to the nature of good and evil, yet one thrives where the other fails. But who can know whether the hand of fate will deal fairly with one man as it does with another. Can Providence be called to question in answering the matter? Laws have been created and instituted by men in so called civilized societies to protect and ensure fairness and equal opportunity in the pursuit of happiness, but when Providence intervenes in the creation of man's laws does it require an understanding of what it is? Can Providence be equated to a man or perhaps a spirit? Can it be attributed to the highest form of governance known to man? Can the one who holds the Divine scepter and rules from eternity be He who can truly define Providence? Only those who seek to know the truth will learn of the answer at the judgment.

The funeral for Norman Miller occurred as planned with Reverend Dumas delivering the eulogy. It was a brief ceremony carried out in the mid morning hours and was not well attended. There were those church members who are obligated to attend all funerals and participate in the service, such as a small choir, a few deacons and others from the missionary guild. Also in attendance as expected were Monica, Trish, Dr. Danforth and Dr. Oniyuki. Surprisingly there were some of Trish's friends other church members who just saw the announcement and decided to come. No great fanfare was given and no large array of flowers was presented.

In his message Rev. Dumas referred to brother Miller as one who had lived much of his life in quiet seclusion in a place where we house the unfortunate souls who have experienced judging by the hand of Providence. But in the end his body like all others will rest in the peace of time before the final judgment is rendered. Monica listened to the words of the preacher and was glad that he was performing the service, but wasn't quite sure of what he was talking about. Even though she had gone to service a few times now with Aunt Trish she was still concerned that his sermons never answered her question.

After the service concluded the body was taken to the church's cemetery where he was interred in a plot near Elena, his wife. There was no repast nor any provision made for anything to take place after the burial so all guests went their separate ways. Monica and Trish however, went back to the church to thank all those who showed up for the service.

"Reverend Dumas I just want to thank you so much for all that you have done not only now for my father, but for my mother a while ago" Monica said.

"We are always here to help those who are in need and God blesses all who use their talents to carry out His word. I'm glad that we were able to provide this service, but now what are your intentions? Do you plan on coming back during our normal service hours on Sunday?"

"I'm going to try, but right now I'm under a lot of pressure with school and other things so it may be hard to do."

"I understand but just remember this. You are never alone in all that you do and there is a Savior you can call on any time night or day who will be able to help and guide you through everything you experience. But you must learn to call on Him."

After that Trish and Monica went back to the apartment.

"Monica you heard the words of the preacher. I just wish that you would really prepare yourself to open your heart and accept the One who can make things alright for you."

"I heard him and I hear you Aunt Trish, but the feeling is just not there yet."

Monica stayed there a little while longer than caught the train back to the university.

Later on that afternoon Trish received a call from Monica.

"Aunt Trish you know I've been doing a lot of thinking about the funeral and what was said by Rev. Dumas. I don't want to end up like my father or my mother so if there is some way that can be avoided like he said maybe I ought to come back there and listen to more of what he has to say. What I'm trying to say is that I will go to church again with you this Sunday."

"Monica you don't know how happy I am to hear you say that. Will you be coming here tomorrow and spend the night?"

"No I need to do some work here so I will catch the early train Sunday morning and if you would please pick me up at the station and we can go straight from there."

"Okay I can do that. Just let me know what time you will be getting there. Remember to allow yourself time with that schedule so that we won't be late getting to church. You know I don't like to walk in late."

"Yes I know and I will make sure I catch the earliest train to avoid that happening."

"Good so I'll see you on Sunday. Goodbye."

"Yes bright and early. Goodbye."

As planned Monica arrived at the station around 10:15 and Trish was there waiting for her. The train was also right on schedule so there was plenty of time to get to the church before the service started. They arrived a bit earlier than usual and as a result were able to get a choice parking space. Inside as more congregants began entering it seemed to Monica like she was seeing more of the same faces she saw at the funeral. Once again the ushers directed Trish to her favorite pew and now Monica understood about this arrangement.

As usual the service started shortly after 11:00 with the choir marching in and taking their seats in the choir loft. The traditional opening prayer of invocation was followed by the reading of a Psalm of thanksgiving and then the rest of the program followed the usual order. By the time the program reached the point where Rev. Dumas was expected to deliver the message for the day the atmosphere in the house was ready to receive it.

"Good morning my brothers and sisters in the Lord. Again I greet you in the blessed name of our Lord and Savior Jesus Christ. This is the day that the Lord has made let us rejoice and be glad in it. Has God done anything for you this week, has He blessed in some special way that you need to give him a praise?"

The hallelujah's rang out from the pews in such a loud response that it was gratifying for the preacher to hear.

"Today we are going to continue our sermon series on the life of our Lord Jesus and it is my hope that you will be blessed by the word coming from above. I will be talking using mainly the book of St. Luke, but from time to time I might quote from one of the other synoptic gospels so please stay with me. Let us pray. Father In heaven, Jehovah my God please allow the Holy Spirit to fall fresh on this your humble servant. Fill me with your presence and let the light that you have placed inside of me shine so brightly that these your people will look at me, but see the light of your son Jesus that emanates from me. Hide me behind the cross so that my ego will not stand in the way of someone seeing Jesus. Let the words of my mouth and the meditation of my heart be acceptable to you oh Lord my strength and my redeemer.

Last week we ended with God having chosen the young girl whose name was Mary to receive His seed through the power of the Holy Spirit. Recall saints that she willingly heeded the message given to her by the arc angel Gabriel and did not reject nor fear. It is important as part of this message that you understand receiving and not rejecting the word from God will guarantee your blessing. Saints we are looking now at chapter 1 verses 29-38. It is important for me to also mention here that another blessed event was taking place around the same time that Gabriel talked to Mary. There was a man by the name of Zechariah, a priest and a chosen man of God whose wife's name was Elizabeth. She was also told she would bear a child, but through natural means and her child would be the one who would clear the way for Mary's baby. His name was John, who became known as John the Baptist because he was the one who started baptizing in the name of the Lord and calling sinners to repentance. It is important to note this because he was the one, when Jesus reached the age of maturity baptized Jesus. Let's not get ahead of ourselves here.

Mary had her baby in the town of Bethlehem, a small town in the region of Judea. I'm sure you all know this story because it is the Christmas story. He was born in a manger because there was no room in any of the inns in the city. Mary's husband Joseph had come to this place because he was responding to a command from Caesar Augustus, who was the emperor at that time, to conduct a census throughout all the land. As part of this Christmas story is also the word that an angel appeared to shepherds in the fields announcing the birth of a Savior and they were the first to go and visit the Christ child while He was still in the manger. Now in Matthew's gospel chapter 2 he refers to another visit by three kings or wise men when Mary and Joseph were no longer living in a manger, but were now in a house. The kings or wise men also known as the magi brought gift to honor the newborn king and thus we have the beginning of the traditional gifts giving at Christmas.

Moving on now Jesus grew and there is not much said in the Bible about His early childhood days, but the story picks up when he reached the age of twelve. Joseph and Mary after fulfilling their obligation to complete the census returned to their home in Nazareth of Galilee. Now every year the family went up to Jerusalem to observe the religious festival the Feast of the Passover. It was there that the first indication of what the Christ child would be all about was given. When Mary and Joseph were returning from the celebration of the feast it was discovered that the child was not among those traveling with them. So they turned around and went back to the city. For three days they searched for him. Now I know all of you mothers out there if you couldn't find you child for three days you would turn that city upside down. When they found him he was in the temple courts sitting listening and questioning the teachers. His understanding of the scriptures at that time amazed the teachers at his acumen at such an early age. Now when He was discovered of course Mary questioned Him about why He had treated them this way by not letting them know where He was. Jesus reply now became the foundational quote for His later actions. He said to His mother "Didn't you know I had to be in my Father's house?' this was the first alert for Mary that even though He was obedient from that time on as we understand it, she knew that this was no ordinary child.

At the age of thirty Jesus was baptized by John the Baptist and after He was baptized the heaven's opened and the Holy Spirit descended on him in the form of a dove. Then a voice from heaven was heard saying this is my son in whom I am well pleased. This was the launching of His ministerial age having been blessed by His father. Immediately after this the Holy Spirit led Him into the desert to be tempted by Satan the devil for forty days. The devil challenged Jesus in three areas. First he was told knowing He would be hungry after His forty day fast, if He was the son of God turn these stones into bread. Jesus not yielding to the temptation the first time said to the devil Man does not live by bread alone, but by every word issued from the Lord's mouth. Then the devil made a second challenge. He was led to a high place and shown all the kingdoms of the world and the devil said I will give you all authority over this for it has been given to me if you worship me. Jesus replied resisting the second temptation, it is written worship the Lord your God and serve Him only. Then the devil persisted in his challenges and made a third one. If you are the son of God throw yourself down from this high point on the temple, for it is written God will command His angels to guard you so that you will not strike your foot against a stone. This lets you know saints that Satan the devil knows the scriptures also so you must be aware of that. After hearing that third challenge Jesus replied "Do not put the Lord your God to the test". After being rejected a third time the devil left Him for now. Saints the important point here is that even Jesus was tempted by the devil not once but three times and each time He did not yield to temptation. That's why He has the power to hold you up when you resist the devil's temptations.

Then Jesus went into the synagogue where he read the scriptures before the priests. When He read from the book of Isaiah the verse that says the Spirit of the Lord is upon me because He has anointed me to preach good news to the poor. He has sent me to proclaim freedom for the prisoners and recovery of sight for the blind, to release the oppressed, proclaim the year of the Lord's favor. When He finished reading and told the priests today this scripture is fulfilled in your hearing referring to himself, they questioned His authority. Talking amongst themselves they said isn't this Joseph's son and we know who he is. Then Jesus replied no prophet is accepted in his hometown. They became furious at Him and drove Him out of the town. They threatened to throw Him down a cliff, but He escaped. There will be other times when He would have to run for His life from those who persecuted Him which we shall see a little later in this sermon.

From here Jesus began His healing ministry as He traversed the countryside. First in Capernaum he drove out a demon an evil spirit from a man in the synagogue. The citizens of Capernaum wanted Him to stay with them, but He told the people He must preach the good news of the kingdom of God to the other towns also. Thus He went on to teach, heal and cast out demons in other cities across the regions. His next task was to gather disciples who would eventually be the spokespersons for His church and the progenitors of the coming kingdom of God message. First to be called was a fisherman by the name of Simon Peter. Now Peter was a kind of strange character which we will talk a little bit more about later. But he was the one who became the first real preacher in the newly formed church of God. Joining him as disciples, whom he also designated apostles were Andrew, Peter's brother James and John, Phillip, Bartholomew, Matthew, Thomas, James the son of Alphaeus, Simon the zealot, Judas son of James and Judas Iscariot who would be the betrayer of Jesus. In all there were twelve of them to begin with. Now He would take these apostles as followers and go about the whole region again teaching, preaching and healing until it became a source of unrest among the Pharisees and Sadducees of the Sanhedrin which was the religious governing body of the Israelites. The Sadducees were the upper class of the Sanhedrin and the Pharisees were of the lower class. But together they considered the acts of Jesus and His apostles as an affront to their authority and consequently something had to be done to stop it. Thus the groundwork was laid for the eventual final act of the one who gave his life to save even them.

Saints I'm going to end this sermon here lest I inundate you with too much information at one time and defeat the purpose of this message. What we have covered today is the birth of Jesus who is the fulfillment of the prophecy of Isaiah and others from the old testament and now we have the beginning of the new testament. Jesus came preaching a message about a coming kingdom of God by which all men could be saved if they would as John the Baptist preached confess their sins repent and believe in Him.

The doors of the church are now open. It is up to you my brothers and sisters whether you want to be a member of the little flock who are called to salvation or risk ending up in the lake of fire at the judgment. No one can answer for you it must be you and you alone who makes the decision which way you will go. But remember the time is growing short when the opportunity will no longer be available to make this choic. Believe me the rapture is coming. Now I don't know when exactly, but as I look around us and you can too and witness the things that are going wrong in the world it is not hard to see that something is happening and it is not good. So come. Come now and be spared from the tribulation by fire that will soon be upon us. Come to the altar of God, give the deacons your hand, but give God your heart. Don't wait too long and be left behind.

Reverend Dumas finished his appeal for new converts to come forward and Trish tried hard not to look at Monica, but she could sense the angst going on beside her. Monica rocked back and forward, side to side as if bordering on a great decision, but did not get up and approach the altar. When the altar call passed she sat like one who was mesmerized by the message, but failed to grasped the gravity of the situation. Trish realizing her dilemma reached out, wrapped her arms around her and just held the rocking child. When the service concluded and the congregants were walking out Rev. Dumas was at the entrance door. He looked at Monica and said: "I saw you today, perceived your struggle and my heart felt for you. I think I know what you're going through, but you and only you must reach that point where you surrender it all to Him and trust in His word. No one can do it for you." With that he grabbed her hand held it for a moment then bid them both a blessed day.

When they reached Trish's apartment and went inside the evidence of the tears that had been welling up in Monica's eyes were still there.

"I don't know what else to say to you or what else to do to convince you which way you need to go, but when I see you struggling like I did today it makes me wonder."

"Aunt Trish I know what you think is best for me and I really and truely appreciate all that you have done for me, but I just can't get past the barrier in my head that seems to be holding me back. The other thing is that he still has not answered my question."

So the conversation ended there and Monica prepared to catch the train and go back to school.

The rest of the school year was uneventful. Monica continued to step lightly around the ones who were constantly tempting her to rejoin the pot gang. Often she had to pretend illness to avoid their excoriation. At the end of the semester and after successfully passing her final exams she wondered where she was going to go for the summer. Certainly she was not going back to the house she ran away from and there was just not enough room at her aunt's place to spend a whole summer in. So the quandary occupied an excessive amount of her time.

At a loss as to what to do and having few options she finally called her former supervisor at Nords told him she would be coming home for the summer and asked if there were any openings she could fill for that time. He was glad to hear from her but said that things were kind of slow right now at the store. He then said he would look into it see what he could do and get back to her. She gave him her telephone number and he promised to do what he could. Now she was getting a little desperate because her scholarship would not cover her staying in the dormitory apartment over the summer. Her last thought was to call on her old friend the musketeer - Reilly.

Ring, ring, ring.

"Hello."

"Hello Reilly it's Monica are you busy?"

"Hey girlfriend where are you?"

"Right now I'm still at school in the city, but I'm going to be coming there very soon."

"That's great can't wait to see you. Where are you going to be staying, I know you're not going back to where you used to live?"

"Well that's my problem. You are absolutely right I will never go back there, but I don't have anywhere to go. I've already inquired about trying to go back to work at Nords and make enough to maybe get a small apartment temporarily, but they said there's nothing open right now. I could hold up in a motel for a very short while, but my money ain't going to last too long that way."

"Oh nonsense girl, you come on and stay with me. I have a two bedroom apartment in one of my father's properties and it's just me. I just have to tidy up a bit to make some room, but it will be fun. When exactly are you coming?"

"Reilly you are a lifesaver. I have to be out of the dorm by Friday of next week so I guess on Thursday I'll go to my aunt's house and get my car then move out that Friday. I can't thank you enough. I'll call you before I come to confirm my plans."

"No need to thank me. We're still musketeers and what are friends for? Okay I'll wait to hear from you when you're ready to move in here. Bye."

"Okay great. Goodbye."

The plan was seemingly going along fine until one day just before all of the roommates were to exit the dorm, CC came in the apartment and announced that she had no place to stay over the summer. Her parents were getting divorced and the house was being sold. There were no other relatives that she said would be able to house her for the whole summer so she was in a bad situation. Monica heard her story and knew exactly how she was feeling even though she had not told either of the other girls what her situation was. Listening to CC's almost tearful plea for help Monica was pressed hard to offer a way out if her friend would have it. The problem was there was only two days left before exiting was a dire reality.

Before calling Reilly and explaining CC's situation to her, Monica asked CC if she had any money to pay rent should her friend be able to take her in for the summer. CC assured her that would not be a problem because her father would pay for it. He just would not pay for her being put up in any hotel or motel for the summer by herself and he certainly wasn't going to sign any lease for an apartment even if it was short term. That part sounded okay to Monica, but then she thought about CC's character and how she was still a member of the pot gang. So she sat her roommate down and had a serious talk.

"CC I've known you for almost a full year now and we've been through some things and had some fun, but my friend who I'm going to ask if she can put us both up for the summer may not be into the stuff you've been doing with Margie and those others. You know what I'm talking about?"

"Yes of course I do, but I'm not hooked on any of that stuff like she is. So if your friend is a real straight arrow I can behave like normal people when I have to do it. Listen I'm in a desperate situation right now and I will do whatever it takes to make it to September when my scholarship will kick in again and I'll move back into the apartment."

Monica did not know that CC was also on scholarship like she was. She thought her parents were paying her school bill. Hearing her plight and recognizing that they had that in common convinced her to make the call and try to impose on Reilly's good heart. After they talked, Monica called Reilly. It was early in the day so she wasn't sure she would even be able to pick up right now because she was probably working, but if she didn't Monica wondered how much of a message should she leave about why she was calling. As it turned out Reilly was at work, but when she saw who was calling she answered.

"Hey girlfriend how's it going? You getting ready to move in here?"

"Hi Reilly well yes and no."

"Oh, oh what does that mean?"

"Are you very busy right now because it's going to take a few minutes to explain it to you?"

"Well I'm at a job site right now, but I'll be able to take a break in about an hour. Are you okay you're not in any trouble are you?"

"No. no I'm fine nothing like that. It's not about me, but someone else. Listen I'll explain it all to you when I call you back in an hour okay?"

"Okay I'll wait for your call. Bye."

"Talk to you later."

A little over an hour passed before Monica called Reilly.

"Hello."

"Hey Reilly it's me. Can you talk now?"

"Yes I have a few minutes. What's up?"

"Well you see one of my roommates from school has the same problem I did before your rescue. Her parents are getting divorced and selling their house so she has no place to stay for the summer. I hate to impose upon your good graces, but she's in a bind just like I was. Can you help her out too by letting her stay with us just for the summer. She has money to pay you rent. Just say what you want to charge. What do you think?"

"Wow Monica that's a real surprise. I wasn't anticipating sharing my place with anybody until you called with an emergency situation. I don't know I have to think about that one."

"The problem with that is as I told you we both have to be out of the dorm on Friday."

"If she has money why can't she stay in a motel like you were going to do?"

"Well when I said she has money what I meant was her father is willing to pay, but not for any hotel or motel."

"How well do you know this girl?"

"We have spent our whole first year together in this apartment so I think I know her fairly well. Now she's not a saint. None of us are, but I don't think she would give you any problems."

"Is she there with you? I'd like to talk to her."

"Yes she is hold on a minute I'll put her on."

"Hello."

"Hi my name is Reilly what's yours?"

"My name is Caroline Clinton but everybody calls me CC."

"Where are you from?"

"Phildelphia."

"I understand your folks are splitting up and leaving you stranded?"

"Yeah I guess you can say that. Can you help me out?"

"I don't know CC. Put Monica back on I want to talk with her."

"I'm here what are we doing?

"Okay I've given it some thought and I'm going to allow it to happen, but only because of you. If she wasn't a friend of yours I wouldn't even consider it."

After thinking about it for several minutes, Reilly finally agreed to allow both Monica and CC to move in with her then she spoke to both of them.

"You know ladies even though I'm going to let you move in with me for the summer, but understand this it's only for those three months. I know you're both non working students, but you're going to have to help out with the expenses, you know like food, cleaning supplies etc, any way you can. I'm not going to set an amount, but I expect to get something for my hospitality."

Reilly laid down the rules and it was immediately agreed to so the move in date was set for that Friday. As they started to move their personal belongings in it became very clear that this arrangement was going to be a bit cramped. Closet space for example was definitely going to be an issue because all of the women had extensive wardrobes. Next there was only one queen size bed in the second bedroom and were the guests going to be comfortable in sharing it became the question? Finally there was only one bathroom - how were three women going to manage its use was decidedly going to be something for negotiation.

The first few days were a little challenging having to compromise on space and bathroom usage, but as grown intellectual ladies they managed to work it out. Within the next two weeks the kinks were ironed out and the flow of activity was like a well oiled machine. In addition the manager from Nords had called Monica to invite her to return there for temporary re-employment. CC was also able to find a job with the city in one of their college summer work programs. So it seemed that everything was going to work out fine.

It was not until William McMahon, Reilly's boyfriend started coming around that the smooth flow of activity got a little bumpy. She had been dating him for months and his coming to her place was not unusual for the couple. However, when the new guests moved in the privacy they once knew disappeared. When Billy, the name he went by, first met the new arrivals he couldn't help but be attracted to one of them. This time it wasn't Monica, who usually got first attention, but CC who caught his eye. Every time he came around and she was there he made some slight move to get closer to her. Reilly didn't pay much attention, at first, to his overtures because she was in love and he could do no wrong.

Over the course of time when his visits to see Reilly became more frequent and sometimes he would stay in her bedroom overnight the inevitable was bound to happen. One Sunday morning while the others slept CC got up and went in the kitchen to get some water. Still dressed in her loosely fitting nightgown she was startled when Billy came in. When she turned around the gown fell partially open exposing a hint of the large beautifully shaped breasts. Instead of pulling the gown together, when she noticed his gaze fixed on them she threw open the garment and gave him a complete view. The exposure didn't last long, but long enough to let him know an invitation was extended. Then she closed the gown wrapped her arms around herself and with an impish smile slowly walked by him back to her room. He stood there awhile caught up in the moment then went back to revisit Reilly.

Later on that morning as each one got up to eat breakfast there was an apparent disturbance in the usually quiet air. Even though by now Billy had left and the three women were together, it was CC who seemed to be a little different in her interactions with the others. Reilly noticed the difference in her and suspected it may have something to do with Billy, but her suspicions were based on the wrong assumption. She thought that CC may be jealous. To add fuel to this thought she began boasting about her lover saying that his friends refer to him as BTB which stands for Billy the bull and she was the only beneficiary of his service. Watching the expression on CC's face however, she was surprised at not seeing the reaction she was hoping for. CC meanwhile just smiled at her innuendo and dismissed the reference.

That night when Monica was visiting with her aunt which she had begun to do on a regular basis since she came home for the summer, during one of their conversations Trish inquired about her love life. Monica tried to sidestep the probe by saying she was working so hard doing extra hours to save money for her return to school she didn't have time for anything else. Trish, the savvy elder, detected the avoidance and was not about to let that reply evade the question.

"You know a young woman at your age even though you are pursuing higher education should not miss out on finding a good man. Now I know what you told me about your experiences with that guy who used you badly, but remember this, if you let your life be closeted because of the behavior of that one man then you're going to miss out on all the good men who are out there waiting for you."

"Yes I know Aunt Trish, but I just don't want to get caught up in another bad love affair right now. Let me move in that direction at my own pace and I think I'll be okay."

"Yes my dear I really believe that. It's just that you are such a beautiful girl with so much to offer I don't want to see you not have the best that life can bring. Okay I've said my piece and that's it."

That conversation ended and they went on talking about a number of other things. In Monica's mind however, Trish may have left the subject, but to Monica she knew that she was still looking for love perhaps still in all the wrong places. She couldn't tell her aunt, but she was frequenting the local bars and nightclubs with CC on many nights during the week. There was no short supply of suitors for both of the lookers so they could afford to be selective about the choice they made to become more than just friends with. Although nothing developed into any long term relationship for either of them, the knowledge that they would soon have to return to school kept them well grounded and benefitting from the experience in learning the habits of many types of men .

The summer months passed quickly and for Reilly the end of her accommodating her visitors couldn't come soon enough. Although the cramped space and bathroom usage had been worked out, it was certainly not like having it all to herself. In addition, every time Billy came around and CC was there something different in his behavior was causing her some anxiety. Nothing was blatantly obvious, but his attentions seemed to be diverted away from her frequently. Billy tried hard to always disguise his intentions, but after a while Reilly's suspicions elevated. She didn't want to confront him directly with what she thought because she believed it was just her imagination and CC never instigated any action to convince her otherwise. So she kept saying to herself in just a few more days the two of them will be gone and things will be like it was before between her and Billy.

Since her two guests moved in the relationship between Monica and Reilly became somewhat constrained. Not because of anything Monica did, but because of the entry of the third party that didn't seem to fit into the musketeer role. Monica sensed this at one point and asked Reilly about it. Reilly however not wanting to reveal her suspicions alwsy evaded the issue and never provided a direct answer to the question. It was not hard to detect Reilly's unwillingness to discuss the matter, so Monica discontinued pursuing it. Even though she knew there was a rift between the two of them, Monica did not want to escalate the difference any more than what it was so she backd off. There had never been, as long as she had known Reilly, any strain on their relationship so it was hard for her to understand what was happening. Even though she surmised the possibility of something to do with Billy, nothing she had ever witnessed would substantiate her conjecture so she dismissed it. She made a commitment to herself that before she left to return to school she was going to get some kind of an answer from Reilly about what was bothering her with their relationship.

It was the day before Monica and CC were to pack up and depart the apartment that Monica decided that now was the time to confront Reilly. Monica had already given Nord's notice of her final day so she left the store early and went to the apartment. Reilly was there when she walked in to her surprise.

'Wow I didn't expect to find you here. I just gave notice at my job that I'm leaving so I thought I would come and get started on packing up my stuff. Are you alright?"

"Well now that you ask no I am not feeling well at all. I've been this way for the last few days and I think I know the reason."

"You want to tell me about it. I need to talk to you about some things anyway before I leave so it may as well be now."

"Okay you can go first" said Reilly.

"You know and I've said this before and now I'll say it again we don't seem to be as close as we were before as the three musketeers. I know Soun Li is gone, but you and me there is something missing from our relationship that I can't identify. It seems ever since I moved in and brought CC we have drifted apart. I'don't know if it was something I did or said but it's different somehow. I can't leave not knowing what changed and if I did something to hurt you in some way. So you want to talk to me and help me to understand what happened?"

"Monica it's not you. I think we'll always be musketeers, but when you brought that girl in here somehow things changed. I really can't say that she's done anything wrong outright, but I get the feeling whenever Billy is around he slyly pays more attention to her than me. Maybe it's just in my mind, but I just can't help myself from thinking it. She's almost as pretty as you are and when I look at her it bothers me. I know you would never do anything to interfere with me and Billy, but I'm not so sure about her. Again she's done nothing so maybe I'm over thinking things and I'm the one who's jealous. But I may have been taking it out on you in my own strange way and for that I'm sorry. Anyway tomorrow you guys will be gone and that part of my life will return to the old normal."

"Reilly you know that you are one of my best friends besides Soun Li and I would never do anything to hurt you. If I had known that bringing CC here with me was going to cause any kind of trouble I would have left her to fend for herself. I wish you had said something earlier to me and maybe we could have worked out a different living arrangement since she got a job."

"Well girlfriend now that part is almost over I didn't tell you the rest of the story why I'm here now. Neither of you may have noticed, but I have been throwing up in the morning and I missed my last cycle. You know as well as I do what that probably means. I haven't gone to get it confirmed yet, but I think I'm pregnant."

"Wow! And I thought this was going to be a great day. I hate to have to leave you not knowing your fate, but both CC and I have to check in on Friday or we'll lose our reservation for the dorm apartment we had last year. When are you going to the doctor?"

"I have an appointment for tomorrow afternoon."

"Have you told Billy?"

"No I want to be absolutely sure before I do that. I don't want him to think that I'm trying to rope him into doing anything he doesn't want. Now please don't tell CC, this is just between you and me right?"

"Of course if that's the way you want it to be."

"Now this is not any of my business, but suppose you are pregnant? How will you tell your father?"

"That's another thing making me sick. I would rather jump off one of his buildings than have to tell him I can't continue on the path he has set for me right now. I may have to do the unthinkable and get an abortion. But let's not jump the gun here yet before I know the results of an examination. Maybe it's just a bad virus."

They both laughed and it was good for Monica to see her do that because even she could feel the tension rising in the room. Just as they were finishing their conversation CC walked in, greeted them both and said she was going to start packing. Reilly then said she was gong to go for a walk and get out of their way so she left. Monica and CC began packing with very little verbal exchange between them.

After a while CC reached the point where she told Monica she was almost finished packing and she was going out. She also said her return would probably be very late. Monica gave this announcement no particular attention and continued her packing. Around 11:30 she finished with her task and had everything ready to go for tomorrow's departure. When she looked at the clock and realized neither Reilly nor CC had come back in she started to wonder. Reilly's state of mind when she went out was questionable, but Monica didn't think that was applicable for CC. Not wanting to become too concerned she went in the living room and started watching television.

When Reilly left the apartment she wasn't sure where she was going, but she knew she had to get out of the apartment while her two guests were still there. The things on her mind were beginning to overwhelm her and not having any concrete answers to the questions was troubling. Driving around with no particular destination in mind she got on the main thoroughfare and just kept going until the warning light on her gas gauge told her she better stop somewhere and refill the tank. When she pulled into the next filling station it dawned on her that she had driven almost to Philadelphia, Pennsylvania. Had she subconsciously headed in that direction knowing it was where CC had come from? If so, what was she planning to do when she got there? The thoughts made no sense to her so after filling up the gas tank she got back in the car and turned around.

It was a beautiful night. The stars were shining brightly and the full moon gave a glow as if the whole world was at peace everywhere. Even the slight chill in the air could not distort the feeling of serenity. For most people the hint of the oncoming fall season was a time to be reflective of the year as it was approaching a new quarter. In Reilly's mind the night however peaceful in its appearance was not comforting nor was it reassuring that everything was going to be alright. When she got back within her neighborhood vicinity rather than go directly back to her apartment she decided to go and see her father. She wasn't sure just why she wanted to see him now, but it never strayed from her psyche even as an adult that whenever her heart troubled her he would be the one to provide a solution to the problem and give her a way out.

She started remembering when she was just a little girl around the age of ten and her mother became ill with a very debilitating disease, up until the time she died he was the one that made sure she was able to withstand the final outcome and endure the separation from the one who she loved deeply. Reilly's mother while she was in good health was her greatest cheerleader and advocate for whatever she wanted to do. It was for her that she excelled in school and brought home outstanding grades at every level. When she passed the trauma could only be eased by a father who understood the close relationship she had with her mother and provide a resource that could not replace her mother's love, but would establish a new bond that could give her the reassurance that her life was not ended and life had so much more to offer her. It was this feeling now that was moving her toward his house even though she wasn't quite sure how much she was prepared to tell him. When she got within two blocks of the house she looked at her watch then suddenly pulled over. The hour was late and did she want to upset him by showing up unannounced. She sat there for several minutes debating the pros and cons of making such an appearance. Was her need for his comforting words at this moment greater than letting him enjoy a good night's sleep without having to wonder about the welfare of his only child? She wrestled with the question and finally decided to move on with her life and withhold telling him anything about her possible pregnancy until she knew for sure that it was true.

Having run out of ideas on where to go now the last place left was to go to the one she had trusted with her love and confide in him what may be happening. She turned the car around and headed for his apartment hoping he would still be up. She had not spoken to him today and wasn't even sure that he would be there. Many times when he didn't know she was coming over he would hang out with his buddies and as a sports fan big time go to many of the local professional or even minor league events. Now she wondered should she call and let him know she was on her way or just drop in and surprise him. She concluded why not just drop in it would be good for her and hopefully for him.

When she arrived at his apartment building there were several cars parked on the street in front of his place. After finding a parking spot, she let herself in through the front vestibule doors and made her way up to the second floor. There was apparently a party or something going on in one of the other apartments because the music was playing at a high volume and you could hear people laughing and talking loudly. So she thought rather than ring his door bell she would use her key and let herself in. Quietly she opened the door and walked in. He was not in the living room so she made her way to the back bedroom and when she opened that door the shock to her eyes was so devastating she almost feinted, but managed to catch herself and run blindly back out the door. Running down the stairs she was having a hard time processing what she thought she saw.

CHAPTER 13

Found And Lost

Seasons change in an orderly fashion and almost everyone can usually tell when one cycle slides into the next. Signs indicating the culmination of one and the beginning of another present themselves in an overt display of nature's ability to transform with dazzling brilliance as the season requires. In the fall the trees transition and become a tapestry for the magnificent array of colors on the leaves that only the master painter could achieve; in the winter the newly fallen snow presents a purity of peaceful calm as it blankets the earth; in the spring the awakening of the planted seeds and the birth of new foliage portends the possibility of good things to come; and finally the summer completes the cycle of life when what has been birthed in the spring gathers strength and rises to greater heights. As the seasons follow a pattern of change that is almost predictable, not so is the heart of man. "The heart is deceitful above all things and beyond cure - who can understand it?" (Jeremiah 17-9 NIV)

As Reilly ran blindly out the door of Billy's apartment with tears streaming down her face her exposure to the deceit of the heart was devastating. No words of consolation or fond embraces at this point could mollify the hurt she felt now. She sat in her car for several minutes trying to unravel the confusion that was going through her mind processing the image she just witnessed. When she finally recovered enough to drive safely she headed straight for her own apartment and went in. The hour was late, but Monica was still up because she was worried about the whereabouts of her friends because neither of them had come home. Reilly threw open the door and boldly entered half crying and half screaming.

"Monica, Monica how could you do this to me? I thought you were my best friend."

Monica totally confused by the vehement declaration tried desperately to calm her down and quickly asked the question.

"Reilly what happened to you, what's wrong?"

"You must have known she was a snake when you brought her into my house. Why did you let her bite me?"

"Please, please tell me what you're talking about I don't understand."

"CC, that's who I'm talking about. I just came from Billy's apartment. I thought I would drop by and surprise him and when I quietly let myself in and opened his bedroom door what did I see, but him screwing CC. No that's not quite right, what I saw was her on top of him riding him like a jockey on a thoroughbred stallion. I've never been so shocked in all my life and it's all your fault. Now what am I supposed to do?"

"Reilly I'm so sorry I don't know what to say. I never thought in my wildest imagination that she was capable of doing such a thing, especially after you were kind enough to offer her a place to stay when she needed it most. What can I do? How can I help right this wrong and make it right?"

After Monica said this, Reilly realized she had nothing to do with CC's behavior she calmed down a bit and sat on the couch gently sobbing.

"I guess she'll be coming here to collect her things before moving out so I guess I'll confront her then " Reilly said.

"Reilly I know you're extremely hurt, but you won't do anything rash like trying to kill her will you?"

"No, that hadn't crossed my mind, but it's not a bad idea. No I think I'll just have it out with her and tell her to get her things out of here along with her body right now whenever she comes in."

It was now about 1:00 am when the door opened and CC sauntered in with a smile on her face. She had no idea that Reilly had seen her with Billy.

"Hey guys why are you still up?"

That's when Reilly lost it and launched herself at CC. Had it not been for Monica pulling her off she may have carried out the thought from a while ago.

"You whore after what I did for you letting you stay here for the whole summer how could you do that to me?"

CC now realizing she had been caught was at a loss for words. Stuttering a bit she offered no apology, but just turned around headed for the door and mumbled she would come back later this morning and get her things. Monica watched her leave and then wrapped her arms around Reilly as they both sat on the couch amazed at CC's attitude.

Later that morning just as she promised CC opened the door threw her keys down on the foyer table and gathered her belongings. Reilly and Monica were there watching her. There was no confrontation, no verbal exchange of any kind just glaring looks of animosity. The wall of silence between all of them was loud enough to be heard for miles around. When CC finished carrying out her things her last words were directed not at Reilly, but at Monica.

"See you at the dorm kiddo."

In response Monica offered.

"Yes I will see you there, but there's no way I will share a room, a couch not even a blanket with you as long as we are in school." .

The brief conversation ended and CC left. Monica stayed long enough after that to try and console Reilly as much as she could, but words would not nor could not undo what had been done to her best friend because of the girl she had brought into her life. Time was running out when Monica had to also be on the road so with her last best offer she told Reilly she would always be her friend and she would call her as soon as she got settled in the dorm. She also let Reilly know that she wasn't sure how she was going to do it at this point, but she was going to find another place to live as far away from CC as she could manage. Reilly through her tear stained eyes embraced her and said goodbye and goodluck.

When Monica finally got to the dormitory apartment building her first stop was to go and see the on site resident advisor. She explained partially, without going into minute detail, the situation between CC and herself and requested another room assignment. The RA answered her and said that every apartment in this building had already been assigned so unless one of the other students was willing to swap with her, there was nothing he could do. Call it fate, Divine intervention, Providence or just plain luck as Monica stood there wondering what else to do another student came in with the same type of complaint about her roommate and seeking an exchange. The swap was made and Monica went to her new apartment to meet her roommates.

From that day throughout the rest of her time at NYU Monica avoided CC like she carried a plague. Even when they had classes together Monica would sit as far away from her as she possibly could. The years went by and both girls were ready to graduate still not speaking to one another. Monica was awarded a fellowship to continue study at the school so she enrolled in the MBA program. CC decided to go elsewhere so the relationship ended. After their sophomore year Margie developed a serious drug problem and was forced to drop out. Monica continued to frequently visit with her aunt and attended church regularly with her. It was on one of those visits right after she returned to school when the spirit finally got through to her.

It was a bright and sunny Sunday morning when the two of them walked into Holy Trinity as they usually did and took seats in the same pews that they usually sat in. The service started at the same time as it usually did and the program followed the same traditional script as it usually did, but today somehow things were different for Monica. She had visited with her old friend Reilly the day before coming to Trish's apartment and they worked out their strained relationship for the better. Reilly's pregnancy scare turned out to be just that and she had forgiven Billy his indiscretion so they were back together and planning to get married. So Monica was feeling good and ready to worship. Reverend Dumas walked to the sacred desk and began.

"Good morning once again my brothers and sisters in the Lord, He has blessed us with another fine sunny day. Remember this is the day that the Lord has made so let us rejoice and be glad in it. I sincerely hope you have been blessed with the messages from above this far and are ready now to receive what more God has to offer. Let us pray. Heavenly father gracious and almighty God I stand before your throne of grace humbly presenting myself as your willing servant wanting to proclaim the good news from the heavenly kingdom. Anoint these lips for preaching and hide me behind the cross so all of God's children may see Jesus. Let the words of my mouth and the meditation of my heart be acceptable to you oh Lord my strength and my redeemer.

In my last sermon I left off at the point where Jesus had been baptized by His cousin John and had His first confrontation with Satan the devil to be tempted by him. After overcoming and not yielding to any of his temptations Jesus began His healing and teaching ministry throughout the region. Along the way He made disciples out of ordinary men who were mostly fishermen and told them they would become fishers of men. As

He traveled the land He began to spread the good news about the coming kingdom of God and what it would mean when they accepted and believed in Him. Today we are going to conclude the sermon series and I will be referencing primarily the gospel according to St. John beginning at chapter 2 verses 1-4. This is the detailed beginning of his performance of miracles throughout the land. The scripture reads: 'On the third day a wedding took place at Cana in Galilee. Jesus mother was there and Jesus and His disciples had also been invited to the wedding. When the wine was gone, Jesus mother said to him, They have no wine. Dear woman why do you involve me? Jesus replied. My time has not yet come.

Even though he said this His mother told the servants do what he tells you to. Nearby there were six stone water pots that were usually used for ceremonial washing. Each pot held about twenty to thirty gallons of water. Jesus told the servants to go and fill the pots with water, which they did. Now when the master of the house tasted from the pots it was new wine and he commented that at weddings it is usual that the choicest wine be brought out first and then the cheaper wine afterward. Remember now at this wedding the choice wine from the master had already run out. Then he marveled saying that the best wine, that which Jesus had made, had been saved for last. Not only did He turn the water into wine, but He made twenty to thirty gallons which was more than enough for the party. Brothers and sisters the point here is that when you call on Him and He blesses you it will not be with anything cheap and it will be more than enough. When you have a need and you call on Him you can expect to receive His best at the right time.

After this He went down into Jerusalem around the annual Passover festival and went into the temple. There He saw the patrons buying and selling sheep and cattle and doves and money changers doing business as if this was a market. He was so angry that He took a whip and drove them all out declaring that my father's house is a house of worship how dare you turn it into a market place.

By now all of the people had seen the miracles He had done and it made the Jewish religious hierarchy angry because the people were turning to Him. But there was one man who though he was part of that hierarchy whose name was Nicodemus came to Jesus by night and said no one could perform the miraculous signs you do unless God is with him. Then Jesus answered him and said unless a man be born again he cannot see the kingdom of God. And Nicodemus bewildered questioned Him saying how can a man be born again when he is old; can he enter into his mother's womb again? Jesus answered no one can enter into the kingdom of God unless he is born of water and the spirit. Flesh gives birth to flesh, but the Spirit gives birth to spirit. Understand this saints you must be baptized to receive that Spirit. It's not too late now, but the time is growing short to allow you to do so.

Let us continue. After His encounter with Nicodemus He went on preaching the word and telling the people that God so loved the world that He gave His only begotten son, Mary's baby, that whoever believes in Him shall not perish but have eternal life. God did not send His son into the world to condemn it, but through Him the world might be saved.

There were many other teachings and miracles that He did which time will not permit me to go into. I will touch on a few more here before I close, but I encourage you to read the entire book of John's gospel so that you get the full understanding of what He did for you and for me. Among some of he other teachings He became known for was His gift to to a Samaritan woman who He met at a well in Samaria. Now at that time Jews and Samaritans were not the best of friends, in fact they didn't even like one another so when Jesus met this woman at a well and asked her to give Him a drink of water, at first she balked saying You are a Jew and I am a Samaritan how can you ask me for a drink? Jesus replied If you knew the gift of God and who it is that asks you for a drink, you would have asked him and He would have given you living water. Then she asked where can you get this living water? Then He told her that whoever drinks from this well will be thirsty again, but whoever drinks the water I give him will never thirst. The water I give will become in him like a spring of water welling up to eternal life. She was so convinced that she went back into town and told everybody about this man and based on her testimony many of them came to believe in Him.

He continued performing miracles throughout the region such as healing a man at a pool in Bethesda who had been crippled for thirty-eight years. The next miracle is one that I believe many of you are familiar with. He took two fish and five loaves of bread and fed five thousand people and had twelve baskets left over. That night after they were finished

His disciples went out into the lake before Him, then He came to them walking on the water. At first they were afraid thinking it was a ghost, but he assured them it was Him then Peter bid Him to let him walk on the water too and Jesus said come. Peter got out of the boat and indeed started walking on the water until he took his eyes off of Jesus and he started to sink. The point here is keep your eyes focused on Him and you will not drown.

There were many other miracles which He performed too many to cover in this brief sermon, but I will continue to touch on those you may be familiar with. For example one day when He was teaching in the temple the Pharisees brought in a woman who was caught in adultery and they made her stand before the group. Then they said to Jesus she was caught in the very act and according to law of Moses she should be stoned to death. They were doing this to try and trap Jesus in a quandary between obeying the law of Moses or not. Jesus cleverly upset their trap by posing to them that if anyone of them could stand there who has not sinned let him throw the first stone. As the accusers went away Jesus asked the woman where are they - has no one condemns you? She answered no and He replied neither do I condemn you go now and sin no more. Another famous one is the healing of a dead man called Lazarus in the town of Bethany. Now this man was a friend who had two sisters named Mary and Martha. One day after Lazarus became sick and died word was sent to Jesus that he had passed. Instead of rushing to his side to recover him Jesus waited two more days where He was. His intent was to prove to the people He had the power over life and death. By the time Jesus got to where Lazarus was entombed he had been dead for four days. Martha got word that Jesus was coming so she ran out ot meet Him and said if you had been here my brother would not have died. There were many Jews at the house comforting the sisters and when they also heard He had come, they also went out to meet Him. When he got to the tomb He said for the benefit of those who do not believe in me I'm going to call him. Then he said: "Lazarus come out." After that Lazarus came walking out and Jesus told the people to remove his grave clothes and let him go. Now this prominent act further infuriated the priests and they feared losing their authority among the people so they began plotting from that time on how to dispose of Jesus.

At this point Jesus knew that His time on earth was nearing an end. It was just before the Passover Feast that He having shown his love for His own who were in the world, now showed them the full extent of His love. That night when the evening meal was being served, He got up poured water into a basin and began to wash His disciples' feet drying them with a towel He had wrapped around His waist. When He finished then he said to them "Now that I, your Lord and teacher have washed your feet you also should wash one another's feet. I have set you an example that you should do as I have done for you." It was at this supper He revealed that one of them was going to betray Him and when Judas Iscariot had been identified, Jesus told him to go and do quickly what you must do.

Later that same night the disciples were told He had to go back to His father, but the Counselor, the Holy Spirit whom the Father will send in my name, will teach you all things and will remind you of everything I have said to you. Soon after that the group assembled in an olive grove in the Kidron Valley where Jesus would go to pray. Now Judas had already carried out his task and alerted the Sanhedrin about where Jesus would be, so Judas came there guiding a detachment of soldiers and officials from the chief priests and Pharisees. They were carrying torches, lanterns, and weapons. When the soldiers asked who was Jesus and He said "I am He" the power of His word knocked the soldiers and the others to the ground.

From this point on Jesus was brought before the religious governing body as well as the Romans. First He was taken to the Jewish high priest, Caiaphas where He was questioned and then taken to the Roman governor Pontius Pilot. Pilot tried to avoid the issue because it was a religious charge and said to the Jews that they should judge him under your own laws. But when the Jews said they had no right to execute anyone then Pilot agreed to question Jesus. Pilot asked Jesus if He was the king of the Jews and He replied "You are right in saying I am a king. In fact for this reason I was born and for this I came into the world, to testify to the truth."

After this the severe punishment was started. Pilot had him flogged, that is beaten and the soldiers twisted a crown of thorns on His head. Pilot made a second attempt to release Jesus, but the Jews adamantly called for Him to be crucified. And so Jesus was crucified, nailed to a cross, pierced with a sword in His side and hung between two sinners while his mother, Mary the wife of Clopas, Mary Magdalene and John the disciple, He loved watched. Later knowing that all was completed so that the Scripture would be fulfilled, Jesus said: "It is finished" and died. However this is not the end my brothers and sisters because on the third day just as He had said He rose from the grave and appeared to many. He appeared first to Mary Magdalene who stood at the tomb where He had been buried crying, and He said to her do not touch me for I have not yet returned to my father, but go and tell them, the disciples, that I am returning to my Father and your Father, to my God and your God. After that He appeared to the disciples twice. The first time Thomas who is called doubting Thomas because he said that he would not believe in the resurrection until he was able to see the nail scars in His hands and place his hand in His side, was not there so Jesus appeared a second time when He was there to allow him to do what he asked for. Then Jesus told him, "Because you have seen me, you have believed, blessed are those who have not seen and yet have believed."

After this Jesus appeared to many others before His ascension back to His Father, but He finally challenged His disciples to go into the world and make disciples of all nations spreading the gospel of the kingdom of God.

This is the end of the earthly life of Jesus the Christ, but the beginning of His heavenly watch over His children and under His watchful eye we who believe will receive eternal life leading to salvation by the gift of the Holy Spirit. My brothers and sisters you heard the word as I have received it and now it is your chance to become true belieers in the Word as it has been presented to you. As you have been told before there is no time left for you to delay. The world is fast coming to an end as you know it. At that time there will be no more opportunity for you to save yourself from the terrible disasters that will befall this earth. Know this that the time is fast approaching when those who have not received the gift of life will not have that opportunity. Come now before the altar of God and of Jesus and receive His blessing. The door is opened. The sacrifice that Jesus made for you is when He shed His blood so that you may not have to shed yours, the gift of God is free, but the cost of rejection will be high. Save yourself now. You have heard the Word now believe the truth that is the Word of God. My sisters and brothers what is about to happen on this earth is called the great tribulation and it will be like nothing you have ever witnessed before in your life. Do not miss the rapture when Jesus returns to receive His people unto Him and be spared the coming calamities and atrocities.

Come now you have been shown the path that leads to salvation, let your heart be your guide and respond to that feeling of spiritual movement in your soul. Let your feet move in the direction that will give you peace and understanding once you accept Him into your life. No longer will you be saddled with the guilt feeling and that has been weighing down on your mind. Come and give your hand to a deacon, but give your heart to God. Don't let this opportunity pass you by. Come now, come now.

When Reverend Dumas finished making his appeal there were many who rose and started toward the altar. Among them was Monica who had been once again wrestling with the idea, and battling with the evil spirit that hovered over her. This time she did not succumb to the fear that held her back, but boldly approached the throne of grace and gave her life to Jesus.

As she walked down the aisle to the altar, the feeling that Trish held in her heart was overwhelming and the tears rained down from her eyes. She was so happy to see that which she had been praying for was finally coming to pass. Monica received the acceptance of the church and was placed on the schedule to receive preparation for baptism.

After the service back at Trish's apartment the celebration was one that Trish had been hoping for some time Even though it came as a surprise Trish was intent on preparing something to acknowledge Monica's new journey. There was nothing in the cupboard worthy of what she had in mind so she insisted they go and enjoy a night out. The restaurant she chose was not the most expensive one in town, but one that was very popular. When they walked in it was not too crowded so the wait time for seating was short. Once they were shown to a table who should be seated near them was Reilly and Billy. Not sure how to react to seeing her back together again with Billy, Monica waved her hand acknowledging them and sat down. There was no further communication between them. Trish and Monica celebrated in high fashion and it seemed like this was the beginning of a new life for the young lady.

From that time on Monica seemed to have discovered what she had been missing in her life. She completed her B.A. Degree in Business then went on to earn an MBA also from NYU. It wasn't long after she graduated that her resume caught the attention of an employment specialist at a highly touted placement agency. The agent forwarded her resume with a glowing recommendation to the hiring manager at one of the world's leading cosmetics companies. Within a few days she was called in for an interview and shortly after that was offered a position in their sales and marketing division in their midtown office in the city. She was so happy that she couldn't wait to inform her aunt which she did that night.

The position seemed to fit perfectly with her background and experience having worked at Nord's and she was quickly becoming acclimated to her assignment. She was being mentored by a training manager named Evelyn Edwards who immediately saw in her the potential for becoming one of the company's best sales managers. Over the course of a short time their close association revealed some common likes and interests and they became more than work associates, but friends. EV as she was called around the office made sure that she was given choice assignments and helped her to avoid the common pitfalls that most new employees at this company fell into. At Brevon Cosmetics it was possible to aspire quickly to higher management if you excelled in sales and showed a propensity to manage large accounts. Monica had both of these skills and it didn't take long for it to be recognized.

She seemed to be moving along at a speedy pace toward entering into the upper echelon of the sales management ranks when things changed. It was at a major sales meeting and to her it was as if fate had arranged for them to meet. When they were introduced by one of their colleagues she was doing all she could to not swoon because of his exceptionally good looks. When he took her hand and held it an unusually long time, she was about to lose all emotional control. To say that he was handsome, in her eyes, would be a gross understatement.

It was after that meeting when he invited her and her female associate Evelyn, out for some after work cocktails that she hoped he would ask her out alone. It seemed as if he could read her mind and when the moment presented itself he made his move. When Evelyn excused herself from the table to go to the powder room, Troy, the man of the hour, seized the opportunity. Apparently, he was as attracted to her as she was enamored of him and the signals were clear on both sides. By the time EV returned, Monica had already accepted his invitation to dinner the following night. It was not hard to sense that something had transpired in her absence because the mood and the conversation took another direction. As Evelyn looked at the face of her associate and protégé then at his, there was no need to guess what had happened. Not that she had any interest in or designs on Troy, but she was still curious about exactly what did happen.

After about an hour and a half of casual drinking and jovial conversation, it occurred to him that none of them had eaten anything so he suggested they all go into the restaurant and order. EV was quick to decline saying she had to go home while Monica hesitated for a moment before also saying she had to leave. He expressed his disappointment at ending the night so soon, but acknowledged their choice. They exchanged pleasantries and wished each other a goodnight and the ladies walked out together.

Once outside Monica told EV what had happened and she was going to call her as soon as she got home because she wanted to know more about him. EV knew him quite well since she had worked with him for a number of years. That night around 9:00 O'clock, much later than the time Monica said she was going to call, EV's phone rang.

Ring, ring, ring.

"Hello."

"Hi EV it's Monica. Sorry to call you later than I said, but you won't believe what happened when I got home."

"Nothing bad I hope."

"Well not really bad, but it required my immediate attention."

"Something you want to talk about?"

"No it's okay I dealt with it. I'll tell you about it some other time. Now I just want to talk about that man you introduced me to. Who exactly is he and what's his status?"

"Monica before we go any further believe me I just introduced you to him because he can help you work wise, not as a potential love interest."

"Yeah okay I got all that, now who is he?"

"One word of warning, you will be playing with fire if you get too involved with him. I would hate to see you get severely burned on my account."

"Wow! Is he that dangerous?"

"He could be if you're not prepared to handle him."

"Okay I've been warned, thanks. Now is he married, engaged, attached - what?"

"Let's start with his full name maybe that will give you a hint. It's Troy Donner and his guys call him TD because he never fails to score. Are you listening?"

"Yes I'm with you go ahead."

"I think when he came to this office about four years ago he had just finished a divorce. He came in with a bravado that impressed everyone around him, even me. I'll tell you this. You won't be the first lady to set their sights on him and come away somewhat damaged. Won't go into details, but again just be aware when you start something up with him."

"Okay - good advice. Now you said that he could help me career wise, what does that mean?"

"Well since you're on that high commission plan for your product line, you know he is one of the district sales managers for your area. He could direct a lot of solid leads your way, if he wanted to. Get the picture?"

"Yeah I got you. Anyway as I told you he asked me out to dinner tomorrow and I said yes so guess I have to go."

"Alright girlfriend go for it, but as I said just be careful."

"I will. Thanks for the tips I'll talk with you tomorrow."

"Okay, goodnight."

"Goodnight."

After that first date, the time they spent together felt like nothing she ever experienced in a relationship before. In all of her twenty-eight years of life, even though she had many suitors, there was never one who made her feel the way she did with him. Being a very attractive and shapely young woman afforded her the privilege of being highly selective about who she chose to allow into her inner circle.

For the first few months it seemed that all would go well forever. They went everywhere together and did most things together. He plied her with a number of small gifts and flowers on a regular basis and she felt like she was on top of the world. He introduced her to his friends and the gang they hung out with was some real party types who enjoyed the best that life had to offer. Taking risks just to have fun was their motto. For Monica it had been a long time since she was a part of that world and she thought she was never going back to that scene, but his charm held sway over her and she was caught up in whatever he said do. Gradually though over many months, very close to their first year together, she began to notice things about him that she had never observed before. Maybe it was because she was initially blinded emotionally by the love bug or perhaps she just didn't want to admit to herself that something could go wrong. In any event when she finally was able to see clearly what he was doing to her, getting away from him was difficult. Whenever she tried to leave him, her strength failed.

They had started living together in a new apartment enjoying the happiness of marital conjugation without the encumbrance of any legal traditional ceremony. Why buy the cow when you can get the milk free was Troy's misguided philosophy. Life seemed to be beautiful for the couple until one day when she came home from work early because she was not feeling well, she walked in and found him with another woman in their bed. The surprising discovery sent her reeling backward and she almost feinted. Before she hit the floor she was able, however, to compose herself to turn around and run out the door.

Later that day after she had called Rev. Dumas who she had become fairly close to and told him about her ordeal, he counseled her and helped her to recover temporarily. She called Troy at the apartment to say she wanted him out of there. He answered and attempted to apologize, but she was not accepting any of it. For a long time she had suspected he was doing something like this before, but had never been able to confirm it until now. Actually catching him, was the final act that she was willing to tolerate and for her it was really over.

Even though she called it quits in her mind, her heart was not cooperating with the thought. She began spiraling downward into an abyss that was placing her in such a depressed state that the thought of ending it all crossed her mind. EV could see what was happening to her and just like the good friend she had become tried to comfort her letting her know that this was not the end of her life. Monica's work also started to slip and attention to her clients became negligent. She had abandoned drinking to any great extent before hanging out with his friends, but now she was prone to go back to the apartment at night and have a drink or two or three to go to sleep. She even stopped calling the reverend for help. Troy was gone from the place, but his presence was still there.

Each day that she arose was like reliving the same nightmare over and over again without a way to wake up. On the job she would show up at her desk, but her attention to even making the little things happen that used to endear her customers to her were now absent. Even her supervisor who was accustomed to praising her for sales acumen and raising the bar for other sales representatives around noticed the difference in her attitude and went to EV to try and find out what was happening. EV who had long since launched Monica on her own was reluctant to reveal the depth of the problem nor even mention that she knew exactly what was wrong. Instead she would cover for her and say that she was going through a slump period just like all of the other super stars in the game. The supervisor accepted this explanation for the time being and backed off confronting Monica.

One night after work and Monica had had one of her worse days since she came to the company she called EV and spilled the content of her heart.

"Hello."

"EV it's Monica did you hear about what happened to me today?"

"No but I imagine it wasn't anything good. So what happened?"

"Well I lost the Vonderbuilt account after a disagreement with Mr. Yeager the CEO."

"Oh my God that was your biggest customer wasn't it? What exactly went wrong?"

'He wanted to place an extremely large order for the Fabuline Facial treatment gift set and I told him it was impossible to get it to him by the date he wanted. In the past I used to be able to persuade him to accept a later date for shipment by either promising him something extra for waiting or do whatever I could swing from production, but this time for some unknown reason I went off and told him he was out of his mind to even expect that. Of course he got angry and told me he was going to find another vendor. Then stupid me, instead of trying to pacify him I got salty too and it just escalated to an argument. He hung up and about fifteen minutes later I received an email from their legal department terminated the account. EV I don't know what's happening to me. What should I do?"

"Monica listen to me very closely. You are taking the breakup with Troy much too hard. I saw him yesterday when he came by here to speak to one of my other trainees and he didn't seem a bit the worse for wear. You know he moved down to the satellite office in Brooklyn that's why we haven't been seeing him around here lately. I'm telling you for this reason he was laughing and smiling as if nothing between you guys had occurred.

He was treating you like just another notch in his gun belt. That's why you have got to pull yourself together, forget him and refocus on your career. You have a bright future here don't blow it on somebody like him. You haven't started drinking or taking drugs have you?"

Monica hesitated answering for several minutes then she replied.

"Well yes, but I'm still in control, I think."

"If you were then what happened today wouldn't have happened would it?"

"No, you're right. I know you're right. Well thanks again for hearing me out and as usual giving me sound advice. I'm throwing away the bottle and the pills now."

"Good! See you tomorrow right?"

"Yeah, right. Goodnight."

"So long."

After they hung up Monica went into the kitchen intending to get herself a cup of coffee, but there on the counter staring her in the face was the half empty bottle of gin from last night. Temptation was challenging her and even now it was funny at that moment she recalled the reverend's sermon about Jesus' confrontation with Satan and Him not yielding to the temptations of the evil one. She laughed and said to herself "Jesus I'm not as strong as you" then picked up the bottle poured a hefty drink and gulped it down. That was the first of a few before she retired to bed on an empty stomach.

The next morning after a fitful dreamless sleep she woke up about an hour after her usual time and frantically scrambled to get ready to go to work. When she got there the message light on her telephone was blinking. With some sense of trepidation she started reviewing them. The first one was from another customer wanting to place an order so she wrote down the name and number and would return the call later. The second one was more urgent because something had happened with a shipment that was supposed to have been delivered yesterday that had not arrived and the customer was not very happy and finally the last one was a veiled threat from another sales rep threatening to expose her about some items missing from the stock room that he knew she had taken. She wasn't in the office more than ten minutes when her day was already off to a very shaky start. Before she sat down at her desk she went to the break room got a very large cup of coffee hoping it would be the medication she needed to get through today. It did help for the moment, but the problems she was facing were still there and she had to decide just how she was going to handle each one. The easiest one was to place the order so she did that. Secondly she went into the computer to see where that missing shipment was and found out that it had been delivered, but to the customer's warehouse instead of their store. It appeared that shipping had miss labeled the shipment. She was able to resolve that one fairly quickly also and re-routed the shipment then called the customer apologized and promised the goods would be in the store today. The last one from the sales rep was not so easily dismissed because she had no idea what he was talking about. She had not taken anything from the stock room or any other place at work so how could they say she did. Whether to call back and confront the caller or wait and see if anything else would happen, because she knew she was innocent, was her dilemma. She decided to take the be patient and see road.

The rest of the today was uneventful and she managed to muddle through it without doing any further damage to any more of her accounts. By the time the work day was over, again she had that bothersome headache that was caused not only by the work stress, but as a result of the sleepless previous night. When she got home she promised not to repeat last night's acts so she fixed herself a good dinner, watched TV and went to bed rather early. It was about midnight when she was awakened by the bright glow in the room. It had been some time now since she had been paid a visit by her grandmother Lois, and she hoped that it really was her. However, there was a distinct difference in the appearance of this glow. It had a strange glimmer which Lois never presented and this time noises coming from inside were eerie and frightening. So she sat straight up in the bed and then it happened.

CHAPTER 14

The Revelation

14 "Do not let your hearts be troubled.
You believe in God[a]; believe also in me.
² My Father's house has many rooms;
if that were not so, would I have told you
that I am going there to prepare a place
for you? ³ And if I go and prepare a place
for you, I will come back and take you to
be with me that you also may be where I am.
⁴ You know the way to the place where I am going
⁵ Thomas said to him, "Lord, we don't know
where you are going, so how can we know
the way?"
⁶ Jesus answered, **"I am the way** and the truth
and the life. No one comes to the Father
except through me. (NIV 14:1-6)

The light shone brightly making it difficult to ignore. It's blinding luminosity should have created a sense of fear and awe because of the brilliance, but even when they glanced at it they refused to cower at it's presence. They continued to act as though it wasn't even there. Moving about haphazardly scurrying around trying to fulfill a destiny that, in the end, they could not begin to imagine what it will be. It was hard to comprehend why they continued to ignore the light when it was there to guide them to their perceived destiny.

Power and majesty was in the light, but they couldn't see it. Strength and courage was also in the light, but they did not perceive it. From time to time one would separate from the masses and declare a reverence for the light. Words, words and more words were spoken and books were written proclaiming the benefits of the light, but the masses did not heed and chose to continually ignore the teachings.

When darkness falls and covers the earth it is nothing but the absence of light. During this time while the masses parade around groping to find their way, many are frustrated because there is no switch to pull or button to press that would restore the light immediately. The timing of the appearance of light is dependent upon where the source is. Daylight in the East does not occur at the same time as in the West. One does not negate the other, but plays a role in support of the timing for its appearance. When one dominates then the other waits patiently for it's turn looking beyond the depths or the height of the horizon. True light cannot be extinguished, but must be seen according to the timing.

* * * * * * *

Monica thought that she had found the true source of light once she got baptized. For a while she no longer stumbled around in life's maze. She truly believed darkness for her was lifted and the path to the source was being made abundantly clear. Now that she could see clearly the direction she needed to go what was stopping her? All the personal baggage she was still carrying caused by a compilation of all of life's trials and tribulations were weighing her down and impeding her attempts to move forward. Backsliding was something she came to know.

Even though she believed she had found the light, shedding the baggage was difficult. When light shines in darkness it illuminates the path, but seeing the Way and moving toward it requires something she was lacking. Years of built up guilt and internal strife was still causing her to be hesitant. She understood that the path before her would lead to salvation, but in her mind there still was a doubt that prevented her feet from taking that next step. She had been told and counseled many times before by Reverend Dumas and each time she was strengthened by his words. But whenever she left him for even a short time, her strength seemed to wane. Looking in the mirror she often asked herself why does this happen to me? For a while she enjoyed a temporary release from the depression that was encumbering her and she was again drawn toward the light with a new sincere commitment to follow it. But then the vicissitudes, the ups and downs of life continued to oppress her. Whenever she looked back over her early life and reflected on all that had been done to her, it was like looking into a historic videotape that was stuck on replay. Even the short periods of happiness which would embrace her periodically were obscured by the persistent shadows.

Leaving behind her former crowd that had been a large part of her refusing to acknowledge even the existence of the light, she was convinced her new start would solve everything. Breaking away from that environment which seemed to have a strangle hold on her, was not easy. Running from what she really believed at one time was the answer to all of her problems, was the most difficult race she had ever entered. Under the tutelage of Rev. Dumas she had gained a sense of priority for her life and sincerely believed that she now had it all under control, but every time she felt comfortable in her new found emotional stability, something would inevitably happen that caused her to relapse. Whenever she thought about Troy and how he had totally drawn her into his web and was in full control of her life, the wall she put up to block him, melted.

Reflections on the beginning of their relationship always seemed to brighten her spirit temporarily, but then as the reverie continued the somber points overtook the joy and the smile turned upside down. No one could ever have convinced her at the start of their relationship that she had not found true happiness, but it was not long before she began to realize that something was out of sorts. The maze of life she was running through seemed to build up more dead ends, as she ran, than it had paths for progress.

EV had warned at the start and even when it became obvious Monica was in deeper water than she was able to tread her warnings became more dire. Monica failed to heed her warnings and at one point felt that the warnings were just a ploy to get her away from Troy so that she could have a shot at him. Blinded by the deep emotional tie she had developed, Monica was unable to see any truth that would be told by anyone concerning her lover. It was not until the affair began to take a deep turn toward the inevitable ending that she finally was able to come to grips with the truth. Her eyes were opened and the scales that had kept her from seeing clearly dissipated and fell.

Now she had to decide what to do next after separating herself from him and believing that the affair had truly ended. Moving on after all she had been through and experienced with him was not easy, but whenever she looked in a mirror and the image that was reflected back to her was frightening enough to make her realize something had to change. Her former beauty and radiance was diminishing rapidly and the more time she had spent in his presence it became obvious what the cause was.

Still it was unclear in her mind what she should do. Successfully running away from the truth is impossible because it will always be there and eventually will overtake you. Avoidance of it only prolongs the time before it catches up. As she continued to go to work and try to salvage some of the mess she created with her accounts she was only mildly successful. Sitting at her desk one day not fully focused on her daily work requirements, she was perusing something she had received in the mail from one of her clients. It was a brochure advertising a number of cruise options boasting that sailing is the best way to relieve stress and relax tensions. The more she read and envisioned herself on one of these luxury ships, with it's elegant staterooms, the more the idea became more appealing to her.

It was not until the end of the workday that she finally concluded this was the answer. Taking a cruise and getting away for awhile seemed like the ideal thing to do and perhaps regain her inner strength and composure. So it was decided. Arriving at her apartment and walking in she noticed the light on the answering machine was blinking. The last thing she was hoping for was a message from him, especially after the last argument they had.

Before listening to the message she hesitated for a moment feeling a sense of fear. When she finally pushed the button it was not until after hearing two spam calls that she heard the one she feared the most.

"Hi, I know you're not there, but I just wanted to leave this with you. Maybe you think I was wrong for what I said and the things I did, but believe me I do love you and never meant to hurt you. I'm leaving the state now and going away so you will not have to see me anymore. When I get settled where I'm going I'll get in touch and let you know. I wish you well and hope maybe one day we can be together again."

After listening to the whole message she had to sit down. Her emotions were betraying her again. The part about his love for her was throwing her balance off as it usually did. Not knowing whether to cry or just dismiss the news she sat still for awhile taking in the message content. Thinking that the wall she had built to block him out was finally holding she was having trouble convincing herself this status was true.

While listening to the messages she was still holding the travel brochure and now it seemed more like a good idea than even before. The call was placed and a travel agent answered.

"Hello - Ideal Cruises this is Michael may I plan a trip for you?"

"Hi, my name is Monica and I'm interested in taking one of your cruises. I'm looking at one of your brochures and I was thinking about using the offer listed for a trip to London England. Is that offer still good?"

"If you're referring to the luxury cruise special that will be departing in two weeks, yes it is still available. However, staterooms for that package are disappearing quickly. Would you like to reserve one now?"

"Before I do that I would like to know a little bit more about what's included and how much will it cost to make a reservation."

The agent sensing that he had a real sale pending began telling her about all of the features included in the package and how this package is one of their best sellers. However, when he came to the part about the costs, Monica had to pause for a minute to let the number sink in. The brochure did not specify some of the additional fees he was quoting and the surprise gave her pause. As he continued to lay out the benefits and the fact that now was a great time to book because of the special offer, Monica was having second thoughts.

When he concluded his pitch the decision question was asked.

"Doesn't that sound like something you want to do?" he asked.

"Well that's a little more expensive than I anticipated. Those extra fees were not given in what I looked at."

Before she could finish her thought, he broke in and said: "Well you sound like a lovely lady so here's what I'm going to do. If you book passage today I will waive the fees and give you the exact price quoted in the book. How's that?" When he said that she was sold. The balance of the conversation was a matter of finalizing the details and getting her a contract. He told her that he would send it via priority express mail so she would have it in two days. Now she was delighted and the excitement began to grow.

As promised, the package arrived on schedule and she reviewed it looking for any hidden clauses. When she finished reading it appeared to be just as he said so she signed and placed it back in the return express envelope he provided. It was done and now she felt a surge of new excitement. Even though she was travelling alone she believed that the trip was going to change her life for the better. Little did she know how right she was in her thinking.

Time passed quickly and after making all of the necessary preparations on her job and buying the new wardrobe she desired one week earlier, the next day was her departure date. While scheduling her transportation pick-up she hoped that there would be no glitches in getting her to the pier on time.

Her ride came promptly and she arrived at the pier an hour earlier than necessary. Going through the check-in process was even easier than she had imagined. Never having taken a cruise before she had been somewhat intimidated by what she thought would be a lengthy and daunting procedure. After she was aboard and guided to her stateroom, upon entry she was thoroughly impressed. The décor was beautiful and now she was really convinced this was going to be fantastic journey. As she looked around and became familiar with what features were available to her, satisfaction became her state of mind.

Completing her inspection of the interior she ventured out onto the terrace and witnessed another eye opening and impressive view of the surrounding landscape and the expanse of the ocean. Feeling good about her decision to embark on this journey she unpacked and put away her belongings then sought the comfort of the beautifully made up bed. She lay there flipping through the documents that had been placed telling her about the dinner schedule and all of the various activities available.

What caught her eye immediately was written in bold letters right at the beginning of the package. It was a notice for the Captain's welcome dinner at 6:30 pm and in parentheses (semi-formal dress requested). She knew that the new wardrobe she purchased for the trip included some very appropriate fashion wear so she was happy that now here was an opportunity to wear it right away.

Since it was early she decided to take a nap and rest before preparing for the affair. Time passed quickly and she was a bit surprised that she had fallen into as deep sleep than she anticipated. The gentle rocking of the ship's motion however had lulled her into a REM state that made her even oblivious to when the vessel actually left the port. When she finally awakened it was later than she realized. Moving with a sense of urgency, not wanting to be late for her first activity, she quickly showered, groomed herself and donned her outfit.

When she arrived at the ballroom she was politely directed to her table where she was seated among six other passengers already there. They were very pleasant and jovial as introductions were made and everyone was anticipating a happy voyage. Some were experienced cruisers and others were first timers just as she was. The conversation was light and convivial so she became more relaxed and was beginning to enjoy it even though she was the only unattached person in the group.

After dinner and having two glasses of wine with the meal, her spirit was elevated and seeking to rise to another level. She noticed on her way to the ballroom that there was a lounge not too far away. As she approached the entrance she could hear soft jazz music coming from inside that seemed to offer an invitation especially for her.

The lighting inside was soft creating a warm and cozy setting. Her eyes quickly adapted and she spotted an empty table just off the bandstand that was somewhat secluded. Since no one was sitting there she made her way over and sat down. Moments later a waiter came over and asked if she would like to order something. Without hesitation she blurted out "I'll have a gin and tonic with a lime twist." She surprised herself at how quickly the words came out of her mouth and it reminded her of her early days at college when Margie first introduced her to the drink and she liked it. This was still her favorite alcoholic beverage and over the years she certainly had many of them. The waiter took her order and disappeared.

The music was soothing as was the drink and she was just getting comfortable enjoying the ambience when a young man, perhaps in his late twenty's or early thirty's approached her table.

"Do you mind if I join you?" he said.

She hesitated at first, not expecting company on the voyage so soon, but then she motioned for him to take a seat. He sat down opposite her and started talking.

"You may not have noticed me at dinner, but I was seated at the table next to yours. I noticed you right away because it seems that like me you were the odd one there."

At that Monica had to stifle a chuckle because what he said she knew was true.

"My name is Kevin Gardner and I'm taking this trip to try and forget about someone. Is that your reason also?"

Monica was a little befuddled at his words since he had only just introduced himself. He hadn't even asked about her name. She stared at him for a few minutes trying to read in his face what could perhaps reveal something about him. His features were nothing extraordinary, nothing like Troy's. but were rather plain and ordinary. She couldn't assess anything from that and with the gin and the wine beginning to make her feel invincible she responded.

"Yes I guess you could say that and I am not looking for a new relationship right now."

He was not offended nor disarmed, but continued to talk.

"I'm sorry please don't misunderstand me I was not making a pass at you, but just revealing my status. What's your name?"

"You know you didn't even ask that when you gave me your name. Didn't it occur to you that you skipped that part?"

"Yes you're right that was rather rude of me. So now that the question has been asked will you give it?"

"Well since I will probably be seeing you at dinner for the next several days I will tell you. My name is Monica Miller and yes I am attempting to erase someone from my mind."

"Now that's done. Have you ever been on a cruise before? I've been told that it is the best way to relax and erase old memories. Is that what you've heard also?"

"I have heard that and no I have not sailed before. I'm going to enjoy this voyage and think about only my well being."

"Me too. Let's drink a toast to our cruise happiness."

They clinked glasses and drank the toast. For some time until well into the night they talked and the conversation was pleasant, but not going into any intimate details about who they were trying to forget. Even though he didn't say it she could tell that he was really feeling depressed and lonely about his situation. As the hour grew late and Monica knew that she had reached her limit on drinks, she politely advised him that it was time for her to retire. When the check came, she offered to split it, but he insisted on paying and signed it to his cabin. Monica noticed when he signed that it was not on the stateroom deck.

He decided to call it a night and said it was time for him to retire also. They left the lounge together, but he went to a lower level as she made her way to one of the upper decks. For a first night she felt that this was a good start and it heightened her expectations for the rest of the trip.

When she returned to her room before actually going to sleep she reflected on how this new acquaintance had entered her life and how in some ways it reminded her of Troy. Although she had promised herself that she wasn't going to do this, her mind began to travel back to the first time she met Troy. She briefly mulled over the idea then caught herself and moved on to other thoughts. Her reinforcement wall against thinking about him was holding and before the melancholy tears started to form the alcohol and late night activity beset her and she got in bed then drifted off into a deep sleep.

The next morning came and Monica felt surprisingly rejuvenated even ignoring the slight twinge of a mild hangover. Perhaps it was because she had subconsciously examined her relationship with Troy and resolved that she was on this cruise because it was her self-prescribed therapy. She arose looked at the clock and decided there was still time to catch the breakfast hour before it closed. Putting on one of her sport outfits she felt good about having purchased the right attire for the trip.

When she arrived at the area serving breakfast she was a bit surprised to see that there was still a line to get in because it was so late. She said to herself "I guess these folks must have done a late night too." While standing in line she had a strange feeling that someone was watching her so she turned around to see. Only a few passengers behind her she saw Kevin also in the line. She nodded her head acknowledging him then turned back around. It did not occur to her at this time that it was anything more than coincidence that he should be there at this hour also.

She moved through the buffet line and availed herself of the vast assortment of breakfast items. After filling her tray with an abundance of food she found a table nearby with just two people there. She asked if the empty seats were taken and upon hearing they were not she sat down. Soon after she did Kevin found her and also sat down.

They exchanged pleasantries and then ate quietly without further conversation until the others who had been at the table got up and left.

"I had a nice time last night and enjoyed every minute. How about you?" he said.

"Yes it was nice the music was just what I needed."

"What are your plans for today?"

At this saying, she was beginning to feel that he was going to be a problem.

"Oh I don't know yet. I'm going to look at the activities schedule and see what seems good."

He didn't pursue the matter any further so she dismissed the idea that he may be pursuing her.

When she got back to her room she looked at the programs and decided to attend the Bingo Tournament which began at 1:00 pm. Before going there she thought she would explore the ship and see where things were. Moving from deck to deck she was amazed at how much was available on this magnificent vessel. Everywhere she turned she was impressed at the décor, the shops, the casino and most of all the restaurants.

Finally it was time to go to the tournament. She was hoping that he would not show up there too so she could really relax and pay attention to the games. He didn't and she enjoyed about three hours of the games even coming away with a modest profit. Once back in her room she decided to take a nap until the dinner call.

This time when she woke up again, not like before, there was plenty of time to leisurely get dressed. At dinner she looked over to where he said his table was and sure enough there he was seated where he would be facing her. Again she nodded to him and he to her and that was all that was said.

After dinner she waited until most of the others had left the ballroom before saying goodnight to her table. She looked over to where Kevin had been sitting and he was gone. She said to herself "good" and made her way through the entrance doors. Back at her room she looked again over the activities schedule and saw there was going to be a Captain's special bonus for all slot machine players. They were giving a free play bonus of up to $250.00. Since it was still rather early she decided to try her luck.

Inside the casino there were several passengers there no doubt with the same intention as she, wanting to take advantage of the free-be. She looked around at the various machines and found one that attracted her attention so she sat down. It was not long before he found her and sat down at the machine beside her.

Now she was really becoming suspicious. Even though she was annoyed, she smiled at him and asked whether he was having a good time. He took that as an invitation to unload and began telling her his life's story seeking some consolation from her. Now she just wanted to get away so she said she had to go to the ladies room and left.

Even though she was disappointed in not staying at her machine long enough to spend the free money, she got the feeling that he was sincerely trying to reach out to her. Feeling a little guilty she planned to apologize the next day when she saw him.

The next day was uneventful and she took advantage of a morning yoga class and then went swimming. She didn't see him all day and began to wonder whether she was over reacting to what she thought might be his intentions.

That night she saw him at dinner and again acknowledged him with a wave of her hand. This night the dinner was special and at the end the waiters put on a show coming in with flaming baked Alaska. Thoroughly enjoying the whole presentation she looked over to his table to see if he was doing the same. It was hard to tell because the expression on his face gave no indication.

After dinner she watched him get up and she caught up with him at the door.

"Are you alright?" she asked. "I watched you during that show and you didn't seem to be enjoying it. Didn't you like it?"

"The show was okay, but I have more on my mind than watching it."

At that point Monica regretted she even approached him because she realized now she had opened the door for him to do another download of his problems. As diplomatically and politely as she could she tried to exit the conversation and move away, but he persisted in talking. Finally she just said: "Listen I know you're hurting so am I, but I'm not a psychologist or a shrink. You really need to find someone qualified to talk with. Have you seen the ship's doctor maybe he can suggest something?"

"No. All I want is someone to listen. I thought it would be you."

"I'm really sorry, but that's just not me."

Then she walked away leaving him standing there.

Following that encounter she went to another room where a comedy show was taking place thinking that might brighten her spirit. She laughed for awhile and at the end of the show felt better. Now it was getting late so she decided to retire.

When she arrived at her stateroom she noticed him a little further away down the corridor. Had he been outside the showroom all this time waiting for her to come out and then followed her here? When he saw her turn around spotting him, he pretended to get ready to enter into one of the other rooms. Now this really sent a red flag up for her because she had seen him sign the check for a cabin on another level so she knew that was not his room.

Once inside she tried to calm herself thinking that it was probably no big deal and not to be too concerned. But something in her mind was telling her to be careful. Confirming not to go out again tonight she decided to relax listen to some soft music, read one of the books she had purchased from one of the ship's stores then go to sleep. Before long she was nodding and no longer reading so she went to bed.

The next morning this time she got up early and was going to have breakfast before the crowd arrived. As she was about to leave she noticed that a note had been slipped under the door.

"I know that you think I'm hounding you, but you're wrong. Since the first night we met I have been trying to find a way to pour out myself to you. I am desperately lonely and have now come to the conclusion that this voyage is not the answer that I'm looking for. I don't believe you should be burdened with my load so I will not contact you or anybody else ever again. This note is just to say goodbye and I hope that you will enjoy the rest of your trip.

Kevin"

The ominous sound of the note frightened her and she wasn't sure at first what to do with it. Finally, she decided to call for her cabin steward and ask him what to do. A few minutes later she heard a knock at the door.

"Just a minute"

"You rang Miss?"

"Yes thank you for coming quickly. When I got up this morning I found this note under my door and I'm not sure what to do with it. It sounds like someone is having a serious problem."

She handed the note to the steward. He looked at it and frowned.

"I see your concern" he said. "Let me get this to the Captain and he will handle it."

"Thank you. I hope the man is alright."

The steward left and she went on to breakfast. This was the fifth day of the voyage and until now there was nothing that had really upset her, but this new thing was troubling. She availed herself of all of the programs she could, even taking a late swim in the pool, but her mind could not dismiss the note. And now that she had not seen him at any of the events all day she began to wonder.

It was not until later that afternoon when she overheard one of the other passengers saying that there was a man missing from the manifest and the Captain was trying to keep it quiet. This passenger was related to one of the stewards and had received the word from him. Monica's mind was now on high alert. Did he jump off the ship was her first thought?

Later that day after she had participated in all of the activities she thought would help her forget about the note, she returned to her room. Upon entering she saw the message light on the telephone blinking. The message was from the Captain asking her to come and meet with him at 6:30. Since that was around the time of her dinner seating she called the number that was left and talked with one of the officers. The officer told her he would call right back after he checked with the Captain. Minutes later the phone rang.

Ring, ring, ring

"Hello."

"Hello Miss Miller this is Lieutenant Anderson I just spoke to you a few minutes ago. The Captain has agreed to meet with you at 5 O'clock if that's okay with you?"

"Yes that would be fine."

"Okay then I'll see you there."

She hung up and began wondering what that was all about. Guessing it must have something to do with Kevin she tried to anticipate the questions. At 4:45 she headed to the meeting place – Captain's quarters. When she arrived she was greeted with a warm welcome and invited to sit in one of his plush easy chairs. He was seated at his desk, but got up and came over to her.

"Thank you for coming Miss Miller. I think you know why I called you here." he said.

"I guess it's about the note I found from Kevin."

"Right! We have become very concerned with not being able to account for his whereabouts. You were the last one to see and speak with him is that right?"

"Well I don't know if I was the last one, but I did see him last night."

"When you saw him did he seem like he was – well kind of out of sorts?"

"What do you mean?"

'You know, did he seem rationale to you?

"Yes, as far as I could tell."

"His note to you seems like he was planning to commit suicide. Did you feel that from his note?"

"I sensed that he might be thinking that way, but that's why I gave it to you."

"Do you think you could have helped him?"

"Captain I'm not a psychologist or any kind of a doctor – what could I do?"

"Probably nothing, but I just had to ask. Okay Miss Miller that it's for now. Again thank you for coming. We'll get back to you if we need anything further."

"Captain can I ask what happens now?"

"Certainly - we'll continue our search of the ship, but if we can't find him the Coast Guard will continue to search the waters for a reasonable amount of time before calling it off. Remember there are over 2,000 passengers aboard who are looking forward to completing the voyage and we have a schedule to meet so we must keep going. You understand that don't you?"

"Yes of course. I was just wondering what the procedure was in a case like this."

"Well now you know. I hope you will not let this spoil your trip. Please go now and enjoy your dinner."

She left the Captain's quarters and decided to walk around for a bit before getting ready for dinner. As she moved about the ship she couldn't help but notice that many of the passengers were talking about the missing man report. The gossip had spread so quickly that it was amazing to her how quickly news like that could travel throughout the vessel. Even though she was aware that an event like a suicide was very important news she pondered why more had not been disclosed by the Captain or his staff to dispel wild rumors from getting out of control. After walking and visiting several new shops for about a half-hour she noticed the time and started back to her room to get ready. Before she got there another passenger walked along side of her and casually started talking. She seemed to be just a very friendly person who loves to talk.

"Did you hear that there is someone missing from the ship?"

Monica looked at her for a moment trying to assess whether she was trying to infer something or just being inquisitive.

"Yes I did. If it's true than that would be a terrible situation if they can't find him."

"You said him. Do you know who it is?"

Caught a little off guard she responded: "No, not really, I just used that expression as a common assumption."

"Yeah you're probably right though. It would be just like a man to go and do something stupid like turn up missing and spoil everybody else's fun."

Monica got the feeling that this woman had some kind of ax to grind and didn't want to get caught up in her story so she politely ended the conversation and continued on to her room.

Around 6:30 pm while she was at dinner, there was the sound of two helicopters circling the ship and searching the waters. Now she knew that something was wrong. Within the next half-hour the Captain's voice came on over the ship's system.

"Good evening travelers this is the Captain speaking. I'm sure you've noticed the aircraft flying around us. There is no danger to the ship and we are in calm waters. However, one of our guests seems to be unaccounted for and we are taking every feasible measure to find him. Please do not be alarmed. We will conduct a thorough search of this vessel and the immediate waters. Continue to enjoy your cruise and do not worry."

After hearing that, it was difficult for Monica to continue to enjoy the trip while it was confirmed what she suspected had been indicated in Kevin's note. It was a suicide note. For the rest of the evening she was trying to decide whether she had been the cause of his decision since he could not get to her. The guilt she was now feeling was unfounded, but she could not shake it.

At dinner she looked again for him, but he was not at his table. She struggled through trying to eat and be jovial with her tablemates, but it was obviously failing. Her tablemates noticed it and asked whether she was okay? She said she was fine and smiled. After dinner she decided to return to the lounge where they first met and perhaps receive some consolation through the music. When she walked in ironically the same table where she first met him was unoccupied so she went and sat down. Just like before the same waiter came over and she ordered the same drink. It was almost as if déjà vu had set in. Even the band was playing the same tune as she recalled. The only difference was that Kevin would not be making his entry into her life. Now the guilt feeling she had been trying to suppress was really rising up to overtake her psyche and spoil any possibility of having a good time from here on out throughout the voyage.

The waiter brought her drink and without any hesitation she gulped it down and ordered another one. Perhaps, she thought if I drink enough of these my mind will be able to enjoy the music. After the third one and sitting alone at the table the positive effect she was hoping for was not achieved, but something else invaded her mind as the alcohol slowly clouded her consciousness. With the dim lighting and now haunting jazz music her mind hearkened back to that night when she received another strange vision. She had become accustomed to visits from her grandmother Lois usually in times of her stressful situations, but this time it definitely was not her. The glow was eerily different, tinged with fiery reds and sulfur yellow and the noise coming from within the image was loud and clanking. When she was finally able to see the image clearly it was grotesques and resembling Satan the devil. It was wrapped in a chain and the noise was coming from it trying to escape from being entwined with steel. Suddenly though from another area in the room another bright glow appeared that resembled Lois, but it was the presence of Michael the warrior arc angel of God who dispatched the grotesque image and then spoke to her.

Still sitting at the table she sat mesmerized as if in a trance listening in her head to the words in her mind..

"Fear not my child for you are protected." Michael said.

"What you have just witnessed is the epitome, the embodiment of pure evil that has been hovering over and around you since you were born. It was because of your earthly father who succumbed to the curse that was placed on him that you were chosen as a target for the continuance of the evil. It was only now that the progenitor of evil was coming to claim his prize. Do not be alarmed that I tell you this now because the time is near when you shall receive a message from on high that will confirm and allay all of your fears and make you realize the true promise for your life."

When Michel finished speaking he disappeared just like the other image. Monica awakened from her trancelike state and realized the band was playing Misty, a song which was her mother's favorite and she remembered it. Not sure what all of this meant, between the drinks, the music, her feeling of guilt and the vision she decided she had enough and was going back to her stateroom. She got up from the table and had just stepped outside the lounge when a loud noise interrupted her forward progress. The ship-wide warning horn sounded for about twenty-five seconds and then a voice came over the system.

"All passengers and crew please listen carefully to the following announcement. This is your Captain speaking again and I have an important message. We have just been informed that there is a major storm just ahead of us and is approaching our current position. There is no need to worry, cause for alarm or panic because this ship is quite capable of riding out any adverse weather conditions we may encounter. However, I am advising all passengers to return now to their cabins and brace for some rough waters. Crew members take your emergency positions and stand by for further orders. I anticipate entering the outer rim of the storm's center in about a half-hour. Again all passengers please heed this message and take proper safety precautions. I will keep you advised of all weather conditions as needed. Thank you for your cooperation."

After hearing the message Monica was feeling less secure now than she had been earlier even during the strange recent experience, but she heeded the warning and continued on to her stateroom. Once inside she decided to enjoy the mellow feeling that the wine at dinner and the drinks afterward had generated so she sat in the easy chair near the bed to reflect on all of today's happenings. She turned on the radio and although there was some static she found a station that provided soft music just as she liked. In a matter of a few minutes she dozed off again into a deep sleep.

Within the hour she was suddenly jolted from her chair and thrown to the floor. The gentle rocking of the ship that she had become accustomed to had now become a violent thrashing about of the whole ship. Being tossed from side to side as the ship encountered the storm she tried to grab onto the bed to stabilize herself. The shaking and bucking went on for about an hour, as she recalled, and it was difficult for her not to be afraid as the Captain had advised.

The time that it finally subsided, she could not remember when it actually ended because she must have either feinted or hit her head on something. It was not until very early the following morning that she woke up and looked out the window. Seeing the dawning of a brand new day and now feeling somewhat relaxed she decided to venture out and see what had happened. She walked forward to the bow and looked out at the magnificent calm ocean.

Imagining a more beautiful sunrise, as she stood on the forward deck, than what was on display right now would be difficult at best. The glorious rainbow, an angelic crown over the rising sun, was a welcome respite after the storm that raged throughout much of the night. The colors were in such a beautiful array that only the Master painter could have achieved such a feat. As the majestic ocean liner continued to sail east to her destined English port, only a very few of the 2,100 passengers aboard were awake or well enough to enjoy the moment and witness the radiant spectacle. Unlike Monica, the others slept now enjoying a peaceful voyage on calm waters after having spent most of the fitful night fearing that some maritime disaster was imminent.

. As the ship sped along the crest of the ocean, Monica was so enthralled, she marveled at the sight. Looking on the vast expanse of the ocean with a sense of wonder, she kept thinking how awesome it is. Could this be a sign that the new day was going to be as beautiful as the view portends? She desperately wanted to believe this as over and over in her mind she recalled the reason why she was even on this cruise. Waffling between the idea of getting away from the daily grind of life's challenges and the need to just go somewhere and relax, she had decided a cruise would be a good option.

While she stared into the cloudless pale blue sky, a thought popped into her head. It was a passage from the Bible, a book she had perused several times over after going to church with her aunt, but had never really read it carefully or appreciated what it was all about. The words "I am the Way, the truth and the life" kept reverberating in her head like a scratched disc. Somehow she knew she was relating to the thought in some fashion, but couldn't put it all together.

"Why now at this moment she asked herself?"

It was too early for her to eat breakfast so she returned to her room and sat in the easy chair staring out the window. Whether it was a wide awake dream or another vision she couldn't tell. An angel dressed in a dazzling white robe appeared before her and started speaking:

"Blessed be the name of the Lord who created the heavens and the earth. He is to be exalted among all men. His mercy endures forever and His grace is sufficient. Your current suffering is not to be compared to the magnificent glory that you will experience in the coming days. Know this that the Lord He is God and it is He that has made you in His own image. He has placed inside of you all that is necessary for you to survive on this planet. Worship Him and He will provide for you.

You have not yet seen Him in His glory, but you must know that He is ever present in your life if you will only acknowledge His existence. There will come a time when you shall know that all things are possible if you only believe that they can be given to you. Believing and having faith that they will occur is part of knowing His presence in your life.

For so many years you have been following a false god that is one of material gain and greed for the things that truly do not matter. The way that you have been traveling is not the one that has been directed for you. Jesus is the Way as your thoughts have been revealing to you. He is not dead, but is alive for evermore. Keep Him in your heart and mind and you will know the compassion that only He can provide for your comfort. Jesus while living among men during His first Advent was able to feel all of the grief that you feel, experience all of the pain that you feel, tempted by all of the trials and tribulations that you experienced and suffering the hurt that you feel, but His resistance to temptation even while in human form did not allow Him to yield to the temptations created by the evil one. Know this beloved, that you are truly loved by the one who can make you whole and will not leave you or forsake you in all situations. Searching for love has evaded your grasp because you did not seek it in the right place. To know true love you must first understand that the one who loves you is the creator of love and gives it freely to all those who love Him. To know the truth is to come before His throne of grace with worship and praise and He shall give you all that you need. Let not your heart be troubled, but learn to call on Him at all times for whom the Son sets free is free indeed from all despair and depression. Your journey is not over and you will continue to have challenges in your life, but know this the hedge of protection that has now been given to you will never fail. The answer to the question that you have been asking all of your adult life, the one that you believed you did not receive an answer to can now be answered. Your question - **Who Am I?** The answer is - You are a precious child of the Most High God the Father and the One who loves you dearly beloved.

During the remainder of this voyage you will begin to know that your life, thus far, has not been lived in vain and that you will find the comfort and love you seek, finally realizing that **Jesus is the Way** and through it all you will be blessed in knowing that you have truly seen the light that has given you clarity of vision and clear understanding. Then you will know that you have been redeemed along with all others who believe when **FINDING THE WAY**.

The New Beginning

ABOUT THE AUTHOR

 Sidney L. Jackson is the founder of El Cid's Books, a website (Elcidsbooks.com) offering published books using his pseudonym El Cid as well as his own name. He is an accomplished novelist and short story writer who brings to the reader wholesome stories that will both entertain and enlighten him or her about the spiritual value of Biblical knowledge. As the reader is engaged in the book's various adventures and challenging situations which mirror real life, the author provides relevant scriptures that deal with the predicament.

Born in New York City in the section of the metropolis known as Harlem, Sidney was exposed, at an early age, to many of the situations that he writes about. He spent his later childhood and young adult years growing up in the city of Newark, NJ where his interests in music and sociology was spawned. Gravitating toward the field of jazz he attended Arts High School, which has become known for producing jazz greats such as Sarah Vaughan, Wayne Shorter and Woody Shaw in addition to several movie and TV sitcom stars.

After high school he matriculated at a southern university where he received the Bachelor of Science degree in Music Education. While studying at this school, during the years of the early Civil Rights movements, he became aware of the disparity between what many religious patrons preached and what they practiced. This led to his interest in Biblical studies and the relevance of scripture to life's journey. With this in mind he furthered his education at the post graduate level studying guidance and counseling and business modeling.

Driven to write about the need for Biblical faith in certain situations using his experience both in the military as a Viet Nam soldier and living in the inner city during some turbulent times, he has penned short stories and completed six novels. The other novels are listed at the beginning of this work. Some of these publications may be found on Amazon and Barnes and Noble as well as on the Elcidsbooks.com website.

Contact information and more about the author may be found on the website (http://www.elcidsbooks.com)

www.ingramcontent.com/pod-product-compliance
Lightning Source LLC
Chambersburg PA
CBHW061141120626
46546CB00005B/1876